OLD WORLD EUROPE 2nd Edition
Teacher's Guide

Fran Rutherford

Illustrated by James Rutherford

Old World Europe, Teacher's Guide
Second Edition, July 2011

Copyright ©2012 Fran Rutherford, Black Forest, Colorado
www.classicstudyguides.com

All Rights Reserved
For permission to use more than short excerpts for critical reviews, contact the author through Aquinas and More, 4727 N. Academy Blvd., Suite A, Colorado Springs, CO 80908/ 800-428-2820

Trademark Notice
Questions for the Thinker™ is a trademark belonging to Fran Rutherford. Materials with this trademark have previously been published by Kolbe Academy and Mother's House Publishing. However, this version is a new, updated and more complete edition and the only one currently authorized. No duplication of content is permitted without written permission from the author.

Original Illustrations, cover design and interior layout by James Rutherford, Colorado Springs, Colorado

Published by Aquinas and More
www.aquinasandmore.com
Colorado Springs, Colorado

ISBN 978-0-9837581-5-0
Made in the United States of America

I dedicate this work to the following:

I dedicate this volume to four teachers who made a difference in my life:

Sister Ita, my second grade teacher from Ireland who loved me and taught me, even though I was left-handed,

Sister Jane de Chantal, who made me welcome in her seventh grade class, even though I was only there for a few months while my dad was in Antarctica,

Miss Claire Canon, who taught me the importance of professionalism in my work,

Mr. Harold Connell, who encouraged me in music, taught me voice, and fought to keep the study of music in the public schools of Virginia.

You were all outstanding teachers because you had a vision which extended far beyond the confines of the schools in which you taught.

Thank you.

Table of Contents

Why Study the Works of Old World Europe?	i
Instructions for the Student and the Teacher	iii
Significant Dates in Old World Europe	v

Unit 1: Poetry — 1

About Dante and the Divine Comedy — 3

The Inferno — 5

Canto I	7
Canto II	7
Canto III	8
Canto IV	9
Canto V	10
Canto VI	10
Canto VII	11
Canto VIII	12
Canto IX	12
Canto X	13
Canto XI	14
Canto XII	14
Canto XIII	15
Canto XIV	15
Canto XV	16
Canto XVI	17
Canto XVII	17
Canto XVIII	18
Canto XIX	18
Canto XX	19
Canto XXI	20
Canto XXII	20
Canto XXIV	21
Canto XXV	22
Canto XXVI	22
Canto XXVII	22
Canto XXVIII	23
Canto XXIX	23
Canto XXX	24
Canto XXXI	25
Canto XXXII	25
Canto XXXIII	26
Canto XXXIV	27

Purgatorio — 29

Canto I	30
Canto II	30
Canto III	31
Canto IV	32
Canto V	33
Canto VI	33
Canto VII	34
Canto VIII	34
Canto IX	35
Canto X	37
Canto XI	37
Canto XII	38
Canto XIII	38
Canto XIV	39
Canto XV	40
Canto XVI	41
Canto XVII	42
Canto XVIII	43
Canto XIX	44
Canto XX	45
Canto XXI	46
Canto XXII	46
Canto XXIII	47
Canto XXIV	48
Canto XXV	49
Canto XXVI	49
Canto XXVII	50
Canto XXVIII	51
Canto XXIX	52
Canto XXX	53
Canto XXXI	53
Canto XXXII	54
Canto XXXIII	56

Paradiso — 59

Canto I	60
Canto II	60
Canto III	61
Canto IV	62
Canto V	63
Canto VI	64
Canto VII	64
Canto VIII	65
Canto IX	66
Canto X	67
Canto XI	67
Canto XII	68
Canto XIII	69
Canto XIV	69
Canto XV	70
Canto XVI	71
Canto XVII	71
Canto XVIII	72
Canto XIX	73
Canto XX	74

Canto XXI	74
Canto XXII	75
Canto XXIII	76
Canto XXIV	77
Canto XXV	78
Canto XXVI	79
Canto XXVII	80
Canto XXVIII	80
Canto XXIX	81
Canto XXX	82
Canto XXXI	83
Canto XXXII	84
Canto XXXIII	85
PARADISE LOST	87
The Verse	88
Book I	88
Book II	89
Book III	92
Book IV	94
Book V	96
Book VI	98
Book VII	101
Book VIII	101
Book IX	104
Book X	107
Book XI	110
Book XII	112
BEOWULF	115
SONG OF ROLAND	127
Prologue	128
The Council of Marsila	128
The Embassy	128
Roland and Ganelon	128
The Treachery	129
The Rear Guard	130
The Paynim Peers	130
The Madness of Roland	130
The First Battle	131
The Second Battle	131
The Horn	131
The Death of Oliver	132
The Archbishop	132
The Death of Roland	132
The Punishment of the Paynims	133
The Lament of the King	133
Alda	133
The Punishment of Ganelon	133
Epilogue	134
THE CANTERBURY TALES	137
Prologue	139
The Knight's Tale	141
The Man of Law's Tale	146

UNIT 2: HISTORY

THE RULE OF ST. BENEDICT	153
Introduction	155
The Rule of St. Benedict	156
Impact of the Rule	157
Prologue	157
Chapter 1	158
Chapter 2	158
Chapter 3	158
Chapter 4	158
Chapter 5	159
Chapter 6	159
Chapter 7	159
Chapters 8 -20	159
Chapter 21	160
Chapter 22	160
Chapter 23	160
Chapter 24	160
Chapter 25	160
Chapter 26	160
Chapter 27	160
Chapter 28	160
Chapter 29	161
Chapter 30	161
Chapter 31	161
Chapter 32	161
Chapter 33	161
Chapter 34	161
Chapter 35	161
Chapter 36	161
Chapter 37	162
Chapter 38	162
Chapter 39	162
Chapter 40	162
Chapter 41	162
Chapter 42	162
Chapter 43	162
Chapter 44	163
Chapter 45	163
Chapter 46	163
Chapter 47	163
Chapter 48	163

Chapter 49	163	XVI	185
Chapter 50	163	XVII	185
Chapter 51	163	XVIII	186
Chapter 52	164	XIX	187
Chapter 53	164	XX	187
Chapter 54	164	XXI	188
Chapter 55	164	XXII	188
Chapter 56	164	XXIII	188
Chapter 57	164	XXIV	189
Chapter 58	164	XXV	189
Chapter 59	165		
Chapter 60	165		
Chapter 61	165		
Chapter 62	165		
Chapter 63	165		
Chapter 64	165		

Unit 4: Novel — 191

Don Quixote — 193
    Part One — 194
    Part Two — 206

Chapter 65	166
Chapter 66	166
Chapter 67	166
Chapter 68	166
Chapter 69	166
Chapter 70	166
Chapter 71	166
Chapter 72	166
Chapter 73	167

Glossary: — 221
Words to Know — 221
Sources Consulted — 233
About the Author — 235
About the Illustrator — 235

The Two Lives of Charlemagne — 169
    Book I — 170
    Book II — 170
    Book III — 171
    Book IV — 173
    Book V — 173

Unit 3: Philosophy — 175

The Prince — 177
    I — 178
    II — 178
    III — 178
    IV — 179
    V — 180
    VI — 180
    VII — 180
    VIII — 181
    IX — 182
    X — 182
    XI — 183
    XII — 183
    XIII — 184
    XIV — 184
    XV — 185

Why Study the Works of Old World Europe?

It would not be completely accurate to title this book "Works of Medieval Literature and History" because it encompasses a wider period of time, from the end of the Roman Empire through the Protestant Revolution. Traditionally, the history of Europe is divided into three basic periods: the classical period of Ancient Greece and Rome, the Middle Ages which roughly fell between the fifth century and the Protestant Revolt in the sixteenth century, and the Modern era. The Renaissance preceded the Protestant Revolt and was characterized by a return to the study of classical learning, art and architecture as well as advances in science.

The early years of this long period are seen as a dark age for the world after the barbarians sacked Rome and terrorized Europe. True, it was a dark age, but not entirely, for it was during this time that the monasteries flourished, grew and preserved culture, art and learning for the future. Secularists would argue that it was a dark age for the Church, but they would fail to understand how important the contributions made through the monasteries of the time were. I would argue that every age has its dark moments, not only in the Church, but in the society as well, but there has been a thread of culture, learning and morality that the Church has managed to weave through the ages. While we cannot gloss over the errors and abuses people suffered at the hands of Church and civil leaders, we cannot fall into the trap of painting all Church and civil leaders with the same brush of corruption and self-indulgence. Through the reading of *The Rule of St. Benedict*, we see the discipline which the monks embraced in order to survive and thrive. We see the inherent goodness in the founders who always urged gentleness as well as firmness in their governance.

It is important to remember that Christianity was spreading in the world, and though some of its proponents were not holy men, many were, and society was gradually civilized through their efforts. Even Charlemagne, though not a religious nor a learned man, was instrumental in establishing the Faith within his sphere of influence.

During the so-called Middle Ages, Christendom was the most influential institution in Europe. Some see that as a negative thing because classical thought of the ancient world was eclipsed and only later "rediscovered" by the humanists at the time of the Enlightenment. What many may not understand is that the ideas and thoughts of this period were themselves influenced by the ancient philosophers, again demonstrating that the Ancients pondered the same questions and faced the same dilemmas that man has experienced throughout his sojourn on earth.

While Christianity was flourishing behind the monastery walls, Islam, which was founded by Mohammed in the 600s, was spreading from the East to the West. It was a conflict, not only of theology, but of how society should be ordered as well. It is interesting to note that the conflict has gone on for 1400 years and does not show any signs of lessening. Readers can understand the hesitancy of writers of the period toward Islam because it was influencing their lives and threatening the survival of what they held dear, much as it is doing in today's world. The period of the Great Crusades, a struggle against the domination of Islam, lasted from 1095-1187, but the conflict has never gone away.

Beyond the spread of Islam in Europe was the Protestant Revolution which turned men of faith into enemies. The Catholic Church split between East and West and Christians divided into denominations. They continue to split, and while many dream of reunification, the realization of that dream seems a long way in the future. The seeds of our experience today were planted centuries ago, and it is helpful for us to study and understand how people thought and dealt with the challenges of their day.

Our society becomes every day more secular. It rejects faith in God, the transcendent, and the idea that there are natural laws which should govern us in every generation. It claims that only science can answer the questions about our existence, and it relies on reason as the only source of knowledge. Yet today, when our educational system largely neglects the thoughtful men of the past, people don't know how to use authentic reasoning skills to form a coherent argument. They have cut themselves off from the great ideas which civilize and humanize them, leading, in essence, to a modern barbarism of living only for the now and for what one can acquire through any means. The moral compass, which the classics show us, is no longer considered a guide by the majority.

The classics of the period covered in *Old Word Europe* manifest goodness and often poke fun at the milieu in which they were written, but that does not make them quaint or irrelevant to us today. Mankind has struggled with the same moral issues since being banished from the Garden of Eden, and will continue to struggle until the end. The virtues of fortitude, honesty, temperance, integrity, bravery and justice are for all ages and generations and are recurring themes in the classics. The endurance of the classics is due to the fact that they engage the readers in thought. They challenge without preaching. They mirror our own challenges, and give us insights into how we can deal with them.

In this work, we are introduced to the compassion and discipline of the monasteries in *The Rule of St. Benedict*; the bravery and fortitude of warriors in *Beowulf*; the ideals of chivalry and the treachery of friends in *The Song of Roland*; the strengths and weaknesses, virtues and vices of Charlemagne in *Einhard's Life of Charlemagne*; the spiritual journey of mankind in *The Divine Comedy*; the humor and imagination of *The Canterbury Tales*; the political thought of what constitutes a good leader in *The Prince*; the humor, idealism and pathos of a seemingly senile old man in *Don Quixote*; and the morality tale of the fall of man in *Paradise Lost*. May you enjoy your discovery!

Instructions for the Student and the Teacher

This book was designed for use by a student and a parent/teacher. Each student should have his own student book in which to write, and the teacher's guide should only be used by the teacher. The student book will facilitate writing the answers to the questions, and it will become a valuable resource for other high school and college classes.

Before reading the assigned books or chapters, the student should look over the group of questions relevant to the assignment so he can have an idea of what the reading will be about. He can jot down the answers to the questions as he comes across them in the reading. The questions are designed to assist the student in understanding the plots and events in the books, the character of the people in the stories, and the thoughts and ideas of the writers. The answers to the questions are found directly within the cited text, annotated with chapter numbers or line numbers, located above each cluster of questions or at the end of the questions. *(Please note: The numbers may not correspond exactly with editions other than those cited, but they are close from one edition to another.)*

As the student reads and rephrases the answers to the questions he will be stimulated to think about other ideas relevant to the upcoming discussion with his teacher. The *Questions for Further Thought* are to facilitate discussion beyond the objective questions and answers. An additional help is the inclusion of research topics at the end of some of the readings. In addition, vocabulary words are listed when they are pertinent to understanding the text.

The question-and-answer method was chosen for the following reasons:

- It helps the student focus on detail. When a student reads a selection and then just reads a summary of that selection he is not challenged to stop and ponder the ideas and truths contained in all the words.

- It introduces the student in a small way to the method used by the ancient philosopher Socrates. This approach to learning is known as the Socratic Method and was used by this great teacher to help his students discover truth. He would ask questions and then respond to their answers with more questions. His goal was to find truth and the meaning of life and to help others discover them as well. Questioning, logical thinking and reasoning were his tools.

- It is a jumping-off point for discussion between the student and teacher.

It is my hope that the thought and discussion that arise from this book will lead a student and his teacher to a greater self-knowledge, a love of the ancients, and an understanding of the works at hand and their relevance today.

Please note: Unlike the answers to the objective questions, the answers to the *Questions for Further Thought* are the opinion of the author. They are presented to provoke thought and reflection. The reader may certainly come to different or additional conclusions.

Note to parent/teacher:
In some sections the author has marked "skip to..." This is either because of sexual content which may be inappropriate for young students or because of extra detail not deemed necessary to understanding the text.

SIGNIFICANT DATES IN OLD WORLD EUROPE

LATE ROMAN EMPIRE

98-117	Roman Empire at its widest extent
313	Edict of Milan
324	Constantine reunites the Roman Empire
325	Christian Council of Nicaea
330	Constantinople founded
375	Huns make inroads into Europe
391	Christianity becomes State religion in Roman Empire
405	St. Jerome completes *Vulgate*
410	Rome sacked by Alaric
	De Civitas Dei by Augustine
	St. Patrick arrives in Ireland
440-461	Pope Leo the Great
455	Rome sacked by Vandal Gaiseric
496	Clovis, King of the Franks, becomes a Christian

EARLY MIDDLE AGES

c. 529	*Rule of St. Benedict*
527	Justinian – Eastern Roman Emperor
537	Hagia Sophia completed
590-604	Pope Gregory the Great
711	Muslim Arabs invade Europe
732	Battle of Tours: Franks defeat Muslims under Charles Martel
672-735	Venerable Bede – Monks guard classical literature
756	Papal States created in Italy
768-814	Charlemagne is King of the Franks
778	Roland's Franks defeated, Roncesvalles Pass, Spain
800	Charlemagne crowned Holy Roman Emperor by Pope Leo III
	Charlemagne begins rebuilding education
814	Charlemagne dies
843	*Treaty of Verdun*: Charlemagne's Empire divides
850	Rise of feudalism
851-91	Viking raids into Germany
910	Cluny Abbey founded in France
989	Peace and Truce of God

HIGH MIDDLE AGES

1054	Schism between Latin Roman Catholic and Byzantine Greek Orthodox Churches
1066	Battle of Hastings: William's Normans defeat Harold's Saxons
1075-1122	Investiture Contest: conflict between Pope and Holy Roman Emperor
1095-99	First Crusade regains Holy Land
	Beowulf
1122	*Concordat of Worms*
1130	*Song of Roland*
1147	First mention of Moscow
	Second Crusade fails to take Damascus
1170	Murder of Archbishop Thomas Becket in Canterbury Cathedral
1189-92	Third Crusade preserves Christian Holy Land possessions
1202-04	Fourth Crusade captures Constantinople and forms Latin Empire
1215	King John of England concedes charter of rights (*Magna Carta*)
1215	Fourth Lateran Council
1215	Dominican Order founded
1218-21	Fifth Crusade (into Egypt)
1228-29	Frederick II's Sixth Crusade regains Jerusalem
1248-54	St. Louis' Seventh Crusade (to Egypt)
1252	Florin first coined at Florence
1270	Eighth Crusade (to Tunisia)
1276	Paper manufactured in Italy

LATE MIDDLE AGES

c:1320	*Divine Comedy* by Dante
1340	Castile and Portugal defeat Muslim threat to Spain
1350	Rise of Italian city states: Italian Renaissance
1378-1418	Great Schism: rival popes in Rome and Avignon
1380	*Canterbury Tales*
1381	Peasants' Revolt in England

RENAISSANCE

1429	Joan of Arc raises siege of Orleans
1431	Joan of Arc burned at Rouen

1456	First printed Bible		
1478	Inquisition established in Spain		
1492	Columbus discovers America		
1492	Last Muslim state in Spain falls to Christians		
1495	*Diet of Worms* abolishes private warfare in Germany		

Protestant Revolution

1513	*The Prince*
1571	Battle of Lepanto
1603	*Hamlet*
1604	*Don Quixote*
1667	*Paradise Lost*

POETRY
Unit One

Unit 1: Poetry

About Dante and the Divine Comedy

During the mid-1200s, Florence was more of a city-state rather than just another city in Italy, with its own army, flag, ambassadors, coinage, etc. Times were turbulent as the upper nobility fought with lesser nobility and artisans, and the lower class triumphed due to increased trade and prosperity. In 1215 a young woman from one family was jilted by a member of another family, leading to the factions known as the Guelphs and the Ghibellines. The Ghibellines were from the old Imperial aristocracy, and the Guelphs were the burghers who in politics were aligned with the pope. There were numerous bloody battles between the two factions and the fate of Florence was caught in the middle. Dante Alighieri was born in 1265 and was only a year old when the matter was settled with the triumph of the Guelphs, the group to which his family belonged.

Only bits and pieces are known of Dante's life. He fought in the battle of Campaldino and the capture of Caprona when he was in his early 20s, and he enrolled in a guild of Apothecaries which led to political activities. He married a woman named Gemma. Florence enjoyed an uneasy peace for 30 years which was broken by another murder, leading to the formation of two parties known as the "Whites" and the "Blacks." Dante, a moderate "White," was elected a prior. In his position he banished his brother-in-law, Corso Donati, leader of the "Blacks" and his friend Guido Cavalcanti, leader of the "Whites." The "Blacks" sought to ally themselves with Pope Boniface VIII whose subsequent actions led to more murders, followed by "purge trials" and the conviction of Dante for graft and corruption. He voluntarily went into exile in 1302 and could not return under penalty of death.

The Guelphs and the Ghibellines as well as the Blacks and the Whites are mentioned often in the *Inferno* and *Purgatorio* and it is helpful to know that bit of background to aid in understanding the frequent mention of one party or the other.

From then on, Dante moved about Italy, spending time with a number of patrons. He died in Ravenna in 1321. *The Divine Comedy* was written between 1308 and 1320, during the time of his exile.

The Divine Comedy

The *Divine Comedy* is composed of three main parts, each known as a *cantica*. According to Archibald MacAllister in the Introduction, the first--*The Inferno*-- expresses the Power of the Father, the second, *Purgatorio*, expresses the Wisdom of the Son, and the third, *Paradiso*, expresses the Love of the Holy Spirit. Each *cantica* consists of 33 cantos, and together with the introductory canto equal 100 cantos which represent the perfect number, or the Unity of God. The structure was to represent Divine Creation and was known for its economy of words, with the choice of words being appropriate for the subject matter.

There are a number of images which are helpful to keep in mind as you read the *Divine Comedy*.
- The sun, known as "that planet," or "the light" represents God
- Virgil represents Human Reason who leads Dante through darkness toward the light
- Beatrice represents Divine Love
- Satan is an unholy Trinity which draws all that is evil to itself

There are four major themes in the work. They are:
- Dante's sinfulness which is not specifically defined but is known in the work as acedia, which is the spiritual failure in the pursuit of Good
- Various levels of understanding the work – narrative (travelogue), allegorical (the guilty conscience of the damned), moral, anagogical (a mystical interpretation of a word or text that detects allusions to heaven or the afterlife and the progress of the soul)
- Moral Universe which is a structure of values and physical laws which exist because of God's will
- Architectonics, or the structural correspondences among the three *cantica*

Each canto is made up of approximately 140 lines and describes the sinner and the punishment. The placement of each reveals Dante's judgment of the seriousness of the sin. This is a journey from sin to repentance and finally to redemption, with the main character being Dante. The work has hundreds of references to historical as well as fictitious figures and events. It was written in the vernacular Italian, and the purpose was to show that man has freedom of choice and is responsible for his moral gain or loss. It should be noted that Hell and Heaven are permanent states while Purgatory is a transitional state. Once a soul has reached Purgatory, its journey to Heaven is guaranteed, while there is no hope for the soul in Hell.

Note 1:
Dante refers to the souls in The Divine Comedy in various ways. Sometimes they are called "shades," other times "spirits," and other times "souls." The meaning is the same. Though he gives them bodily attributes, the reader should keep in mind that the suffering, while very real and in an apparent body, is actually spiritual. As Dante discovers in trying to touch or embrace some of these souls, there is no physical entity for him to grasp.

Note 2:
In Questions for Further Thought™ I have sought to pull enough from the end notes of each canto to aid the student in understanding the context of the poem, but I have refrained from pulling too much, less the beginning student lose heart. I encourage the student who is so inclined, to read the notes as his interest dictates. There are many notations about figures from the Bible, from mythology, and also from history which are of interest.

The Inferno
The Divine Comedy: Part 1
by Dante Alighieri
Translation: John Ciardi
New American Library

Dante begins his work by describing his age, but it is in poetic language. The student is encouraged to stop and figure out his age and the day the poem begins. Being under the sign of Aries represents creation and the dawn of the Easter season.

The *Inferno* opens with Dante in a dark wood, having lost his way. His path up the mountain is blocked and he is frightened. He encounters the ghost of Virgil whose task it is to lead him up the mountain and through Hell. Above the entrance to Hell is the admonition "Abandon all hope, you who enter here." That admonition sets the tone for the *Inferno*. It is a place of intense suffering and pain, utterly without hope of escape. Dante has placed both political and religious figures in Hell, and his placement reflects his judgment of the seriousness of the sins they committed while on earth. One can assume that he saw them as his enemies!

The primary theme of *Inferno* is God's justice. The punishments are related to the sins which were not repented of. It isn't that God is vindictive, but rather that the sinner has chosen his eternity by the choices he made in life. Dante experiences sympathy for many of the souls he meets, but he is corrected in this—it is not his place to question God's justice.

Note: Pay attention to the punishments. They are related to the sins.

Unit 1: Poetry

Canto I
The Dark Wood of Error

1. How old is Dante?
    As the poem opens he is "midway in our life's journey." The expected lifespan was three score and ten, so he is 35 years old.
2. What is the dark wood?
    The dark wood is the world of sin.
3. What had Dante done?
    He had left the straight road of virtue.
4. What gave Dante courage?
    He saw the rays of the sun over a little hill.
5. What is the first beast he encounters, and what does it symbolize?
    He encounters a spotted leopard, which symbolizes malice and fraud.
6. What is the second beast he encounters, and what does it symbolize?
    The second beast is a lion, symbolizing pride and ambition.
7. What is the third beast he encounters and what does it symbolize?
    The third beast is a she-wolf, symbolizing greed and lust.
8. Who was the son of Anchises?
    His son was Aeneas.
9. Whom does Dante meet?
    He meets the poet Virgil who had written the *Aeneid*.
10. Who was Dante's inspiration as a poet?
    Virgil was his inspiration.
11. What does Virgil tell Dante?
    He tells him that he must take another course, because the one he is on will only lead to damnation.
12. What does Virgil propose?
    He proposes that he lead Dante through Hell, which he must go through before he can find salvation and then through Purgatory.
13. What does he promise him if he wants to climb even higher?
    He promises him a worthier spirit to guide him.
14. Why can't Virgil lead him to the "blessed choir?"
    He rebelled against God's law.

Question for Further Thought

What is Christian teaching on salvation, and would this explain why Virgil could not enter Heaven?
    Christian teaching is that salvation comes through Christ alone. Virgil lived before the time of Christ, so he could not enter Heaven.

Canto II
The Descent

1. Whom does Dante invoke?
    He invokes the Muses.
2. Who was the father of Sylvius?
    Aeneas was his father.
3. What was Rome ordained for?

Unit 1: Poetry

       Rome was ordained to house the seat of the Catholic Church.
4. What does he say is the door to eternal life?
   Faith is the door.
5. What does Virgil tell Dante he suffered from?
   Virgil says he suffered from cowardice.
6. Why does Virgil go to Dante?
   He goes to Dante because he had been asked to go by Beatrice, a woman who loved Dante and feared that he would be lost forever if he were not led away from his sin.
7. Who sent Beatrice to Virgil?
   The Virgin Mary, St. Lucy and Rachel sent her.
8. What does Beatrice say about fear?
   She says that one need only fear that which can harm him.

Canto III
The Opportunists

(The Vestibule of Hell)
1. What does the sign on the gate indicate?
   The sign on the gate indicates that they are entering Hell.
2. How do you know?
   The sign says to abandon hope, all who enter here.
3. Who made Hell?
   Hell was made by a Divine Architect.
4. How is the Creator described?
   The Creator is all powerful, all loving and possesses ultimate intellect.
5. When was Hell created?
   It was created before man, because "only those elements time cannot wear were made before me…"
6. What kind of souls do Dante and Virgil first encounter?
   They encounter the souls of those who stood for nothing, who lived for themselves.
7. What is their fate?
   They are doomed to wander in the darkness, forgotten and envious of everybody else.
8. What does Charon say to Dante?
   He tells him to go away, because he is still alive and cannot be taken across Acheron.
9. What have the souls waiting to cross lost?
   They have lost the fear of God.
10. What happens to the fear of Hell in those who are damned?
    Their fear turns to desire.
11. What happens to Dante?
    He swoons.

Questions for Further Thought

A. Who was Pope Celestine V?
   He was pope in 1294. Though he was a holy man, in fear for his soul he abandoned the Papacy. The priest who had advised him became Pope Boniface VIII, and he became the symbol of Church corruption to Dante.
B. What did the King of the Dead in the dead mountain in Tolkien's *Return of the King*, say to Aragorn when he, Legolas and Gimli entered the paths of the dead?
   He said "this path was made by those who are dead, and the dead keep it. The dead do not suffer the living to pass."

Canto IV
The Virtuous Pagans

(Circle 1: Limbo)
1. When Dante awoke from his swoon, where was he?
    He was on the abyss of Hell.
2. How does Virgil explain his pale appearance?
    He attributes it to the pity he feels for those in Hell.
3. What sounds do they hear in the first circle?
    They hear untormented sighs of sadness.
4. Who is in the first circle?
    In the first circle are those sinless people born before the time of Christ.
5. How do they suffer?
    They suffer by living in desire but without hope.
6. How does Dante feel when he sees these souls?
    He feels a weight upon his heart.
7. Whom had "a Mighty One" (Christ) taken from this place?
    He had taken Adam, Abel, Noah, Moses, Abraham, David, Jacob, Rachel and many others.
8. Whom do they meet?
    They meet Homer, Horace, Ovid and Lucan.
9. What do they all possess?
    They all possess wisdom.
10. What do we learn about Virgil?
    We learn that he was here as well.
11. How do we know that?
    The other poets greet him by saying "honor the Prince of Poets; the soul and glory that goes from us returns…"
12. How do they receive Dante?
    They receive him by honoring him as one of their own number: the sixth.
13. Who are some of the others they see here?
    They see heroes, heroines, philosophers, scientists and commentators: Electra, Hector, Aeneas, Caesar, Camilla, King Latinus, Lavinia, Brutus (who drove Tarquin from power), Lucretia, Aristotle, Socrates, Plato, Cicero, Seneca, Euclid and Hippocrates.

Question for Further Thought

What might the Citadel represent?
    The Citadel represents philosophy as exemplified by the pagan Greeks and Romans. They had the light of human reason but did not have the light of God, thus, the Citadel was a light in the darkness of Hell. The brook seems to separate those in the Citadel from the rest in Hell.

Word to Know:

wraith: ghost, spirit, phantom particularly the spectral image of a person in his exact likeness

Unit 1: Poetry

Canto V
The Carnal
The Sins of the She-Wolf, Incontinence

(Circle 2)
1. What sound is heard as they enter the second circle?
    They hear moaning.
2. Who guards this circle?
    Minos guards it and upon examining each soul, declares the sentence.
3. Who is in the second circle?
    In the second circle are those who had abandoned reason and sinned in the flesh—those who did not control their carnal lusts.
4. What is their punishment?
    They are tossed about in the winds.
5. Who are some of the souls here?
    In this second ring are Dido, Cleopatra, Helen, Achilles, Paris, Tristan, Paolo and Francesca.
6. What does Dante feel upon seeing these damned lovers?
    He feels pity and confusion.
7. What led Francesca and her lover to Hell?
    They were reading the story of Lancelot and were caught up in passion by what they read.
8. How did they die?
    They were murdered by a relative.
9. How does Dante respond to their story?
    He weeps with pity, and then he swoons again.

Questions for Further Thought

A. How serious did Dante think sexual sin was? How do we know?
    Sexual sin, while sufficient to be the cause of damnation, was the least serious of the sins leading one to Hell, because it was one of the easiest for man to fall into. We know that because of his placement of these sinners near the "top" of Hell, rather than near the bottom or the pit of Hell.
B. How do we know that Francesca and Paolo were murdered by a kinsman?
    We know they were murdered by a kinsman because Dante says "Caïna waits for him who took our lives." Caïna is the part of Hell reserved for those who commit treachery against their kin.

Canto VI
The Gluttons

(Circle 3)
1. What conditions exist in the third ring?
    In the third ring are perpetual frozen rain, hail, dirty water, black snow, putrid air and slush.
2. Who guards the entrance?
    Cerberus, the three-headed dog guards the entrance.
3. Who recognizes Dante?
    A fellow-citizen from Florence named Ciacco recognizes and calls to him.
4. What was the sin of those in the third circle?
    Those in the third circle were gluttons.
5. What ability do the people in this ring have?
    They have the ability to tell the future.

6. What future does Ciacco see for Florence?
   He predicts war between the Blacks and the Whites in which the Whites will initially win, but within two years the Blacks will rise and oppress the Whites.
7. How does Dante feel?
   His soul is weighed down by the agony of the souls here, and he is full of tears.
8. What does Ciacco ask of Dante?
   He asks to be remembered to his friends.
9. What does Virgil tell Dante about the time after the final judgment?
   He tells him that the torments will be greater and so will the pleasure.
10. Whom do they meet as they are leaving?
    They meet Plutus, the god of wealth.

Canto VII

The Hoarders and the Wasters, the Wrathful and the Sullen

(Circles 4 and 5)
1. How does Virgil comfort Dante?
   He tells him that Plutus cannot harm him nor can he hinder his progress on his journey.
2. What are the souls doing here?
   They are rolling weights back and forth while howling at each other.
3. How does Dante feel?
   His heart contracts with pain.
4. What sinners are here?
   In this fourth circle are avaricious priests, popes and cardinals who either hoarded or squandered what they had.
5. Why is it impossible to discern who they are?
   In life these sinners did not discern, now they are indistinct.
6. What does Virgil tell Dante about Fortune?
   Some people have more of it, and some have less, but the balance is always shifting.
7. What is the Styx?
   The Styx is a vaporous, dark swampland.
8. Who is mired in the swamp?
   Those who were overcome with anger and hate are mired here.
9. What causes the bubbling water?
   It is caused by the sighs of the sullen souls who inhabit it.

Word to Know:

tonsure: ceremonial shaving of the head of a monk, sometimes in the form of a cross

Questions for Further Thought

A. What is the time of day as they cross over to circle 5?
   It is past midnight of Good Friday.
B. Does Dante express pity for the sullen souls?
   No. For the first time he does not indicate pity for those he sees.

Unit 1: Poetry

Canto VIII
The Wrathful, Phylegyas, The Fallen Angels

(Circle 5: Styx, Circle 6: Dis)
1. Who is the boatman?
    The boatman is Phylegyas.
2. What does Virgil tell him?
    He tells him that he is to take them to the other side of the swamp.
3. Why didn't the boat continue to skim across the top of the water?
    It now carried Dante's living weight.
4. When one of the shades speaks to Dante, how does he respond?
    Dante responds with contempt for him and praises God that he is dragged back down into the mire.
5. Who is this man?
    He is Filippo Argento, an arrogant soul, whom Dante knew.
6. How does Virgil describe Dis?
    He calls it "Hell's metropolis."
7. What is seen for the first time in Hell here in Dis?
    Fire is seen for the first time.
8. What structures does Dante see?
    He sees mosques made of iron.
9. What did they have to cross to get to Dis?
    They had to cross a moat.
10. Who is above the gates?
    The spirits purged from Heaven (the fallen angels) are there.
11. What do the condemned souls demand?
    They demand that Virgil enter without Dante.
12. How does Dante feel?
    He feels frightened and hopeless about returning to the world.
13. Is Virgil allowed to enter?
    No he is not.
14. Will they enter, and how do you know?
    They will, because they see somebody coming who needs no guide, "and at his touch all gates must spring aside."

Questions for Further Thought

A. Who was Filippo Argenti?
    He was a political enemy of Dante. Dante used this portrayal of him as an insult to his family. Dante's enemies appear in various circles of Hell.
B. Why would Dante use mosques as the buildings in Hell?
    The mosques represent Islam which was seen as a heretical sect, and therefore, an enemy of the Church.

Canto IX
The Heretics

(Circle 6)
1. What is Dante feeling as they wait for help?
    He is feeling fear.
2. What does Virgil tell Dante in answer to his question about whether or not those from the first ring of Hell ever come

this far down?
   He tells him that once before he (Virgil) had crossed through Hell and returned to the first ledge.
3. What does Dante see in the tower?
   He sees three Furies.
4. Why did Virgil tell Dante to turn and close his eyes?
   He feared that if the Gorgon appeared and he saw her she would turn him to stone.
5. Who comes through the smoke toward them?
   A Messenger from God's Throne, an angel, comes to guide them.
6. What does Dante see as they follow the angel?
   He sees fields of open tombs, each tomb surrounded by flames.
7. Who are the suffering souls here?
   They are heretics.
8. What direction did they leave this area?
   They bore right.

Questions for Further Thought

A. What were the Furies and where have they appeared in ancient literature?
   The Furies were malignant female spirits whose purpose was to hound and torment those people who had violated the conventions of the society such as murdering kin or desecrating temples. They were prominent in the story of Orestes.
B. What did the heretics deny?
   The heretics denied the existence of God, and thus immortality. Their punishment reflected dead souls.

Canto X

1. What does Dante request?
   He asks to see who is in the tombs.
2. What does Virgil tell Dante about the tombs?
   He tells him that after the final judgment all the souls will return to these tombs with their bodies, and the tombs will be sealed.
3. Who rises from the flames?
   Farinata, a bitter enemy from Tuscany (a Ghibelline), rises up to speak.
4. What explanation does Dante give Guido about why his son is not with him?
   He says that perhaps Guido's son scorned Virgil (and human reason).
5. What observation does Dante make?
   He observes that the dead here can see the future but do not know what is happening in the present.
6. Why are the shades here able to see the future?
   They are able to see the future because God's light shines on them.
7. What will the Sweet Lady reveal to Dante?
   She will reveal the journey of his life.

Question for Further Thought

Who were the Epicureans?
   The Epicureans followed the teachings of Epicurus who taught that the good life was attained by reliance on the senses, not in a belief in a supernatural being. They held that pleasure, or the absence of pain, was the only good.

Unit 1: Poetry

Canto XI

1. How many circles are below where they are now standing?
    There are three smaller circles.
2. What sin is most hated by God?
    Malice, the sin which wills to injure others, is most hated by God.
3. Why is fraud particularly offensive to God?
    Fraud is particularly offensive because only men engage in it.
4. Who are in the lowest of the next three circles?
    In the lowest circle are those who engaged in fraud.
5. To whom is violence done?
    Violence is done to God, self and our neighbor.
6. Who is in the first circle?
    Murderers, robbers and plunderers are there.
7. Who is in the second circle?
    The suicides, and those who waste their own things are there.
8. Who is in the third circle?
    In the third circle are those who blaspheme or deny God and His creation.
9. Who is in the smallest circle?
    In the smallest circle are those who betray others, breaking the bond of love. These would be simoniacs, sycophants, hypocrites, sorcerers, pimps and cheats, among others.
10. Who is at the very center?
    At the very center are the traitors.
11. What does Dante ask about the incontinent?
    He asks why they are not punished here in the fire.
12. How does Virgil respond?
    He says that incontinence offends God less than malice and bestiality.
13. What does Virgil say about usury?
    He says it prevents one from advancing in life, thus interfering with God's plan.

Word to Know:

simoniac: one who sells spiritual things such as relics, sacraments, church offices, etc.

Question for Further Thought

What is Dante referring to when he talks about the wheel, the Wain over Taurus, and the Fish?
    He is talking about the time of day and where they are in relation to the signs of the Zodiac. It is now about two hours before dawn, or 4:00 in the morning of Holy Saturday.

Canto XII
The Violent Against Neighbors
The Sins of the Lion, Violence and Bestiality

(Circle 7: Round 1)
1. Who guards the first round of Circle 7?
    The Minotaur guards it.
2. Why does the ground beneath Dante shift?
    It shifts because of his living weight.

3. Who was He "who took the souls from Limbo?"
    He was Christ.
4. What is the punishment for those who committed violence against others?
    They are damned to an existence in boiling blood.
5. What do the Centaurs do?
    They patrol the top of this pit and shoot arrows at any who try to rise above the boiling blood.
6. What does Chiron notice about Dante?
    He notices that what he touches moves.
7. Why does Dante need help across the ford?
    He has to be carried because he is alive and does not float through the air like the spirits.
8. Who are some of the violent who are punished here?
    Being punished here are Alexander the Great, Dionysius, Azzolino (a Ghibelline tyrant), Attila, among others.
9. What does the Centaur reveal to Dante and Virgil?
    He reveals that even in the same part of Hell, the punishments vary in degree. For instance, some of the violent damned boil in blood up to their throats, while others only up to their ankles.

Canto XIII
The Violent Against Themselves

(Circle 7: Round 2)
1. From the boiling river of blood, where do they go next?
    They go to a pathless wood where the foliage is black instead of green.
2. Who inhabits the wood?
    The Harpies, bird-like creatures with human faces, inhabit the wood.
3. Why does Virgil encourage Dante to break off a twig?
    He encourages him to do so because Dante would not have believed him if he told him that the trees were souls, as Dante had not previously believed what Virgil had written.
4. How does Dante feel when he realizes he has broken part of a spirit in the twig?
    He feels fear.
5. Why does Virgil want to know the name of the soul?
    He wants to make amends for having had Dante break off the twig.
6. What will Dante do?
    He will seek to restore the good name of the soul.
7. What does this soul blame his fate on?
    He blames it on the envy people had toward him because he shared confidences with Frederick.
8. How does Dante feel upon hearing the story?
    His heart is choked with compassion.
9. How do the souls of suicides get to this circle?
    They are assigned here by Minos and take root wherever they fall. Then they are constantly fed upon by the Harpies.
10. Why will these souls not exist in their bodies after the final judgment?
    They threw away their bodies through suicide and will not have them here.

Canto XIV
The Violent Against God, Nature, and Art

(Circle 7: Round 3)
1. How did Dante react to the Florentine's tale in the last canto?
    He was moved to tears.

Unit 1: Poetry

2. What is the land like in round three?
    It is a wasteland of burning sand with flakes of flame falling from above.
3. In what position are the condemned?
    Some are supine, some are squatting, and others are just roaming.
4. What is the sin of the souls here?
    Their sin is pride, or scorning of God.
5. What are the tears of the giant which flow into Acheron, Phlegethon and Styx?
    They are the sins of the world that lead to Hell.
6. Why have they not come to Lethe?
    Lethe is the place where the souls are cleansed because they have repented. Therefore, it is outside of Hell.

Words to Know:

supine: lying on the back, face up

rill: rivulet, brook

Question for Further Thought

Can you conjecture what the meaning of the ancient giant, the Old Man of Crete might be?
    According to the notes at the end of the canto, the metals each represent an age of man, each deteriorating from the Age of Innocence represented by the gold head. The giant's shoulder faces Egypt (Damietta, representing the past) and he looks toward Rome (the future). Dante represents the Holy Roman Empire with the Age of Iron and the Roman Catholic Church as the foot of terra cotta.

Canto XV
The Violent Against Nature

1. Why can't Dante stop to visit in this round?
    If he stops he will be stuck here for 100 years in the intense heat.
2. Who is punished in this place?
    Sodomites (homosexuals) are punished here.
3. What does Brunetto mean when he tells Dante he will walk at his hem?
    Dante is walking on a ridge above the sands where Brunetto is, so Brunetto's head is at the level of Dante's ankles (more or less).
4. How does Dante answer Brunetto's shade as to why he is here?
    He tells him that he had gone astray and was rescued by Virgil.
5. What does Brunetto advise Dante to do?
    He advises him to continue his work.

Note about Fiesole:
Fiesole was an ancient city which had sided with Catiline in his war with Julius Caesar. Caesar had destroyed the city and established Florence, settling both Romans and Fiesolans there. The Romans as the aristocracy were always at odds with the rest. These were yet more factions which plagued Florence during her long history. The scorn shown by Dante reflects the fact that he traced his lineage to the Romans.

6. What does Brunetto predict?
    He predicts that Dante will be maligned because of the good that he does by those who are envious and proud.

7. How does Dante feel about Brunetto?

    Dante admires him and seems to love him. He had learned much about his art from him and feels grateful to him.
8. How will Brunetto be remembered?

    He will be remembered by his book of prose called *The Book of Treasure*.

Canto XVI
The Violent Against Nature and Art

1. What does the waterfall signal?

    It signals the proximity of the next circle, number 8.
2. What did the shades recognize about Dante?

    They recognized his Florentine dress.
3. What does Virgil tell Dante about these souls?

    He tells him to do as they ask because respect is due them.
4. What has Borsieri reported?

    He has reported that courtesy and valor have disappeared from Florence.
5. What does Dante confirm?

    He confirms that new people and quick wealth have caused pride and excess.
6. What signal does Virgil use to get to the next level?

    He throws Dante's waist cord down the precipice and a monstrous shape rises from the pit.

Canto XVII
The Violent Against Art; Geryon

(The Sins of the Leopard, Fraud and Malice)
1. What does the beast Geryon represent?

    He represents fraud.
2. What is his appearance like?

    He has an innocent face and the body of a reptile, with paws, hairy armpits, bright knots and subtle circlets on his body and a forked tail.
3. What does Virgil instruct Dante to do?

    He instructs him to go see who the shades are here while he negotiates passage to the next circle.
4. How are the shades here identified?

    They have pouches hanging around their necks which have their coats of arms.
5. What sin have these shades committed?

    They have committed the sin of usury.
6. How does Dante react when Virgil tells him to mount the beast?

    He trembles with fright; then he feels shame.

Note:
Questions 2-4 in Canto XI explain why frauds are in this circle.

Word to Know:

usury: the practice of lending money at an exorbitant rate of interest

Unit 1: Poetry

Canto XVIII
The Fraudulent and Malicious, The Panderers and Seducers, The Flatterers

(Circle 8 (Malebolge) Bolgiae 1 and 2)
1. How does Dante describe this Circle?
    He calls it a sloping ground of stone forming a giant pit, with ten descending troughs connected by narrow cliffs.
2. What is the meaning of *malebolge*?
    It means evil pouches.
3. What do these stone pouches surround?
    They surround the pit of Hell.
4. What are these souls doing?
    They are moving quickly, being driven by horned demons with lashes.
5. What sinners are here?
    Here are the souls of panderers—people who traded in women, seducers and deceivers and flatterers.
6. What famous figure is here?
    Jason, who stole the Golden Fleece, is here.
7. Going the next step lower to *bolgia* 2, what sinners does Dante find and in what condition?
    He finds those who flattered for personal gain now living in excrement.

Word to Know:

pander: cater to or profit from the weaknesses of others, such as procuring clients for prostitutes, etc.

Questions for Further Thought

A. Notice that the spirit which Dante sees in this *bolgia* "thought to hide his face." How is this different from the spirits Dante has encountered up to this point?
    The spirits before have asked to be remembered, now it seems they wish to be forgotten.
B. What does Venedico Caccianemico imply in talking to Dante?
    He implies that Bologna is a city of panderers and that there are presently more Bolognese in Hell than living.
C. Is there a difference in Dante's choice of words as he moves closer to the pit of Hell?
    Yes. His language is less refined and vulgar at times.

Canto XIX
The Simoniacs

(Circle 8: Bolgia 3)
1. What does Dante express to Sovereign Wisdom?
    He acknowledges the justice of Wisdom in judging and assigning punishment.
2. How are the simoniacs being punished?
    Their heads are down in stone holes the size of Baptismal fonts, their legs sticking out and twitching, and the soles of their feet burning.
3. Whom does Dante notice twitching more than the others and who seems to be in a hotter fire?
    He notices a pope.
4. When he speaks to the pope, what does the spirit say, and what does that imply?
    The spirit asks if it is Boniface (another pope) who is there, implying that he too was a simoniac.
5. What will the arrival of Boniface mean for this pope?
    It will mean he will leave this stone hole and descend into the pit.

6. How do we know he is a pope?
   We know he is a pope by the "Great Mantle" which hung upon him.
7. What question does Dante ask of the pope?
   He asks if Jesus had required any payment by Peter before making him pope.
8. What is Dante's attitude toward these popes?
   He believes they are justly punished.
9. How does he feel about the Papacy?
   He feels reverence for it.
10. How does Virgil react to Dante's words toward the pope?
    He approves.
11. What does Dante say about Constantine?
    He says that when he brought his wealth to the Church, evil entered in.

Canto XX
The Fortune Tellers and Diviners

(Circle 8: Bolgia 4)

1. How does Dante refer to this first Canticle?
   He calls it the Canticle of Pain.
2. What is the appearance of the souls here?
   Their faces are reversed on the necks so that they stare backwards, unable to see forward, and their tears flow down their backs.
3. How does Dante react?
   He weeps.
4. Why does Virgil rebuke Dante?
   He rebukes him for weeping at the punishment instead of the sins of augury and for questioning the judgment of God.
5. What does Virgil say about the founding of his city of Mantua?
   He says that when Manto settled there she no longer practiced augury. He wants Dante to reveal that fact in his writing in order to wipe away the image of Mantua as a city of augury.

Word to Know:

augury: the art of telling the future by reading signs or omens; fortune-telling

Questions for Further Thought

A. What might Dante be referring to when he talks about the days when there were so few males in Greece that even the cradles were empty of sons?
   He is referring to the period when the Greeks were away fighting at Troy.
B. What time of day is it?
   It is the morning of Holy Saturday, 1300 A.D.

Canto XXI
The Grafters

(Circle 8: Bolgia 5)
1. How is this *bolgia* described?
    It is a sink of boiling pitch which coats the bank with "gluey mire."
2. What sin had the souls here committed?
    They had abused their positions to enrich themselves through dishonest dealings.
3. Why are the souls kept below the surface of the pitch?
    They are below the surface and unseen because in life their dirty dealings were done in secret.
4. Why does Virgil emphasize to Dante that he had best not be seen by the demons until Virgil has secured safe passage for them?
    He says that because Dante had been accused of graft and was banished on pain of death.
5. How does Dante feel in the presence of the many demons?
    He feels fear and stays very close to Virgil for protection.
6. What does Dante refer to when he says "in just five hours it will be, since the bridge fell, a thousand two hundred sixty-six years and a day; that was the time the big quake shook all Hell."
    He is referring to the earthquake that occurred when Christ died.
7. What does Malacoda tell them when they notice that the bridge is broken?
    He tells them that there will be another cliff beyond by which they can cross.
8. What are some of the names of the demons here?
    Some of the names are Grizzly, Hellken, Deaddog, Grafter, Pigtust and Catclaw.

Question for Further Thought

When Dante refers to the time "in just five hours…" what time of day will it be and what time of day is it now?
    Dante believed Christ died at 12 noon, so it will be noon on Holy Saturday, meaning it is now 7:00 in the morning. (Most Christians believe Christ died at 3 P.M.)

Canto XXII

1. What happens to one of the souls who dares rise up out of the pitch?
    He is hooked by a demon and savagely clawed.
2. What does Dante ask the soul from Navarre?
    He asks if there are any souls here from Italy.
3. What does the Navarrese soul account for?
    He accounts for his dishonest dealing. This is ironic because in life, his dealings were hidden.
4. What happens as the fiends are fighting?
    The poor soul from Navarre escapes back into the boiling pitch.

Word to Know:

graft: to acquire money by unfair or dishonest means

Canto XXIII
The Hypocrites

(Circle 8: Bolgia 6)
1. What does Dante fear?
    He fears the rage of the demons from whom he and Virgil have just escaped.
2. What does Virgil admit?
    He admits that he, too, has been afraid.
3. How does Virgil treat Dante?
    Virgil treats him as a mother protecting her child.
4. Why can the demons not pursue them to the next pit?
    They cannot leave their assigned place in Hell.
5. How are the souls in *bolgia* 6 dressed?
    They are dressed as monks in dazzling cloaks which are heavy like lead, symbolizing the weight of the sin of hypocrisy they carry.

Note:
The Jovial Friars were an order of monks from Bologna, and their mission was to serve as peacemakers, keep order and protect the weak. They became lax in the observance of the rule of their order and were suppressed by a Papal decree.

6. Whom does Dante see nailed to the ground?
    He sees Caiaphas.
7. Who else is here?
    The father-in-law (Annas) of Caiaphas and other members of the council which condemned Christ to death.
8. When they inquire about how to move on, what are they told?
    They are told that the bridge is broken, but they can climb through the ruins.
9. Why is Virgil annoyed?
    He realizes that Malacoda had lied to him about the bridge.
10. What does the Friar tell Dante and Virgil about the Devil?
    He tells them that he had heard that he is a liar and the father of lies.

Question for Further Thought

What is the significance of Caiaphas who "must feel the weight of all through all eternity?"
    Caiaphas had decreed that it was better for Christ to die for all the people than for the nation to perish, so he is here feeling the weight of all who pass.

Canto XXIV
The Thieves

(Circle 8: Bolgia 7)
1. How does Virgil help Dante pass to the next *bolgia*?
    He lifts him up and tells him to test the slab he places him on to see if it will hold his weight.
2. What physical state does Dante find himself in?
    He is physically exhausted by the climb and wants to rest.
3. What advise does Virgil give Dante?
    He tells him to get up on his feet, control his feet and "call upon the strength of soul that wins all battles…"

Unit 1: Poetry

4. What is the condition of the souls in this *bolgia*?
    The souls are naked, their hands are bound behind their backs by serpents which are knotted between their legs. The souls are bitten by the serpents, burn up and turn to ash, and then are reborn for continuous torture in this manner.
5. What sin had Vanni Fucci committed?
    He had stolen Church treasure from the sacristy and allowed others to be blamed for the crime.
6. What does Vanni Fucci predict?
    He predicts that the Blacks and the Whites (see introduction) will battle again and the Whites will lose. His intention is to cause Dante grief.

Canto XXV

1. What does the thief do as this canto opens?
    The thief curses God.
2. What happens to the thief?
    He is punished for his blasphemy by the serpents and centaur.
3. What happens to a soul in this *bolgia*?
    The lizard attacks the soul of a human thief and transforms that thief into a reptile. After this happens, the "new" lizard attacks another human form and transforms that one. It is fitting that here in Hell, the souls who were thieves on earth have to steal their very form. The cycle is endless from man to reptile and back again.

Canto XXVI
The Evil Counselors

(Circle 8: Bolgia 8)
1. How does Dante feel at seeing so many of Florence's citizens here?
    He feels shame for his city.
2. What does Dante see as he approaches the next *bolgia*?
    He sees flames which contain the souls of the evil counselors.
3. What famous souls are here?
    Ulysses (Odysseus) and Diomede are here.
4. Why are they here?
    They are here because they masterminded the Trojan Horse.
5. Why does Virgil say Ulysses and Diomede would scorn Dante's speech?
    They were Greeks and would scorn his more "Roman" speech.
6. What does Ulysses acknowledge about his life?
    He acknowledges his lust for worldly experience as being stronger than the joy of being with his family.
7. What does Ulysses relate?
    He relates the experiences of his journeys.
8. How did Ulysses die?
    He went down with his sinking ship.

Canto XXVII

1. When does Ulysses' spirit depart?
    It departs when Virgil dismisses it.
2. What does the next flame/spirit ask Dante?
    He asks him if there is peace in his home of Romagna.

3. What is Dante's answer?
   He answers that Romagna is perpetually at war, even though there was no open conflict when he recently left.
4. Why is the spirit willing to speak?
   He is willing to speak because he believes nobody will return to the world to tell the truth.
5. What does the spirit relate?
   He relates the story of how Boniface VIII made war on his own Christian people and corrupted this man who had become a monk.
6. What persuasion did the pope use to gain his counsel?
   He said that he held the Keys to Heaven and would absolve him in advance of his sin.
7. Who came to meet his soul when he died?
   St. Francis came to meet him.
8. Who intervened and why?
   A Black Angel intervened because of his complicity with Boniface in the destruction of Palestrina and his failure to repent before death.

Canto XXVIII
The Sowers of Discord

(Circle 8: Bolgia 9)
1. What does Dante introduce at length?
   He introduces the idea of the terrible mutilations the souls in the 9th *bolgia* suffer.
2. What does Virgil say about Livy?
   He says that Livy's reporting of the spoil of the golden rings (taken by Hannibal at Cannae) is true.
3. Which soul does Dante see with his entrails hanging out?
   He sees Mohammed.
4. What sin had these souls committed?
   They had sown discord, scandal and schism.
5. What is the punishment for these who have sown discord?
   They are cut up by the demon, and as they walk around the pit their wounds heal in time to be cut up again when they come back to where they started.
6. What does Pier da Medicina request?
   He requests that he be remembered and that Guido and Angiolello be warned of coming treachery.
7. Whom else does Dante meet?
   He meets the tribune Curio who had advised Caesar to cross the Rubicon, thus starting the Roman Civil War.
8. What does Dante see next?
   He sees a body carrying its own head by the hair.
9. Who is this wretched soul?
   He is Bertrand de Born, who had caused division between a king and his son.

Canto XXIX
The Falsifiers
Class I, Alchemists

(Circle 8: Bolgia 10)
1. How had Dante felt in the last *bolgia* where the sowers of discord were?
   He wanted to stay and weep.
2. What does Virgil say to him?
   He asks him why he can't pull himself away from there and then tells him they still have much to see in very little

Unit 1: Poetry

       time. The next valley is 22 miles around and is not yet the end.
3. Whom does Dante think he saw there?
   He thinks he saw a kinsman there, and he mourns for him.
4. Why does Dante feel shame?
   The violent death of his kinsman was never avenged, so that has brought shame on the family.
5. To entice the two souls to speak, what does Dante say to them?
   He says "so may the memory of your names and actions not die forever from the minds of men…"
6. What does Capocchio say about his skill?
   He was such a good alchemist that he mimicked nature.

QUESTIONS FOR FURTHER THOUGHT

A. If the moon is under their feet, what time is it now?
   It is noon on Holy Saturday, because the sun would be overhead.
B. What might be a "companion" art to alchemy which would merit burning at the stake?
   Witchcraft would be a companion art, and both were punished by burning at the stake.
C. How does the punishment of the falsifiers here relate to their sins on earth?
   They corrupted others by their deceptions while they lived, and here they are corrupted by loathsome conditions and by each other without relief.

WORD TO KNOW:

alchemy: any apparently magical process of changing ordinary materials into something valuable, such as metal to gold

CANTO XXX
The Falsifiers
The Remaining Three Classes: Evil Impersonators, Counterfeiters, False Witnesses

(Circle 8: Bolgia 10)
1. What sin had the shade who ran with Myrrha committed?
   He had disguised himself as a dying man in order to dictate a false will so that he would benefit from the death.
2. What had Master Adam done?
   He had counterfeited money.
3. What would he like to see?
   He would like to see his partners-in-crime here with him.
4. Who charged Joseph with wrongdoing?
   Potiphar's wife, as told in *Genesis* 39:6-23, charged Joseph with trying to commit adultery with her. Her sin, in addition to trying to seduce him, was to lie (bear false witness against him), and for that sin she is in this pit.
5. What sin had Sinon committed?
   He had convinced the Trojans to take the Horse into Troy, and that brought about the end of Troy.
6. Why does Dante grieve?
   Virgil has scolded him for staring at the souls who are fighting with each other.
7. How does Virgil respond to Dante's shame?
   He forgives him and tells him that less shame would have cancelled out a greater sin.
8. Why does Virgil want to discourage Dante from getting too involved in the quarreling of the souls?
   He says that wishing to hear these things is degrading.

Questions for Further Thought

A. What could you likened the fascination with other's quarrels to?
      You could liken it to the enjoyment of gossip or defamation of another's character. Virgil is trying to instruct
      Dante throughout this journey by showing him the consequences of every class of sin imaginable.
B. What is the irony of Master Adam's punishment—to be full of dropsy but perpetually thirsty?
      Dropsy is a condition in which the body is full of fluid; so he was full of fluid but could not satisfy his thirst.

Canto XXXI
The Giants

(The Central Pit of Malebolge)
1. What are the "towers" that Dante sees?
      They are giants, and they guard the pit of Hell.
2. Why are giants more fearful than elephants or whales?
      Giants are more fearful because of their intelligence and their evil wills.
3. Who is the first giant Dante sees?
      He is Nimrod, the one who built the Tower of Babel.
4. What is the irony of Nimrod's speech?
      The irony is that nobody understands it.
5. Ephialtes had warred against the Olympian gods. What is his punishment?
      He stands in Hell with his arms and hands bound.
6. How do Dante and Virgil get down into the pit?
      The giant Antaeus sets them down into it.
7. How does Virgil describe Cocytus, the pit of Hell?
      He calls it "the bottom of all guilt."
8. How does Virgil convince Antaeus to help them?
      He tells him that Dante can preserve good memory of him because he still lives.
9. Whom do they see in the pit and what is it like there?
      They see Judas and Lucifer, and it is freezing and icy.

Question for Further Thought

Are you surprised that it is freezing at the pit of Hell? What did you expect?
      Answers will vary.

Canto XXXII
Compound Fraud
The Treacherous to Kin, The Treacherous to Country

(Circle 9: Cocytus, Round 1: Caïna, Round 2: Antenora)
1. Whom does Dante call upon to help him describe the pit of Hell?
      He calls on those "Ladies of the Heavenly Spring" who are known as the Muses.
2. How does Dante describe the pit of Hell?
      It is a lake frozen like glass, and it is very thick.
3. What is the punishment for the souls here?
      They are caught in the frozen lake with their teeth chattering, eyes tearing and their heads bent.
4. What is the significance of the name Caïna?

Unit 1: Poetry

It is named for Cain, who slew his brother Abel, thus committing treachery to a kinsman.
5. What does Dante demand of the soul whom he kicks?
    He demands to know his name, but the soul will not reveal it.
6. What does Dante do?
    He grabs him by the hair and yanks it out.
7. What does he observe in seeing two souls frozen in the same hole?
    He observes that one is eating the other's neck.

Canto XXXIII
Compound Fraud
The Treacherous to Country, the Treacherous to Guests and Hosts

(Circle 9: Cocytus, Round 2: Antenora, Round 3: Ptolomea)
1. Why does the soul who is gnawing at the other's neck agree to speak to Dante?
    He hopes to reveal the other's sin.
2. Who are the two souls?
    One is Count Ugolino, and the one he is gnawing at is Archbishop Ruggieri.
3. What story does the Count relate?
    He had trusted the Archbishop who then turned on him and had him imprisoned with his four sons. They were starved to death in a tower, one by one.
4. What does Dante say about the Count's sons?
    He says they were innocent.
5. What is the significance of the name Antenora?
    It is named for Antenor, who betrayed Troy to the Greeks.
6. What is the irony of the Archbishop being gnawed by Ugolino?
    He starved Ugolino and his sons to death and is doomed to be food for Ugolino in death.
7. What consolation do the weeping souls in the next round lack?
    Due to their supine position, their tears freeze and cannot be shed.
8. What does Friar Alberigo tell Dante about the soul?
    He tells him that as soon as one betrays another, his soul is snatched away to Hell and inhabited by a demon, even though the body may go on living.
9. Does Dante feel pity for these souls?
    No he does not, saying "to be rude to him was courtesy."
10. What is the significance of the name Ptolomea?
    It is named for Ptolomey, whose story is told in *Maccabees* (1 Mac:14-7). He invited his father-in-law and his sons to a banquet, and then murdered them all, thus betraying hospitality by harming his guests.

Questions for Further Thought

A. In telling the story of Ugolino Dante shows pity. Does he seem to believe Ugolino should be here? Why or why not?
    Answers will vary. The pity he shows seems to have more to do with the fate of Ugolino's sons than with his own fate. Ugolino had betrayed Pisa, so he belonged here.
B. What is Ugolino's overriding emotion?
    His overriding emotion is hate.

The Inferno

Canto XXXIV
Compound Fraud
The Treacherous to Their Masters, Satan

(Circle 9: Cocytus, Round 4: Judecca, The Center)
1. What is the condition of the souls in the center of Hell?
    They are solidly frozen in the ice, their condition made worse by the icy wind.
2. What does Dante feel?
    He feels extreme terror, feeling deprived of life and death.
3. How does Dante describe the Devil?
    He is a hideous giant with three heads of different colors, two bat-like wings under each head which beat furiously and are the source of the great wind of Hell. He weeps from all six eyes, the tears being bloody and full of pus. In each mouth is a sinner. The central mouth holds Judas Iscariot, the other two hold Brutus and Cassius.
4. What are the colors of Satan's faces?
    One is red, another is black and the other is yellowish.
5. What name does Dante give Satan?
    He calls him Dis.
6. What time is it when they pass by Cassius?
    "The night is coming on" means it is the evening of Holy Saturday.
7. How do Dante and Virgil leave Hell?
    They climb down Satan's body into a cave, then begin their ascent by a little road, leaving the center of the earth.
8. What time does Virgil say it is when they emerge?
    He says it is "middle tierce" meaning it is 7:30 a.m. They have gone through the center of the earth and have moved ahead twelve hours.
9. What does Dante see when they are out of the pit?
    He sees Satan's legs projecting upward.
10. Where are they when Dante sees this?
    They are under the "other hemisphere."
11. What can be heard but not seen coming from Satan's tomb?
    A little stream is heard.
12. How does Dante end the *Inferno*?
    He and his guide climb out of the darkness and walk out beneath the stars.

Questions for Further Thought

A. What sin does Dante consider to be the greatest and how do you know?
    He considers treachery toward God and others to be the greatest sin. We know that by his placement in Hell of the traitors closest to Satan, and by his naming of the central point of hell Judecca, for Judas.
B. What do you think the colors of Satan's faces symbolize?
    One possible explanation would be that the red face symbolizes hate, the black face ignorance and darkness, and the yellow face represents impotence, jealousy and envy.
C. What is the meaning of the little stream?
    It is the stream called Lethe, which is the river of forgetfulness. Dante describes it as flowing from the "peak" which is Purgatory, meaning that the memory of the sins of those in Purgatory is flowing to Hell, which draws all evil.
D. Would you rank the sins in the same order that Dante did? Why or why not?
    Answers will vary.
E. Is it coincidence that Satan is like an unholy trinity, or do you think Dante deliberately portrayed him that way?
    It is likely that Dante wanted to show Satan in exact opposition to the Triune God who represents perfection.

Satan represents all that is evil, deficient in harmony and imperfect, so the triune Satan is a fitting opposite of God.

For Further Research:

The citadel in Limbo is parallel to the Great Citadel in Minas Tirith in *The Lord of the Rings Triology* by J. R.R. Tolkien. Read and compare the passages describing Minas Tirith and compare them with this citadel.

Purgatorio
The Divine Comedy: Part 2
by Dante Alighieri
Translation: John Ciardi
New American Library

Dante and Virgil have emerged from Hell and are climbing toward the Mount of Purgatory. Dante believed that only the Northern Hemisphere was inhabited and that the Southern Hemisphere was covered with water except for the Mount of Purgatory. This mount was on an island in the ocean.

The Mount had three major divisions:
- Ante-Purgatory which was at the base of the mountain
- The Mountain of Purgatory which is opposite Jerusalem
- The Summit, or Earthly Paradise

In contrast to Hell, where the souls are being tormented and not purified, the souls in Purgatory willingly accept their sufferings in reparation for their sins. The penances relate to the sins they are purging, and despite the sufferings, hope prevails because once purified, the souls will be released to Paradise.

The primary theme of *Purgatorio* is the role of Free Will and individual responsibility. The souls in Purgatory put themselves there by their choices in life. Their purging, or purification, results from understanding their sins and being freed of the concupiscence (tendency) toward those vices which led them to sin. They suffer willingly.

Unit 1: Poetry

Canto I
Cato of Utica

(Ante-Purgatory: The Shore of the Island)
1. What is the second kingdom given for, according to Dante?
    It is given as a place for man's soul to purge his guilt before ascending to Heaven.
2. To whom does Dante pray for inspiration?
    He prays to the Muses, especially Calliope who is the Muse of epic poetry.
3. What time is it?
    It is the dawn of Easter ("Sweet azure of the sapphire of the east was gathering…The planet…was making all the east laugh with her rays…"
4. What does Dante see in the sky?
    He sees four stars "unseen by mortals since the first mankind."
5. What does Cato ask?
    He asks how Dante and Virgil have escaped from Hell and if the damned are now allowed to wander here.
6. What does Virgil instruct Dante to do?
    He instructs him to show reverence to Cato.
7. What does Virgil explain to Cato?
    He explains that he was sent by "A Heavenly Lady" to guide Dante away from the road he was on which surely would have led to his damnation.
8. Where does Virgil tell Cato he is from?
    He tells him he is from that "Round not ruled by Minos, with your own Marcia…" meaning that he came from Limbo, the first round of Hell where the souls of the philosophers and noble pagans reside without having to pass by Minos for judgment.
9. What does Cato tell Virgil to do?
    He tells him to proceed but to first tie a green reed around Dante's waist and clean his face.
10. Where must they go to find the reed?
    They must go to the low point of the plain around the Mount of Purgatory.
11. What marvel does Dante behold?
    When Virgil pulls a reed from the ground, another grows immediately in its place.

Questions for Further Thought

A. How many times is Cato's name mentioned in this canto?
    It is not mentioned at all.
B. How can we know it is Cato?
    We can know it is Cato by the references to his suicide in Utica and his wife Marcia. (See the notes for a further explanation of Cato and Marcia).
C. What do the four stars represent?
    They represent the Cardinal Virtues of Prudence, Justice, Fortitude and Temperance.
D. What does the reed represent, and why does it grow at the lowest point of the plain?
    The reed represents Dante's humility, and he must start his ascent of the mountain from the very bottom, not missing any part of Purgatory, just as he didn't miss any part of Hell.

Canto II
The Angel Boatman, Casella, Cato of Utica

(Ante-Purgatory: The Shore of the Island)
1. How does Dante describe the time?
    The sun's highpoint of its meridian circle covered Jerusalem while it was night over the Ganges, and "Aurora in

her passage" indicates that it is now past dawn where he is.
2. What does Virgil tell Dante to do as they see the boat approaching?
    He tells him to get down on his knees because God's Angel is approaching.
3. What must Dante do when he sees the Angel's face?
    He must look down because of the brightness.
4. How do the souls leave the boat?
    After the Angel makes the sign of the cross they "cast themselves, at his signal, to the shore."
5. What do the souls ask Dante and Virgil?
    They ask them to show them the road up the mountainside.
6. How does Virgil describe himself and Dante?
    He says they are pilgrims.
7. Why are the souls amazed?
    They are amazed to see Dante breathing.
8. What happens when Dante tries to embrace one of the souls?
    All he feels is empty air.
9. What puzzles Dante?
    He doesn't understand why it has taken so long for Casella to get here, because he had died months earlier.
10. While they are listening to Casella sing, what does Cato tell them?
    He hurries them off, reminding them that they must climb the mountain to God.

Questions for Further Thought

A. What mood is immediately sensed as this canto opens?
    One can immediately sense relief and hope.
B. What color is mentioned that we have not seen in the Inferno?
    The color white is mentioned.
C. How did Dante describe the arrival of the souls in Hell? See Canto 3, line 113.
    "The evil seed of Adam in its Fall cast themselves, at his signal, from the shore…"

Canto III
The Late-Repentant, Class 1: The Contumacious Manfred

(Ante-Purgatory: The Base of the Cliff)
1. What does Dante say about the Mountain of Purgatory?
    He says it is "where Reason spurs and Justice picks us clean."
2. What does Dante say about a noble conscience?
    He says that the noble conscience is aware of even the slightest fault, and he says Virgil has such a conscience.
3. Why is Dante afraid?
    He realizes that he only sees one shadow and fears Virgil has left him.
4. How does Virgil explain why he has no shadow?
    He says that only his earthly body could cast a shadow, a spirit does not.
5. What does Virgil say about reason?
    He says that it cannot penetrate the mystery and power of God.
6. What does he say about Aristotle and Plato?
    He says that they couldn't understand God even though they sought the understanding of intellect.
7. How does Dante describe the souls here?
    He says they are meek and dignified, walk very slowly, like sheep in a flock and already among the elect.
8. What startles the souls?
    Dante's shadow startles them.

Unit 1: Poetry

9. What does Manfred want Dante to do?
    He wants him to let his daughter know that he sought God's pardon before he died from his wounds.
10. What power do those on earth have regarding the repentant souls?
    They can pray and reduce the time of the dead in Purgatory.

Questions for Further Thought

A. Is it a practice among Christians to pray for the dead?
    Praying for the dead is one of the Spiritual Works of Mercy taught by the Catholic Church.
B. Is there an Old Testament precedent for praying for the dead?
    Yes there is. In *2 Macabbees* 12:44-45, we read about the soldiers who had fallen in war and were found to have been carrying idols. Judas took up a collection of 2000 drachmas of silver and sent it to Jerusalem as a sin offering. "For if he were not expecting that those who had fallen would rise again, it would have been superfluous and foolish to pray for the dead. But if he was looking to the splendid reward that is laid up for those who fall asleep in godliness, it was a holy and pious thought."
C. Why have the souls here been made to wait to begin their ascent of the mountain?
    They waited until the end of their lives to repent, and so they have to wait to begin their journey to Heaven.

Words to Know:

contumacious: flagrantly disobedient or rebellious; refusing to appear in court

indolent: lazy, sluggish

Canto IV
The Late-Repentant, Class 2: The Indolent Belacqua

(Ante-Purgatory: The First Ledge)
1. What does Dante say about the soul?
    He says that man only has one soul and it can only be engaged in one thing at a time.
2. What is it that gives Dante the strength to make the difficult climb?
    He has a great desire and a good guide.
3. Whom does Virgil tell him they will meet?
    They will meet someone who will guide them upward.
4. Why is the sun on Dante's left side in the morning?
    It is on his left because he is in the Southern Hemisphere.
5. What does Virgil explain about the difficulty of the climb?
    He says that it is much more difficult to begin the climb than to finish it.
6. What was Belacqua's sin?
    He was lazy and indifferent.
7. How long must he wait here before he begins his climb and why?
    He must wait as many years as he lived on earth because he delayed seeking salvation.
8. What could help shorten his time?
    His time could be shortened by the prayers of the living.

Note:
Plato believed that man had three souls and for a time, Dante believed that as well. This is his statement that he no longer believes that, and it shows his spiritual progress.

Questions for Further Thought

A. What time was it when Dante realized time had passed while he listened to Manfred?
    It was about 9:00 am on Easter.
B. What might Dante be referring to when he refers to "God's Bird above the Gate?"
    He is referring to God's Angel at the Gate of Purgatory.
C. As Virgil leads Dante away from Belacqua, what time is it and how do you know?
    It is noon because Virgil says "the sun has touched the very peak of day above the sea…"

Canto V
The Late Repentant, Class 3: Those Who Died by Violence Without Last Rites

(Ante-Purgatory: The Second Ledge)
1. What does the soul notice here about Dante?
    Again, the soul notices that he casts a shadow "as if he were alive!"
2. What does Virgil want Dante to do?
    He wants him to stay focused on his task of climbing the mountain and not to be distracted by the idle whispers of the souls.
3. What are the souls singing?
    They are singing the *Miserere*, which is Psalm 50.
4. How did these souls die?
    They died by violence.
5. How were they saved?
    A light from Heaven reminded them to repent and forgive others right before death.
6. What do the souls request?
    They request prayers from the living.

Canto VI
The Late Repentant, Class 3: Those Who Died by Violence, Sordello

1. To whom does Dante compare himself at this moment?
    He compares himself to one who has just won a gamble, because the people are following him hoping for a share.
2. What was the prayer of the shades?
    Their prayer was that others would pray for them.
3. What is the difference between the prayers of these souls and those of the ones Virgil had written about?
    The ones Virgil had written about were from souls whose sins had not been atoned for, and therefore their prayers were ineffective.
4. Who will clarify things for Dante?
    Beatrice, who will appear at the summit of the mountain, will clarify things for Dante.
5. Why does the shade of Sordello agree to speak to Virgil?
    He agrees because Virgil tells him he is from Mantua, the same place Sordello was from.
6. What does Dante accuse the priests of doing?
    He accuses them of meddling in temporal affairs instead of seeking after holiness.
7. Which emperor has neglected Italy and allowed it to become embroiled in feuds?
    The Holy Roman Emperor Albert has neglected Italy.
8. Who is Dante referring to when he says "O Supreme Jove, for mankind crucified…?"
    He is referring to God.
9. Is Dante praising Florence?
    No, he is speaking sarcastically, because Florence was always embroiled in warfare.

Note:
Dante continues to refer to the strife between the two parties of the Ghibellines and the Guelphs. He blames a lack of central authority for the strife, and even refers to strife within the Ghibelline party between the Montagues and the Capulets of *Romeo and Juliet* fame. Because of these feuds, Italy was in chaos while the northern part of the Empire enjoyed the attention of the emperor and relative peace.

Canto VII
The Late-Repentant, Class 4: The Negligent Rulers

(Ante-Purgatory: The Second Ledge, The Flowering Valley)
1. Why had Virgil lost Heaven?
     He lost Heaven for lack of faith.
2. How does Virgil describe the abode of his soul?
     It is a place of untormented gloom where one hears the sound of hopeless sighs and where there is no hope of seeing God.
3. Besides the noble pagans, who dwells there?
     Babies who died before baptism dwell there.
4. What are the three Sacred Virtues?
     They are Faith, Hope and Charity.
5. Who resides in this valley where they will spend the night?
     The shades of monarchs who neglected their duties reside here.
6. What does Dante say about virtue?
     He says that it is rarely passed on from father to son. Only in rare cases does the son have more virtue than the father, as in the case of Henry III of England.
7. Why are these rulers waiting here before they begin their ascent?
     They made God wait for their repentance, so now they must wait.

Note:
The student interested in the significance of the various rulers mentioned should take time to read the notes at the end of the chapter.

Questions for Further Thought

A. Virgil says those in Limbo were not dressed in the Three Sacred Virtues, but practiced all the rest. What is he referring to?
     He is referring to the Cardinal virtues of Justice, Temperance, Prudence and Fortitude referred to in Canto I, lines 23 and 31.
B. What does the light of the day (the Sun) represent?
     It represents God, without whom one is lost.
C. Why does Dante place Henry alone?
     He is alone because England was not part of the Holy Roman Empire.

Canto VIII
The Negligent Rulers
Ante-Purgatory: The Flowering Valley

(Nightfall, Easter Sunday, The Guardian Angels, The Serpent)

1. What do the souls do as night falls?
    They sing a beautiful hymn.
2. Why do the Angels come?
    They come to guard the souls in the valley from the Evil One, the Serpent.
3. What does Dante feel?
    He feels "icy-cold with fear."
4. What does Judge Nino say about his wife?
    He says that she stopped mourning for him (the weeds and white veil were a sign of mourning) because she was soon to marry another who would also die.
5. What indictment does he make about women?
    He says they only stay faithful if their love is rekindled often by sight and touch.
6. What does Nino ask Dante to do?
    He asks him to tell his daughter Giovanna to pray for him.
7. As Dante is watching the stars, what does Sordello see?
    He sees the approaching serpent.
8. What is the center point at which the stars are slowest?
    It is the South Pole.
9. What happens to the serpent?
    He is driven off by the Angels.
10. What was the Malaspina family known for?
    They were known for their generosity and bravery.
11. What does Malaspina predict?
    He predicts that within seven years Dante will benefit from his generosity.

Questions for Further Thought

A. How could the serpent still be a problem to these souls?
    These souls are not yet in Purgatory, but are only in Ante-Purgatory. They can still be tempted and lose salvation.
B. Why are the Angels there?
    The Angels are there to guard them and help them to reach Heaven because they have repented.
C. What does Nino mean when he says that his wife's tomb will bear a Milanese viper instead of Gallura's cock?
    It was the custom to put the husband's coat-of-arms on the tomb of his deceased wife.

Note:
The hymn the souls sing is *Te lucis Ante*, which is a prayer that they will be protected from the evil that prowls the night. They know that they are still vulnerable and need God's protection.

Canto IX
The Angel Guardian

(The Gate of Purgatory)
1. Why had Dante slept?
    He was worn down by bodily fatigue.
2. What happened while Dante slept?
    He was carried to the Gate of Purgatory.
3. Who had carried him here?
    A lady named Lucia carried him. (Lucia means Divine Light).
4. How does Dante feel?
    He feels confident and happy.

Unit 1: Poetry

5. What does Dante note about the three steps leading to the Gate of Purgatory?
    Each step is a different color.
6. What has Dante had to do each time he has seen an Angel?
    He has had to look away because of the radiance.
7. What is the first step like?
    The first step is white polished marble, reflective like a mirror.
8. What is the second step like?
    The second step is very dark, cracked and made of a rough "fire-flaked" stone.
9. What is the third step like?
    The third step is like porphyry and is bright red.
10. What posture does Dante assume before the Angel?
    He is prostrate at his feet.
11. What does the gatekeeper Angel do?
    He inscribes seven "p's" on Dante's forehead and tells him to remove them before he leaves. The "p's" are for *peccata* (sins).
12. How many keys does the Angel use to open the gate?
    He uses two, a silver and a gold one.
13. What does the Angel warn Dante about?
    He warns him not to look back, as he will find himself outside if he does.
14. What does Dante hear as the gate is opened?
    He hears the singing of *Te Deum Laudamus* which is a hymn in praise of God.

Questions for Further Thought

A. The entrance to Purgatory is symbolized by the Rite of Reconciliation, or Confession. Knowing that, what might the three steps symbolize?
    The white step might symbolize perfect contrition or sorrow for the sins of one's life; the dark step actual confession of sins, and the third step the satisfaction for sin which results from deeds of love and works of penance. This is the basic form for the Sacrament of Confession.
B. What does the Angel's question about where their guide is imply?
    It implies that one must have a guide to enter Purgatory.
C. What does the Angel represent?
    The Angel represents the Church as being responsible for the ministry of Confession. Christ had told his apostles "whose sins you bind are bound in Heaven, whose sins you loose are loosed in Heaven." (*John* 20:22-23)
D. There are Seven Deadly Sins. What are they?
    The Seven Deadly Sins are Pride, Envy, Wrath, Sloth (Acedia) Avarice, Gluttony and Lust.
E. If Dante has just confessed his sins, why can he not just go straight to Heaven?
    He has still not been purified of concupiscence, which is the tendency or inclination to sin.
F. What do the two keys symbolize? (They are the keys in the Papal Seal)
    The gold key symbolizes the authority of the Church and the confessor to forgive sin. The silver key represents the thought and deliberation of the confessor in determining whether or not to grant absolution for sin.

Words to Know:

porphyry: purple stone

prostrate: face down

Canto X
The Proud
The Needle's Eye, The First Cornice

(The Whip of Pride)
1. What does Dante mean in saying the threshold of the gate is seldom used?
    He is saying that many are damned because they follow the crooked path to Hell.
2. Why is the path called a "needle's eye?"
    It is called a "needle's eye" because it is narrow and difficult to maneuver.
3. After passing through the opening, where are Dante and Virgil?
    They are on a ledge.
4. What is the circling bank constructed of?
    It is constructed of white marble and carved with scenes of the Annunciation and other depictions of humility.
5. Why is Dante confused?
    He cannot distinguish between the sculpture and reality.
6. What emperor is portrayed here?
    Emperor Trajan is portrayed here with the widow to whom he promised justice.
7. How do the proud pay for their sin?
    They must crawl on their hands and knees carrying heavy burdens on their backs. Those burdens are the weight of pride they carried on earth.

Question for Further Thought

What is the significance of the title "the Whip of Pride?"
    The panels of the first cornice depict scenes which illustrate how great people have chosen the path of humility over pride, and they serve as a whip by example.

Words to Know:

censer: vessel which holds charcoal and incense and hangs on the end of a long chain, used during the Mass and other liturgical services and symbolizing the sending of prayers up to Heaven

cornice: molding or ledge which projects along a wall

Canto XI

1. What prayer are the souls here praying?
    They are praying an extended *Lord's Prayer* or *Our Father*, asking help for themselves and their loved ones still on earth.
2. What was Aldobrandesco's sin?
    He had excessive pride in his ancestry and the deeds of his ancestors.
3. What was Od'risi's sin?
    He had claimed credit for his art which rightfully belonged to another.
4. What does Od'risi say about earthly fame?
    It is short-lived as a breath of wind, because one artist betters another and each one's fame dims with the rise of the next.

5. Salvani was presumptuous while he lived, but he did something before he was dying that earned him merit in God's eyes. What did he do?
   At the peak of his glory, he turned beggar to raise the ransom for his friend who was being held by King Charles.
6. How does the canto end?
   The canto ends with Salvani's prediction that Dante would suffer at the hands of his neighbors.

Canto XII
The Rein of Pride, The Angel of Humility

1. What posture had Dante assumed as he walked along this level?
   He had assumed a stooped posture in order to talk to the souls as they moved along.
2. What was carved on the slabs?
   The carved slabs showed how the people looked when they were alive.
3. What is on the track where they walk?
   There are stone figures carved which depict mythological and *Old Testament* examples of the consequences of pride.
4. What does the Angel of Humility do to Dante and why?
   He strikes his forehead with his wing to remove one of the "p's."
5. What does Dante hear as they move on?
   He hears a hymn *Beati Paupers Spiritu*, "Blessed are the Poor in Spirit," which is one of the Beatitudes.
6. How does Dante contrast the entrances to the different levels of Hell and Purgatory?
   In Hell the sounds are wails and anguish, here they are joyous songs.

Question for Further Thought

How do the scenes depicted on the floor differ from those on the walls where Dante entered?
   The scenes on the wall show scenes of humility, beginning with the Virgin Mary, and those on the floor depict the results of pride, or the lack of humility.

Words to Know:

pedagogue: teacher

abjure: give up, reject

Canto XIII
The Envious
The Second Cornice

(*The Whip of Envy*)
1. How does Dante describe the track of this cornice?
   It is dark, bare and level, and there are no carvings.
2. Since they have no Angel to guide them, who is their guide?
   God (the sun, Blessed Lamp) is their guide.
3. What do they experience?
   They hear invisible spirits flying by speaking of love for others.
4. What is the "Whip of Envy?"
   The "Whip of Envy" is Love (Charity).

5. The first thing they hear is *vinum non habent*. Why is that significant?
   Mary again is the first example of Love here, and that is what she told her Son at the Wedding of Cana—"they have no wine." (*John 2:1-10*)
6. Who was Orestes?
   Orestes avenged the death of his father Agamemnon by killing his mother. He was a character in the *Oresteian Trilogy* by Aeschylus.
7. Who said "Love your enemies?"
   Christ commanded that we love our enemies.
8. What do they see on the inner cliff?
   They see spirits dressed in dark cloaks, the color of the cliff, praying to Mary, St. Michael and all the Saints.
9. How does Dante feel when he gets close enough to see the spirits?
   He feels great anguish.
10. Why?
    The souls are dressed in haircloth cloaks and their eyes are sewn shut with wire. Being thus blinded, they lean on each other for support.
11. How do the souls respond when Dante asks if there are any Latin souls there?
    They reply that they are citizens of Heaven, not of an earthly city.
12. What was Sapia's sin?
    She rejoiced in the bad fortune of others.
13. What does Dante say about his own sin of envy?
    He says that he will not spend a long time on this ledge because he was not overly envious.
14. What sin burdens him?
    His sin of pride burdens him.
15. What does Sapia request?
    She asks Dante to restore her good name to her kin.

Questions for Further Thought

A. The first three examples of Love are heard in the voices of the spirits. What do these examples generally tell us?
   They tell us to love others, to love our friends and to love our enemies.
B. Why are there no pictures here as in the first terrace?
   There are no pictures here because the souls cannot see with their eyes sewn shut. That is why the sounds are so important.

Words to Know:

livid: the color of a bruise; ashen blue-black, here symbolizing envy

absolution: the forgiveness of sins

Canto XIV
The Envious
The Second Cornice

(*The Reign of Envy*)
1. What do the two spirits ask Dante?
   They ask his name and where he is from.
2. How does Dante respond to their question?
   He describes his home as the bank of a river which flows out of the mountains through Tuscany. He does not name it and declines to name himself, saying he has won little fame.

Unit 1: Poetry

3. What does the spirit say about the Arno Valley?
    He says the area should perish because there is no longer any virtue there.
4. To what kinds of beasts does the spirit liken the people who live along the Arno?
    He likens them to swine, curs, dogs, wolves and foxes.
5. What kinds of vices do these animals represent?
    They represent indecency, contempt and fraud.
6. What does the spirit predict?
    He predicts that the grandson of the other spirit will terrorize the people of his homeland, bringing dishonor to the family name, and that Dante will suffer and leave his home as well.
7. Why do the spirits agree to tell Dante their names?
    They see God's favor in him.
8. What has become of the descendants of the numerous people for whom the shades grieve?
    They have fallen into decadence.
9. What does Virgil lament?
    He laments the fact that Satan lures people away from Heaven.

Questions for Further Thought

A. Why is it ironic that the shade of Guido del Duca praises the good people of the Arno?
    It is ironic because he is in this ring where envy is punished. Envious people do not generally praise others as he is now doing.
B. Dante and Virgil hear two voices rolling by like thunder. They are the voices of Cain and Aglauros, both of whom envied a sibling. What does Virgil tell Dante about what they have just heard?
    He tells him that those voices serve as a warning to keep men in control of their envy. Those voices are the "reign of envy."

Words to Know:

cur: person who is seen as mean or cowardly; mongrel

chivalry: gallantry, courtesy, graciousness, loyalty

Canto XV
The Envious, The Angel of Caritas, The Wrathful
The Second Cornice: The Ascent, The Third Cornice

(The Whip of Wrath)
1. By Dante's description, what time of day is it?
    It is 3:00 p.m.
2. What causes Dante to have to shield his eyes?
    He has to shield his eyes from the bright light of the Blessed Angel of Caritas (Love of others).
3. Where do we find the saying "Blessed are the merciful?"
    It is one of the Beatitudes found in *Matthew 5:7*.
4. What concept does Dante find difficult to understand?
    He finds it difficult to understand the idea that the more people who share in a good, the richer they are than if just a few share in it. The envious do not want to share what they have, and this concept is what they must learn.
5. Is Virgil talking about material goods?
    No, he is talking about spiritual goods, particularly *caritas*, or love of others.

6. Who will elaborate further on this idea?
    Beatrice will elaborate further.
7. What do we learn about the marks on Dante's forehead?
    Two of them have now been erased.
8. What happens to Dante?
    He goes into a trance and sees a vision.
9. What is the first vision?
    It is the Blessed Virgin Mary gently saying "My son, my son, why do you treat us so?" This refers to the story in *Luke* 2:41-52 when Joseph and Mary became separated from Jesus, and three days later they found him in the Temple.
10. Who is the boy Dante sees being stoned and asking forgiveness for his murderers?
    He sees St. Stephen, the first martyr, who was not a boy, but a man and the first deacon.
11. What have Dante's visions been about?
    He has seen examples of wrath tempered by mercy.
12. How does Virgil explain the visions?
    He says they are given to Dante so that he will open his heart to the waters of peace offered by God to release his own anger.
13. What do they see as they leave this cornice?
    They see billowing black smoke.

Note:
This experience is relevant for Dante because of his banishment from Florence and the anger he harbored toward those who were responsible. He cannot ascend further until he lets go of the anger he feels toward them.

Word to Know:

wrath: anger, rage

Canto XVI
The Wrathful, Marco Lombardo

(The Third Cornice)
1. What prayer does Dante hear?
    He hears the *Agnus Dei* or "Lamb of God."
2. Does it sound like a chorus singing?
    No, all are in unison as if with one voice.
3. How has Virgil been directing Dante to deal with the souls so far?
    He has been telling him to be respectful.
4. What does Dante ask Marco?
    He asks where the fault lies that the world is so evil.
5. What does Marco say about free will?
    He says that it is a gift from God, not controlled by the Heavens. The light of reason helps man to tell right from wrong. When men fall away from God's laws, it is because they choose to: the blame is within themselves.
6. What does Marco say about the soul?
    He says that in its youth and innocence it follows whatever gives it pleasure. The soul is gradually guided to seek higher things.
7. What does he say man needs?
    He says man needs restraint of law and a good shepherd.

Unit 1: Poetry

8. What does he say about the current pope?
   He says that he is worldly and failing to lead the people as he should.
9. What does he say about Rome?
   At one time Rome had two "Suns" or rulers, the emperor and the pope, but now one man is both emperor and ruler.
10. What does Dante see as he concludes his conversation with Marco?
    He sees a ray of light through the once opaque smoke.
11. Why is it not fit for the Angel to see Marco?
    He is not yet purified of his wrath.

QUESTIONS FOR FURTHER THOUGHT

A. What does the *Agnus Dei* prayer request of God?
   It asks for mercy and peace.
B. Dante holds one particular pope up as his example of corruption. We met him in the *Inferno* and he is mentioned again here. Who is he?
   He is Boniface VIII.
C. Why can Dante not see anything here?
   He cannot see because he is guilty of the sin of anger which is purged here.

WORDS TO KNOW:

kalends: in Rome, the first day of each month

swathing: wrapping of a person in bandages or cloth

CANTO XVII
The Wrathful, The Angel of Meekness
The Fourth Cornice, The Ascent

(The Rein of Wrath)
1. What time is it?
   It is sunset of the second day on the mountain, Easter Monday.
2. What do Dante's visions illustrate as he is leaving the third cornice?
   They are examples of the actions of wrathful people: Procne, from Greek Mytholgy, Ahasuerus from the *Book of Ester*, (*Old Testament*) and Amata from the *Aeneid*.
3. What does the Angel of Meekness do?
   The Angel bids them to ascend before they ask.
4. When Dante felt the Angel's wing fan his face, what happened?
   The Angel was removing one of the marks from his forehead as he heard "Blessed are the peacemakers..." He was cleansed of his wrath.
5. What sin is purged here?
   The sin of sloth is purged here.
6. How does Virgil explain sloth to Dante?
   He says that natural love is perfect, but love which comes from the mind can err toward evil through too little or too much vigor. The slothful fail to love enough to pursue the ultimate Good which is God. Another spiritual term for sloth is lukewarmness.
7. What forms does bad love take?
   Bad love takes three forms:

- Pride—desiring to better others and see them fall
- Envy—desiring the ruin of others due to a belief that their success is tied to one's failure
- Anger—desiring vengeance on others

Words to Know:

sloth: apathy, laziness, indolence

acedia: another name for sloth

parse: to analyze grammatical structure of a word or sentence

rue: regret, lament

Canto XVIII
The Slothful
The Fourth Cornice

(The Whip of Sloth, The Rein of Sloth)
1. What does Dante want Virgil to do?
    He wants him to continue his explanation of love which is the source of all good and evil acts.
2. What does Virgil say about love?
    He says that the mind creates an image of something from the physical object and focuses on it. The soul is naturally drawn toward Love and cannot rest until it finds Love. The three cornices they have visited have shown them that not all love is good.
3. What question does Dante have?
    If Love is not from within, how can one earn merit or blame for the direction his love takes?
4. How does Virgil reply?
    He says that he can explain the answer from the standpoint of Reason, but Beatrice will have to explain the mystery that is tied to faith.
5. Does one have power over the innate liberty with which he is born?
    Yes he does, once he has the power of Reason, and it is up to himself to control it.
6. What does Virgil term this moral sense that man has?
    He calls it Free Will, and that is what Beatrice will expound upon.
7. Dante doses off. What wakes him?
    He is awakened by a mob of spirits running as if in a frenzy.
8. What examples of spiritual zeal (the opposite of sloth) are experienced by Dante as the "Whip of Sloth?"
    As the spirits are running past, he hears the refrain "Mary ran to the hills" and "Caesar, to subdue Ilerda struck at Marseilles, and then swooped down on Spain."
9. Why do the spirits run without stopping?
    They are filled with the desire and zeal to purge themselves of sloth.
10. "The Rein of Sloth" is represented by runners crying with examples of those who were slothful in life. Who are the examples?
    The first is the Jewish people who muttered against Moses when they met hardship in the desert. The other is the group of Trojans who preferred to end their journey in Sicily rather than continue on with Aeneas (Anchises' son) to found Rome.
11. What does Dante do as the canto ends?
    He falls asleep.

Unit 1: Poetry

Question for Further Thought

What physical events occur on this cornice to Dante?
> Dante's weakness causes him to doze and dream as he approaches the last step. These are physical manifestations of sloth which is here purified.

Canto XIX
The Slothful, The Angel of Zeal, The Hoarders and Wasters, the Avaricious
The Fourth Cornice, The Ascent, The Fifth Cornice

(Dante's Dream of Sirena)
1. Who is the seductress that Dante dreams about?
   > She is the Siren whom Odysseus encountered.
2. Who else appears in his dream?
   > A saintly lady appears who helps drive the Siren away.
3. What Beatitude does the Angel of Zeal express here?
   > The Angel expresses the Beatitude "Blessed are they that mourn."
4. What does Dante mean in speaking of the witch "for whom…those above us weep?"
   > He means the souls on the cornices or ledges above were seduced by her.
5. What is the safeguard against the temptations of the Siren?
   > The safeguard is to gaze upward to God.
6. What does Dante see on the fifth ledge?
   > He sees the spirits weeping as they lie outstretched with faces down, crying "My soul cleaves to the dust." (Psalm 119)
7. The soul tells Dante "*scias quod ego fui successor Petri.*" Can you guess what he meant?
   > He meant "I was a successor of Peter" or a Pope.
8. How long was he pope?
   > He was Pope Adrian V for a month and a few days.
9. Why is the pope here?
   > Because he had been greedy for worldly things and for failing to turn his eyes heavenward, he is now being purged by groveling in the dust.
10. Why does Dante kneel to the pope?
    > He kneels out of reverence for his office and dignity.
11. What does the pope tell him?
    > He tells him to stand, because he is just an ordinary person who serves God.
12. What does the pope request of Dante?
    > He asks him to tell his niece Alagia to avoid the path he and others of their family have taken.

Questions for Further Thought

A. What does the Siren represent?
   > She represents the temptations of the world which can lead us away from God.
B. What does the soul imply who tells Dante that the nearest way to the next cornice is to the right if he has not been sentenced here in the bitter dust?
   > The soul implies that not everyone bears the guilt of all of the sins purged in Purgatory, and so they may pass by certain ledges if they are free of those specific sins.
C. The pope says "*Neque unbent*" which means "they never marry." Why does he say that to Dante?
   > He says it to reflect the passage in Scripture (*Matthew 22:30*) in which Christ is asked to which man a previously

44

married widow would be married in Heaven. Christ tells her that there is no marriage in Heaven. Likewise, the pope is telling Dante that titles and positions will not exist in Heaven, so he has no need to treat him as a pope now.

Words to Know:

geomancer: one who predicts the future based on patterns made by throwing handfuls of dirt on the ground

crone: a term which insults the age or appearance of a (usually older) woman

prone: lying face-down

avarice: greediness, materialism

Canto XX
The Hoarders and Wasters, The Avaricious
The Firth Cornice

(The Whip of Avarice, The Rein of Avarice)
1. The she-wolf was seen in the *Inferno* (Canto 1, line 48). What vice does she personify?
    She personifies greed (avarice).
2. How does Dante feel on seeing the spirits here who weep and lament?
    He feels compassion.
3. What is the first thing Dante hears on this cornice?
    He hears the souls crying out a prayer to Mary about her poverty and her child being born in a stable.
4. What do we know about Fabricius?
    We know that he refused wealth in order to maintain his honor and live without vice.
5. Who is the third holy one spoken about?
    The third is St. Nicholas.
6. The words Dante hears proclaim which virtue?
    They proclaim generosity to God and man by accepting humility and preferring honor to wealth, even if it means accepting poverty.
7. What does Hugh Capet relate?
    He relates the greediness and treachery of French royalty. (According to the notes, some of the history is not quite accurate, but the point is clear. The French royalty became degenerate through the generations).
8. Who is the Vicar of Christ?
    The Vicar of Christ is the pope, and Dante is talking about the pope being abused by members of his dynasty.
9. What is the "Reign of Avarice?"
    The Reign of Avarice is the reciting at night of examples of the downfall of figures from Mythology, Scripture and history as a result of greed.
10. What happens as they are leaving this cornice?
    An earthquake and then a loud shout of "Glory to God in the Highest!" occurs.
11. What puzzles Dante?
    He cannot figure out the source of the earthquake and subsequent shout.

Unit 1: Poetry

Note:
Fabricius was a Roman Consul in 282 who refused the bribes and prerogatives of his office. He lived in poverty by choice.

Questions for Further Thought

A. What is St. Nicholas known for?
   He was the Bishop of Myra who rescued the daughters of a minor official from a life of prostitution by providing dowries so they could marry respectably.
B. The pope abused by Capet's dynasty is none other than Boniface VIII. Why would Dante lament that when we have seen his disgust for him in the *Inferno*?
   Dante had great respect for the Papacy, the office of the pope. Even though Bonifice VIII was corrupt, he was still Christ's Vicar, and as such, he was due the honor and respect of a pope.

Words to Know:

rapacity: greed, selfishness, miserliness

parricide: murder of a parent or close relative

Canto XXI

(Statius)
1. How does Dante feel?
   He grieves on seeing the suffering the spirits must undergo for purification.
2. What does Virgil mean when he tells the shade that he is relegated to eternal exile?
   He refers to the fact that his final resting place is in Limbo, not in Heaven.
3. How far will Virgil lead Dante?
   He will lead him only as far as his knowledge (Reason) allows.
4. What does the soul say is the source of the earthquake?
   It is caused by the release of a soul from Purgatory into Heaven.
5. What allows the soul to be freed?
   The soul is freed once the will is free of the desire for sin.
6. Who is being freed now?
   This spirit, named Statius, who is speaking to Virgil and Dante, is being freed.
7. Whom does Statius credit with inspiring his poetry?
   He credits Virgil and says that to have lived in Virgil's time would have been worth another year spent in Purgatory.
8. Why does Virgil tell the shade not to kneel to him?
   Virgil reminds him that they are both shades and have no bodies to embrace.

Canto XXII
The Gluttons
The Ascent to the Sixth Cornice, The Sixth Cornice

(The Tree, The Whip of Gluttony)
1. What had the Angel who directed them to the Sixth Cornice done?
   He had removed another mark from Dante's forehead, and in quoting the Beatitude, said "Blessed are they who thirst for rectitude…" instead of saying "who hunger…"

2. Why is Dante able to move quickly now?
   He has been purged of the tendency to many sins now, and his spiritual burden is much lighter.
3. What was the sin of Statius?
   His sin was prodigality—he spent too freely.
4. What mistake does Statius make regarding Virgil?
   He thinks he is a Christian, as seen in his question about following the Fisherman.
5. What does Statius credit Virgil for?
   He credits Virgil for bringing him to the Christian faith and for making him a poet.
6. Why had Statius kept his faith a secret?
   He was afraid of persecution.
7. For his lukewarmness, how long did he spend on the Ledge of Sloth?
   He spent more than 400 years.
8. What does Virgil reveal to Statius about other poets, philosophers and mythological persons?
   He reveals that they are with him in Limbo.
9. What do they encounter on their way off this ledge?
   They encounter a tree with an inner voice which warns them not to eat of its fruit.
10. What is the "Whip of Gluttony" as the voices here recount?
    They recount Mary's concern for the couple at the Wedding of Cana, the noble women of Rome who drank water, Daniel who acquired wisdom by refusing rich food, and John the Baptist who only ate locusts and honey.
11. What virtue do these voices illustrate?
    They illustrate moderation and abstinence.

QUESTION FOR FURTHER THOUGHT

How are greed and prodigality related?
   They are related in that they both consume the sinner with material goods, either the acquisition of them or the lack of prudence in their use.

CANTO XXIII
The Gluttons

(The Sixth Cornice)
1. What does Dante hear?
   He hears *Labia mea, Domine*, "Open my lips, O Lord" (Psalm 51).
2. How do the shades here appear?
   They are emaciated, have scabby skin and dark hollow eyes.

Note:
During Dante's time, people believed that God had signed His creation OMO DEI, or Man of God. The eyes formed the Os, the brows, nose and cheekbones formed the M, while the ears formed the D, the nostrils the E and the mouth the I. Because of their emaciation, the only prominent part of the faces of the shades was formed by the bones of the face.

3. From their appearance and knowing how the punishments here relate to the sins, what was the sin of the souls on this cornice?
   Their sin was gluttony.
4. How does Dante recognize his friend?
   He recognizes his voice, not his face.
5. What is the effect of the fragrance of the tree and the running stream?
   They increase the desire for food and drink in the souls, but the souls cannot partake.

Unit 1: Poetry

6. How does Forese describe the pain he feels?
    He describes it as a "gift of grace" which is renewed each time he passes the tree.
7. How has Forese's time in Purgatory been shortened?
    His time has been shortened by the tears and prayers of his wife.
8. What virtue did Forese's wife exemplify?
    She was chaste.

Note:
Barbagia was a region in Sardinia where a clan of bandits lived. They were a wild tribe and their women went about naked. Dante is saying that these women were more virtuous than the women of Florence.

9. What does Dante say about Moslem women?
    He says they do not require coercion to dress modestly.
10. What does Forese predict?
    He predicts disaster for Florence within a few years (about 15, if young men begin to grow beards at that age).
11. How long will Virgil accompany Dante on his journey?
    He will accompany him until they meet Beatrice.

Canto XXIV

(The Tree of Knowledge, The Rein of Gluttony)
1. Where is Forese's sister Piccarda?
    She is in Heaven (High Olympus).
2. What inspires Dante to write?
    Love inspires him.
3. What does the poet note about his poetry?
    His poetry fell short of the "sweet new style" of Dante's poetry because it lacked the inspiration of Love.
4. What does Dante lament to Forese?
    He laments the decline of virtue and goodness in his city of Florence and the coming bloodshed.
5. After speaking with Forese, what do Dante and his guides encounter?
    They encounter a tree laden with fruit, in front of which stand many souls begging to eat.
6. What is the origin of this tree?
    It has sprung from the root of the Tree of Knowledge in the Garden of Eden.
7. What is the "Rein of Gluttony?"
    It is the voices speaking of the results of gluttony: Eve's gluttony for knowledge rather than for God; the drunkenness of the Centaurs which led to their deaths, and the Gideons who lost victory because they drank without moderation and caution (*Judges* 7:5-6)
8. What does Dante suddenly hear?
    He hears the Angel of Abstinence direct them to ascend to the next ledge.
9. What Beatitude does the Angel proclaim?
    He proclaims "Blessed are those who hunger for righteousness" (in very elaborate words)!

Words to Know:

presage: foretell, portend

ambrosial: tasting delicious, as food of the gods

Canto XXV
The Ascent

(The Discourse of Statius)
The Seventh Cornice (The Lustful, The Whip of Lust)
1. Why do they have to hurry in their ascent?
    Because they cannot climb at night.
2. How does Dante feel?
    He alternates between feeling strong and weak and hesitates to speak.
3. What puzzles Dante?
    He doesn't understand why the shades appear so thin when here they do not need nourishment.
4. Whom does Virgil ask to answer Dante's question?
    He asks Statius to answer.
5. How would you summarize Statius' answer?
    After conception the embryo has no intellect; rather it moves and feels as a lower animal; then as it grows the brain organizes the intellect and there the soul is enlivened by God's breath. When the body dies the soul is freed and goes to the bank of Hell or Purgatory where it is formed as it was on earth, only as a shade.
6. What remains after the body dies?
    Memory, understanding and will remain.
7. What does the soul do of its own free will?
    It chooses either the bank of Purgatory or Hell.
8. From what is the shade formed?
    The shade is formed from air.
9. As they mount the next ledge, what do they see?
    They see flames, with only a narrow path to walk along the edge.
10. What does the choir sing?
    The choir sings *Summae Deus Clementiae*, "God of Clemency Supreme," a hymn begging for the grace of chastity.
11. What do the souls cry out?
    They cry out "*Virum non cognosco*," "I know not man," said by the Virgin Mary when the Angel Gabriel announced that she would be the Mother of God (*Luke* 1; 26-38).
12. What do the voices here praise, and thus, what is the "Whip of Lust?"
    "The Whip of Lust" is the cry of praise for chastity as exemplified by the Virgin Mary, Diana, and faithful husbands and wives.

Questions for Further Thought

A. Why does Dante say they had to climb the narrow passage one at a time?
    He is signifying the fact that each soul makes its way to Heaven alone as it is purified of its sins.
B. What do the flames symbolize?
    The flames symbolize the passion of lust.

Canto XXVI
The Lustful

(The Seventh Cornice, The Rein of Lust)
1. What does Dante note about the effect of his shadow?
    It makes the flames appear to be a darker red, and the shades take note.

Unit 1: Poetry

2. How do the shades process through this ledge?
   They are in two circles, one clockwise, the other counter-clockwise.
3. What do the shades do as they meet?
   They greet each other with a brief kiss.
4. What is the "Rein of Lust?"
   It is the shout of "Sodom and Gomorrah" and other cries which recall indecent or lustful behavior.
5. What sins do these shouts speak of?
   They speak of unnatural lust (homosexuality and bestiality).
6. What do Dante and the poets he meets speak about?
   They speak about poetry and praise other poets.

Canto XXVII
The Angel of Chastity

(The Seventh Cornice)
The Wall of Fire
The Angel Guardian, The Earthly Paradise

1. To express the time of day, Dante makes references to three places. Can you name them?
   The three places are:
   - Where his Maker's blood was shed – Jerusalem
   - The scales of Libra ride above the Ebro – Spain
   - While Ganges' waters steam – India
2. What does the Angel of Chastity sing?
   The Angel sings *Beati mundo corde*, "Blessed are the pure in heart," one of the Beatitudes. He tells them they must pass through the flame in order to be purified.
3. How does Dante feel?
   He is afraid, frozen, and holds his breath. He wants to go through but his body resists.
4. How does Virgil reassure Dante?
   Virgil tells him that he has guided him safely in far worse places and though the flames may bring torment, they won't bring death, and he should enter in peace.
5. What finally convinces Dante to risk the fire?
   He is assured by Virgil that Beatrice is waiting on the other side.
6. What guides them through the fire?
   They hear a paean and follow it to the ascent.
7. After they have passed through the flames what does Dante see?
   He sees a light that is so bright he has to look away. This light is the Angel Guardian of the Earthly Paradise.
8. What do they hear?
   They hear *Venite Benedicti Patris Mei*, which is "Come ye blessed of my Father."
9. Do they complete the ascent?
   No, they do not, because the sun sets and they cannot climb at night. So Dante sleeps while Statius and Virgil keep watch on the steps.
10. How many days have they been on the mountain?
    This is the end of the third day.
11. In Dante's dream, what do Leah and Rachel do?
    Leah weaves garlands of flowers, and Rachel sits at her mirror staring into her own eyes.
12. When they reach the summit, what does Virgil tell Dante?
    He tells him that he has led him as far as he can and has now reached the limit of his understanding. He has led him by "grace of mind and art," which is reason, and Dante now has a sound and free will which no longer needs his guidance.

13. What is the final thing Virgil tells Dante?
    He says "lord of yourself I crown and mitre you."

Questions for Further Thought

A. What might the activities of Leach and Rachel symbolize?
   Leah symbolizes the active life, while Rachel symbolizes the contemplative life.
B. What does Virgil mean when he tells Dante he is past the steep ways?
   He is telling him that he is no longer in danger of sinning, so he is free to wander at will.
C. What does Virgil's crowning and mitering of Dante mean?
   Dante is as close to being master of his body and soul as he can be through the use of reason, which Virgil has taught him.

Word to Know:

paean: expression of praise or joy

Canto XXVIII
Lethe

(The Earthly Paradise)
1. What phenomena of nature does Dante note as he enters the divine forest?
   He notes a gentle breeze and the singing of birds.
2. What does Dante say about the stream he finds?
   He says it is purer than the purest waters of the earth, and though it is in constant shade, it is so clear that nothing could hide in it.
3. Whom does he see on the opposite side of the stream?
   He encounters a lady singing and picking flowers.
4. What does Dante feel?
   He feels hatred for the stream which divides him from the woman.
5. Why is the lady here?
   She is here to answer Dante's questions.
6. What does the lady explain about the garden?
   This is the garden where Adam and Eve sinned; the wind is not an earthly wind but rather a heavenly wind which carries the pure air of Heaven.
7. What does she say about the earth?
   She says that the earth contains the sacred soil which holds the source of many fruits and flowers which man has not yet experienced.
8. What does she say about the water?
   She says that it comes from an eternal fountain by God's Will and has two branches. One branch, Lethe, removes the memory of earthly sins and the other, Eunoe, restores memory of all the good deeds one has done in his earthly life.
9. What does she say about the poets of the Golden Age?
   She says they had an awareness of this garden, though they placed it incorrectly.
10. How do Virgil and Statius react to her words?
    They smile.

Unit 1: Poetry

Questions for Further Thought

A. Dante states "I started out…" What does this indicate?
   It indicates that he is now leading Virgil and Statius.
B. What is the "nest of humankind?"
   It is the Garden of Eden, where man was created.

Canto XXIX
The Banks of Lethe

(The Earthly Paradise)
The Heavenly Pageant
1. What does the lady sing?
   She sings *Beati Quorum Tecta Sunt Peccata*, which is "Blessed are those whose sins are forgiven."
2. What does Dante feel toward Eve?
   He feels reproach at her for delaying his enjoyment of what he now sees.
3. Whom does Dante invoke for help in relating what he sees?
   He invokes the Muses.
4. What do they hear approaching?
   They hear the chant of "Hosanna", which was shouted when Christ entered Jerusalem.
5. The people and things Dante sees are from the *Book of Revelation*. Do you know what they symbolize?
   They symbolize:
   - 7 golden candelabra: Gifts of the Holy Spirit (Wisdom, Understanding, Counsel, Knowledge, Fortitude, Piety, Fear of the Lord)
   - People in white: purity
   - 24 elders: books of the *Old Testament* or the 12 Patriarchs and 12 Apostles
   - 4 living creatures crowned with green leaves and with wings and feathers full of eyes: 4 Evangelists (Matthew, Mark, Luke and John)
   - Griffon: Christ in the form of God and Man
   - Chariot: the Church Triumphant
   - 3 ladies: Theological Virtues (Faith, Hope and Charity)
   - 4 ladies robed in purple: Cardinal Virtues (Prudence, Justice, Temperance, Fortitude)
   - Old man who was a follower of Hippocrates: St. Luke, the Physician
   - Old man with a blade: St. Paul, writer of the Epistles
   - 4 of humble aspect: Peter, James, John and Jude, writers of the Minor Epistles
   - One who moved in a trance: St John, writer of the *Book of Revelation*
6. How does Virgil respond to what they are seeing?
   He is silent and in awe.
7. What happens as the chariot nears Dante?
   There is a clap of thunder and the procession stops.

Words to Know:

acolyte: cleric's assistant

pennon: long narrow flag carried on a lance

caparison: ornamental covering for a horse, saddle decoration

Canto XXX
Beatrice

(The Earthly Paradise)
Virgil Vanishes
1. What is the Septentrion?
    The Septentrion refers to the seven stars of the Big Dipper. Here, Dante is using the term to refer to the seven candelabra in the procession.
2. What does the prophet cry?
    He cries *Veni Sponsa, de Libano*, "Come, Spouse of Lebanon."
3. What are Powers and Principals?
    They are types of Angels.
4. What are they saying?
    They are saying *Benedictus qui Venis*, "Blessed are You Who Come."
5. Who comes into view?
    A veiled lady dressed in green, red and white--Beatrice--comes into view.
6. How does Dante know it is Beatrice?
    He knows because of a force he had experienced in his soul when he was a boy, and which he now feels.
7. What does Dante realize when he turns to speak to Virgil?
    He realizes that Virgil is gone.
8. How does Dante respond to the realization that Virgil is no longer there?
    He weeps.
9. Dante turns when he hears something. What does he hear?
    He hears his name spoken (it is the only time his name appears in the *Divine Comedy*).
10. What does Beatrice tell Dante?
    She tells him not to weep, because he will soon be weeping for something else.
11. How does Dante feel at her reproach?
    He feels ashamed.
12. The angels sing "In You Lord, I put my trust" (*Psalm* 31:1-8). Why do they sing?
    They sing to show their compassion for Dante and to move the lady to compassion.
13. What does Beatrice reveal about Dante?
    While she was a girl, he lived a virtuous life. After she became a young woman, he was influenced by others who led him astray, and he forgot about her.
14. How did she try to influence him after she died?
    She prayed for him and tried to inspire him through dreams.
15. How was she able to save him?
    She had him taken through Hell and Purgatory.
16. What must Dante do in order to proceed?
    He must drink of the water of Lethe to finish wiping out his guilt.

Canto XXXI
Lethe, Beatrice, Matilda

(The Earthly Paradise)
1. How does Dante feel as Beatrice continues to demand that he speak?
    He is speechless, confused and terrified.
2. How does Dante behave while Beatrice tells him that nothing should have led him away from her influence?
    He stands with his head bowed, feeling ashamed.

Unit 1: Poetry

3. What does she tell him to do?
    She tells him to lift his beard and look at her.
4. What is "the beast which is one person in two natures without division?"
    That is the Griffon (Christ).
5. As Dante recognizes his guilt, what does he do?
    He swoons.
6. What does the lady who helps him to the stream say?
    She says *Asperges Me*, "Wash Me."
7. Then what does she do?
    She helps him to drink from the stream.
8. Who are the Four Maidens who dance?
    They are the Cardinal Virtues—Justice, Prudence, Fortitude and Temperance.
9. In order to see the light in Beatrice's eyes, whom must Dante see first?
    He must see the Theological Virtues of Faith, Hope and Charity, represented by the three ladies.
10. What is Beatrice looking at?
    She is looking at the Griffon.
11. What do the three ladies ask of Beatrice?
    They ask her to unveil her mouth so that Dante may discern yet another beauty in her (her smile).

Questions for Further Thought

A. What different manifestations of the Cardinal Virtues have we encountered in the *Divine Comedy*?
    They have appeared as stars and as nymphs. The Virtuous Pagans had these virtues, but alone, they were not enough to save them. Missing was faith in Christ.
B. What is the first vision Dante sees?
    He sees the two natures of Christ, shifting back and forth through the eyes of Beatrice.
C. What does Beatrice represent here?
    She represents the authority of the Church.
D. What is the Second Beauty?
    The Second Beauty is the joy of Divine Love as it receives a purified soul, represented by Beatrice's smile.

Words to Know:

swoon: lose consciousness, faint

Canto XXXII
Beatrice Unveiled

(*The Earthly Paradise*)
Departure of the Heavenly Pageant, Transformation of the Chariot
1. How long has it been since Dante saw Beatrice?
    It has been ten years.
2. What happens to his sight?
    He is temporarily blinded as if he had looked at the sun.
3. What does he see when his sight is restored?
    He sees the procession moving away.
4. What do Dante and Statius do?
    They follow the procession, led by Matilda (the lady who had led him through Lethe).

5. Who was she "who heeded a forked tongue?"
   She was Eve, who heeded the serpent.
6. What do they hear?
   They hear the murmuring of "Adam."
7. What does the procession do?
   It circles a huge tree which has no foliage, obviously the Tree of the Knowledge of Good and Evil.
8. Why is the Griffon praised?
   He is praised because he does not eat of the wood of the tree.
9. How does he respond?
   He responds that only by avoiding that wood (corruption) can goodness be preserved.
10. What does the Griffon do?
    He binds the tree to the chariot's pole.
11. What happens to the tree?
    It grows beautiful foliage and flowers.

Note:

The chariot represents the Church Triumphant. The tree represents the Civil Authority of the Holy Roman Empire. Beatrice approaches the tree on foot in an act of humility to show the humility the Church should have before the legitimate civil authority. Dante is showing his ideal of the Church which had become corrupt, as he demonstrated in the *Inferno*. The cross on which Christ was crucified was believed to have come from the Tree of the Knowledge of Good and Evil. By tying the tree to the chariot pole, Dante symbolizes that the cross draws the Church forward.

12. What does Dante do after he sees this vision?
    He falls asleep and dreams again.
13. To what does he compare his falling asleep and awakening?
    He compares it to the Apostles at Christ's Transfiguration (*Matthew* 17:1-8).
14. Where is Beatrice?
    She is sitting under the tree on the ground with her attendants, guarding the chariot.
15. Where have the others gone?
    They have followed the Griffon to Heaven.
16. What does Beatrice tell Dante to do?
    She tells him to note well what he sees so that he can write about it when he returns to earth.
17. What happens as Dante sits with Beatrice?
    A great bird swoops down over the chariot, attacking it with force and causing it to rock. It is followed by a thin fox which Beatrice drives away. The bird returns, leaving behind some of its feathers, and a voice exclaims "Oh what a load you bear, my little ship!"
18. What happens next?
    A dragon rises from the earth under the chariot, ripping the floor with its tail, and then it wanders away.
19. What happens to the chariot?
    It is covered with the feathers from the bird and sprouts seven heads.
20. What appears on the chariot?
    A harlot appears.
21. What stands at her side?
    A giant stands at her side.
22. What does she do, and what is the result?
    She looks at Dante with lust, and the giant beats her.
23. What does the giant do next?
    The giant unties the one-time chariot from the tree and drags it through the woods.

Unit 1: Poetry

Note:
The symbolism here may not be obvious to the modern reader. Following is one interpretation, found in the notes at the end of the Canto. The fox represents the heresies which threatened the early Church (and still does). The bird which descended and left its feathers is the Eagle of Imperial Rome. The grief expressed is for the corruption the "little ship," the Church, would experience as a result of the wealth it would acquire. The woman in the car (the harlot) is found in *Revelation* 17:3, and represents the Seven Deadly Sins which are opposed to the Virtues. The "ungirt harlot" represents the Papacy of Boniface VIII, mention of whom has appeared numerous times in the *Divine Comedy*, and Clement V. The giant is the French monarch which controlled the Papacy. As the harlot looks at Dante (representing Italy), she is seen to represent Philip IV of France who humiliated Boniface VIII. Boniface was in league with various rulers and neglected his spiritual charge in pursuit of worldly plunder. Dragging the chariot off could represent the removal of the Papacy to Avignon by Philip.

QUESTIONS FOR FURTHER THOUGHT

A. The procession generally represents what?
   It represents the Church, which has come to meet the repentant sinner.
B. The tree which is encircled by the procession represents Law. Why is Adam's name murmured here?
   His name is murmured because he broke the law by eating from the tree.
C. What do the purple blossoms on the tree signify?
   They signify the empire (royalty).
D. If by joining the pole to the tree, neither was damaged, what could that signify?
   It could signify the peaceful coexistence of the empire with the Church.
E. What could be another interpretation of the large bird attacking the chariot?
   It could symbolize the persecution by the empire of the early Christians.
F. The dragon breaks the floor of the chariot. What could this signify?
   It could signify schism in the Church.
G. What are the Seven Deadly Sins?
   They are pride, envy, sloth, lust, greed, intemperance and anger.

Canto XXXIII
Eunoe

(The Earthly Paradise)
Dante's Purification Completed
1. What do the "Holy Seven" chant?
   They chant *Deus Venerunt Gentes*, "The Heathens are Coming into Thine Inheritance" (*Psalm* 79).
2. What is the mood?
   It is one of grief.
3. How does Beatrice respond?
   She responds with Christ's words *modicum, et vos videbitis me*, "A little while and you shall see me no more,… because I go to the Father" (*John* 16:16).
4. What does Beatrice ask Dante?
   She asks him why he doesn't ask her any questions.
5. How does he respond?
   He says that she knows his needs so he doesn't have to voice them.
6. How does she respond to that?
   She tells him that he has to shed his fear and shame because he has been purified.
7. What does Beatrice say about her prophecy?
   She says that it is obscure, but it will come to pass soon.

8. What must Dante remember to report?
    He must report that the tree of the garden has been twice despoiled and that God is offended.
9. What does Beatrice say about the tree?
    She says that there is a particular reason that it is so tall and has an inverted crown (it is wider at the top than at the bottom), and its form has a moral meaning.
10. What troubles Dante?
    He is troubled because he cannot understand what Beatrice is talking about.
11. What is her explanation?
    She says the school of thought (Philosophy, Reason) which he has followed as an end in itself is far from the Divine Truth.
12. What has Dante forgotten and why?
    He has forgotten his estrangement from Beatrice because he has drunk the water of Lethe.
13. What does she promise Dante?
    She promises to speak so that he will understand.
14. Who is to lead Dante to the River Eunoe?
    Matilda, the woman who led him to Lethe, will lead him.
15. Who accompanies Dante and Matilda to the River?
    Statius accompanies them.
16. Why does Dante not tell more about the water he has drunk?
    He does not tell more because there is no more room in his plan of the work for more verses.
17. How does Dante end the *Purgatorio*?
    He ends it by indicating he is now ready to journey to Heaven because he has been purified, "…perfect, pure, and ready for the Stars."

Questions for Further Thought

A. What does Beatrice mean when she quotes Christ's words announcing his Resurrection?
    She means to comfort the virgins with the assurance that the Church will triumph.
B. Beatrice tells Dante that the one who broke the cart will know God's wrath. She uses a quaint expression " …God's wrath will not be calmed by soup, however hot." What does that mean?
    She is referring to a custom in Ancient Greece whereby a murderer could escape punishment if he ate soup over the victim's grave for nine consecutive days. In Florence the grave was guarded to insure that nobody ate soup over it.
C. The eagle will not be without an heir forever. What does the eagle represent?
    It represents the Roman Empire.
D. What is the moral meaning of the form of the tree?
    The tree is so tall and wider at the top, symbolizing how little is man's understanding of Good and Evil as compared to Divine Truth. Man is just too limited to understand through Reason alone.
E. What does Matilda mean that "Lethe could not have washed that memory away?"
    Lethe washes away all memory of sin, so that memory was not sinful.

Word to Know:

Eunoe: memory of good

For Further Research:

The eagle returns and leaves its feathers to cover the chariot. This refers to the Donation of Constantine. What was the significance of this Donation?

Briefly, this was a supposed document of Constantine which recognized the spiritual dignity of the Pope in the spiritual order and gave him certain privileges in the world as well as the wealth of the empire. This document is considered the most famous forgery in the history of Europe. In the *Divine Comedy*, the aid from the eagle (his feathers) is seen as a burden for the Church which led to its corruption.

Paradiso
The Divine Comedy: Part 3
by Dante Alighieri
Translation: John Ciardi
New American Library

Dante has repented of all his sins and can now enter Heaven. He has been loved by Beatrice since they were children, and out of love, she has led him to repent. Now, he is entering Love itself. In *Paradiso*, the language is mystical rather than common as in the previous parts of *The Divine Comedy*. Heaven is composed of the universe—the moon, the sun, the stars, etc. On each are to be found different souls (points of light) who are enjoying paradise. They seem to move in and out, back and forth before him in continual motion. He finally understands all that he has sought to know, and with his will in conformity with God's love, he can see God.

Unit 1: Poetry

Canto I
The Earthly Paradise, Ascent to Heaven

(The Invocation, The Sphere of Fire; The Music of the Spheres)
1. Whom does Dante invoke for help in telling this part of his story?
    He invokes Apollo along with the Muses.
2. What does Dante say about the intellect as it gets closer to Heaven?
    It grows in understanding.
3. What does Dante do after he sees Beatrice do it?
    He looks straight into the sun.
4. What term does Dante use for what has happened to himself?
    He says he has been trans-humanized.
5. What is the "last created part" of his being?
    The "last created part" of his being is his rational soul.
6. Why does Dante have a difficult time understanding his experience?
    He is full of misconceptions and tries to understand through his mortal eyes.
7. What is happening to Dante?
    He is rising effortlessly toward Heaven.
8. What does Beatrice explain to Dante about his ascent?
    She explains that it should not surprise him because now that he has been purified, his soul is drawn quickly to God.

Questions for Further Thought

A. What is the goal of our intellect (our mind, our will, etc)?
    The goal of our intellect (our mind, our will, etc) is the understanding and knowledge of God.
B. When Dante expresses a wish to be crowned with bay, what does he mean?
    He hopes his poetry will be worthy to be awarded the laurel (bay) wreath which was given to poets.
C. Dante says that it seems as if day is added to day. What does he mean?
    He means that it is so bright that it is as if there were another sun giving yet more light.

Word to Know:

Empyrean: the sky or heavens, the celestial sphere, believed to be the highest part of Heaven and the dwelling place of God

Canto II
Ascent to the Moon, The First Sphere: The Moon

(Warning to the Reader; Beatrice Explains the Markings on the Moon)
1. What does Dante advise his readers?
    He advises them to turn back because the book will be very difficult to understand.
2. Where do Dante and Beatrice find themselves (the first star)?
    They are on the moon.
3. What is it like?
    It is dense, pearl-like and smoothly polished.
4. What did he note as they entered the elements of that body?
    He noticed that there was no disturbing of its substance when they entered.

5. That observation prompts him to think of what mystery?
    He thinks of the mystery of God-become-Man.
6. What does Dante want to know?
    He wants to know what the black spots on the surface of the moon are.
7. To what does he attribute the spots?
    He attributes them to varying degrees of density on the moon's surface.
8. How does Beatrice explain the spots?
    She says that energy and light are transmitted through the universe from the Prime Mover who is God, and they appear different on the various heavenly bodies, depending on the qualities of those bodies.

Questions for Further Thought

A. Not only does Dante call on Apollo, but also on Minerva to help him. What does Minerva represent?
    She represents wisdom.
B. What might Dante mean in referring to the "bread of angels?"
    He is referring to the knowledge of God and expressing the fact that only those with faith will be able to comprehend what he is to reveal.
C. Who are the Blessed Movers from whom must flow the motion and power of the circling spheres in the heavens?
    The Blessed Movers are the Angels and Intelligences given command over each.
D. What is Dante generally expressing in this long discussion?
    He is generally expressing the view of the universe as understood during the Middle Ages.

Canto III
The First Sphere: The Moon

(The Inconstant: Piccarda, Constance)
1. How do the faces appear to Dante?
    They appear as mirrored images.
2. Why are the souls here?
    They are here for inconstancy, or failure to keep their vows.
3. What does Dante ask Piccarda?
    He asks her if the souls here long to be in a higher point in Heaven.
4. How does she respond?
    She says that all she longs for is here—to wish for more would put her will in opposition to God's will.
5. How had her vow been broken?
    It had been broken by force from men who had forced her out of the cloister.
6. Who is with Piccarda?
    The Empress Constance is with her.
7. How does this canto close?
    It closes with Dante turning to Beatrice who is so radiant he cannot endure it.

Questions for Further Thought

A. Who was Piccarda?
    She was a nun, the sister of Corso and Forese Donati whom we met in Purgatory. Corso took her from the cloister and forced her to marry in order to form a political alliance.
B. What is the love which is often mentioned?
    That love is *caritas* or charity, which is the love of others.

Unit 1: Poetry

C. Why is the moon considered inconstant?
   It is inconstant because it is ever changing in relation to the earth. It waxes, it wanes, it is full and then it is dark.

WORDS TO KNOW:

limpid: calm, transparent

pallid: pale, ashen

inconstancy: unfaithfulness

puissance: power

CANTO IV

(Beatrice Discourses: The True Seat of the Blessed, Plato's Error, Free)
(Will, Recompense for Broken Vows)
1. Does Dante state his questions to Beatrice?
     No. She knows them before he speaks.
2. What does he wonder?
     He wonders why the bliss of one who is faithful to a vow and is violated is diminished.
3. What else does he wonder about?
     He wonders if the soul returns to the star from which it came, as Plato believed.
4. How does she explain the position of the souls in Heaven?
     She has to use physical expressions to help him comprehend spiritual realities; all are before God but enjoy His "eternal breath" in varying degrees.
5. What had Piccarda and Constance failed to do?
     They had failed to return to the convent at a later time when they were free to do so.
6. What was the difference between the wills of the two women as contrasted with that of Lawrence?
     The two women had consented because of a dread of further harm, while Lawrence had allowed himself to be burned on a grill rather than give in.
7. What does Dante ask as the canto ends?
     He asks if one can make satisfaction for defective vows.
8. Why does Dante have to look away rather than straight into Beatrice's eyes?
     He cannot yet take in the magnitude of love that she reveals.

QUESTIONS FOR FURTHER THOUGHT

A. Why would the idea of a soul returning to the star from whence it came be heresy?
     It would imply predestination and deny free will.
B. Who was Lawrence?
     St. Lawrence was a deacon in Rome in 258 who, when ordered to produce the Church's treasure presented the poor of Rome. As a punishment he was martyred, being roasted on a grill.
C. Who was Mucius?
     He was a young man in ancient Rome who had vowed to kill Porsenna. He did not succeed and so he held his right hand in fire till it burned. As a result, he only had one usable hand--his left--and was known as Scaevola (left-handed).

Word to Know:

heresy: dissent, unorthodoxy

Canto V
Ascent to the Second Sphere, the Second Sphere: Mercury

(Beatrice discourses, The Seekers of Honor, The Emperor Justinian)
1. How does Beatrice explain her brightness?
    As love increases, so does her brightness.
2. What does Dante want to know?
    He wants to know if an unfulfilled vow can be satisfied in a way other than the original promise stated.
3. What is God's greatest gift to man?
    God's greatest gift to man is his free will.
4. What happens once a man has made a vow to God?
    He gives up his free will to God, so deeds cannot fully compensate.
5. What can the Church do?
    The Church can dispense one of the vows he has made.
6. What two parts constitute a vow?
    A vow is made up of a covenant and the things promised.
7. Which part cannot be cancelled?
    The part which cannot be cancelled is the covenant.
8. What is the significance of the turning of both the white and yellow keys?
    It is the authority of the Church to dispense one from a vow.
9. What does Beatrice say about the vow of Jephthah?
    The vow was bad in the first place and worse in the keeping.
10. What had he vowed?
    He had vowed that if his army were victorious he would sacrifice the first living creature who greeted him when he returned home. That turned out to be his daughter.
11. Who was Iphigenia?
    She was Agamemnon's daughter who was also sacrificed because of a bad vow made by him.
12. What does Beatrice counsel?
    She counsels Christians to be guided by the Scriptures and the Church and not to take vows lightly.
13. What is the second sphere?
    The second sphere is Mercury.
14. In addition to the radiance of the light, what else does Dante sense here?
    He senses joy.
15. Why can't Dante see the spirit that speaks to him?
    The light that surrounds the spirit is too bright.

Word to Know:

covenant: promise, pledge

Unit 1: Poetry

Canto VI
The Second Sphere: Mercury

(Seekers of Honor: Justinian, The Roman Eagle)

Note:
Constantine moved the headquarters of his empire to Byzantium, and the Roman Eagle, which was the symbol of the Roman Empire, flew east. Dante believed that Rome was the center of the Church and the Empire and that Constantine's Donation led to the corruption of the Church.

1. Who was the new son of the Latian king?
    The new son was Aeneas, who left Troy to fulfill his destiny of founding Rome.
2. Who is the spirit who talks to Dante?
    The spirit is Justinian who was emperor in the 500s.
3. What did Pope Agapetus do for Justinian?
    He instructed him in Christ's Divine and Human natures.
4. What is Justinian known for?
    He codified Roman law.
5. What was the symbol of the Roman Empire?
    The eagle was its symbol.
6. What does Justinian recount?
    He recounts the history of the empire.
7. What happened during the reign of the third Caesar (Tiberius)?
    Christ was crucified.
8. Under Titus, the eagle "avenged the vengeance taken for that crime of old!" This refers to what?
    This refers to the destruction of Jerusalem which Dante saw as vengeance for the death of Christ in that city.
9. With what does Justinian end his history?
    He ends it with the present strife between the Ghibellines and the Guelphs.
10. What spirits inhabit this "star" (Mercury)?
    Mercury is inhabited by those who sought fame and honor while working for the Good.
11. Are the souls content to be here?
    Yes they are, and they realize that their state is in proportion to their merit.

Note:
The translator points out the parallel structures between the Canticles of *The Divine Comedy*. In the *Inferno* VI he related what was happening in Florence, in *Purgatorio* VI he related the conditions in Italy, and in *Paradiso* VI he related the conditions in the Roman Empire.

Question for Further Thought

What is Justinian's attitude toward the empire?
    He reveres it as part of God's plan.

Canto VII
The Second Sphere: Mercury, Ascent to the Third Sphere

(Seekers of Honor: Justinian; Beatrice Discourses)
1. What is Dante's question at this point, which Beatrice knows before he asks?
    He wants to know how a just vengeance could be justly avenged.

2. Who was the man not born?
    The man not born was Adam.
3. What did the man in question 2 do?
    He failed to control his own free will and being damned, damned all his offspring as well.
4. What did God do?
    Through Christ, God united himself with Adam's nature and suffered to atone for men's sins.
5. What is Dante's next question?
    He wonders why God chose the crucifixion as the way of redemption.
6. What is Beatrice's answer?
    She says man was incapable because of sin to make satisfaction for himself, so God, in His Divine Goodness, humbled himself to take up the cross.
7. With what attributes did God endow humankind?
    He endowed it with immortality, freedom and likeness to God.
8. What alone can take away man's freedom and likeness to God?
    Sin can take those attributes away.
9. What else puzzles Dante?
    He doesn't understand how God's creation came to be corrupted.
10. How does Beatrice explain the puzzle?
    She says that the angels and heavens which were created by God are incorruptible, but secondary forces use created things to create earthly elements which are corruptible.
11. How can Dante infer proof of his resurrection?
    His life (and the life of all of mankind) was created directly by God and was filled with love for the Creator. The Creator draws all life to Himself.

Canto VIII
The Third Sphere: Venus

(The Amorous: Charles Martel)
1. What influence was Venus thought to have on men?
    It was thought to influence their passions, particularly those relating to love.
2. How does Dante know they have reached Venus, even though he was unaware of the ascent?
    He sees that Beatrice has grown even more radiant.
3. From where do the souls come to speak to Dante?
    They come from the Empyrean.
4. What does Dante long to hear?
    He longs to hear the "Hosanna."
5. What do these souls come to do?
    They come to bring joy to Dante.
6. What does Dante ask Charles Martel?
    He asks him how bitterness can come from sweet seed (or why children do not always inherit the good virtues of their parents).
7. How does Charles answer?
    He says that even though men are created good, they are influenced by the stars and through free will, can choose evil.
8. How does Charles explain diversity?
    He says that men are created for various things in order to provide society with what it needs.
9. When do problems occur?
    Problems occur when the individual does not follow the natural inclinations and abilities he is given (when one has the intellect to be a priest becomes a king instead, or one who is born to be a soldier becomes a priest).

Unit 1: Poetry

Question for Further Thought

Does Dante's thought reflect a vision of a world of chaos or a world of order? Explain.
> Dante's vision is definitely a world of order. That is reflected in the physical construction of the *Divine Comedy* and in the thoughts he expresses. Nothing happens by chance—rather God has created the world in order and allows for the natural consequences to occur for mankind because of the great gift of free will. There should be no surprises, then, when men are either punished or rewarded according to their choices in life. Order demands the results which happen.

Canto IX

(The Amorous: Cunizza, Folquet, Rahab)

1. What does Charles predict?
   > He predicts attacks and deceptions on his house in Naples.
2. Does Cunizza have any regrets about her life?
   > No, she does not.
3. What does Cunizza predict?
   > She predicts a blood bath for her people and treachery on the part of the bishop.
4. What does Dante realize about the spirits here?
   > He realizes that they know his mind—he doesn't have to ask his questions because they already know them.
5. Why are the spirits here so happy?
   > They are happy because of the power and mercy of God who has forgiven their sins. They no longer have to repent because they no longer think of their sins. Their thoughts are now fixed only on love (charity), and their joy is compounded by the experience of each others' joy.
6. Whom does Folquet point out?
   > He points out Rahab who was the first soul called to this Sphere of Heaven.
7. What had Rahab done?
   > She had helped Joshua to win at the battle of Jericho. After the Crucifixion, she was the first soul taken up to Heaven.
8. What pope does Folquet refer to who has lost his sense of mission?
   > He refers to Boniface VIII, whom we previously met in Hell.
9. What is the accursed flower of gold?
   > It is the lily on the florin, which was the money of Florence.
10. What is implied about the pope?
    > He has caused corruption by seeking profit rather than spiritual goods.
11. What does Folquet predict?
    > He predicts that the Vatican and Rome will soon be freed of this corruption by the moving of the Papacy to Avignon.

Words to Know:

decretal: papal decree relating to Church law or doctrine

decree: official order

Paradiso

Canto X
Ascent to the Sun, The Fourth Sphere: The Sun

(Doctors of the Church, The First Garland of Souls: Aquinas)
1. In what way does Dante mention the Trinity?
    He says that the ineffable First Presence contemplated His Son with that "Third Essence of Love breathed forth forever by Them both." The Third Essence of Love is the Holy Spirit.
2. What does Dante marvel at?
    He marvels at the perfection of creation.
3. What does Dante ask the reader to do?
    He asks the reader to stay with him and feast on the joy he is experiencing. It is a demanding exercise because Heaven and God's ways are not to be grasped easily.
4. What eclipsed Dante's devotion for Beatrice?
    His love for God eclipsed his devotion for Beatrice.
5. Does the first soul to speak identify himself by name?
    He doesn't introduce himself until he introduces Dominic and Albert, his teachers.
6. Who are the inhabitants of this Sphere of the Sun?
    They are men known for their wisdom and teaching.
7. Who is the spirit for whom "men hunger for any news" and within whose mind "were shone such depths of wisdom…?"
    He is Solomon.
8. How many souls does Dante see here?
    He sees twelve.

Canto XI
The Fourth Sphere: The Sun

(Doctors of the Church, The First Garland of Souls: Aquinas, Praise of St. Francis, Degeneracy of Dominicans)
1. Who were the two princes of the Church about whom Aquinas speaks?
    He speaks of Dominic who in wisdom "walked the earth bathed in the splendor of the cherubim," and Francis who "In his love, shone like the seraphim."
2. Who was the Lady who, like death knocks on no door that opens to her gladly?"
    That is Poverty, which Francis embraced before the diocesan court when he renounced all his possessions.
3. Who was Poverty's "First Groom?"
    Her "First Groom" was Christ.
4. What did the venerable Bernard do?
    He joined St. Francis in poverty (in fact, he was his first follower).
5. What was the humble cord?
    It was the rope the followers of Francis wore around their waists. It was also worn by the poor, who used it as a belt.
6. What did Francis receive from Pope Innocent?
    His order was recognized by the pope (only conditionally, however, because he thought Francis' Rule was too harsh).
7. What did Honorius do?
    He gave full approval to the Order which St. Francis founded.
8. What does his going to preach to the Sultan imply?
    It implies that he went to convert the Moslems. He was not successful.
9. What is "Christ's final seal, the holy wounds of which he wore two years?"
    The wounds are known as the stigmata.

Unit 1: Poetry

10. Who was his "fellow helmsman?"
    His "fellow helmsman" was St. Dominic.
11. What does Dante (through Aquinas, himself a Dominican) say about the followers of St. Dominic?
    He says they became worldly and did not bear fruit the further they got from his leadership.

Words to Know:

aphorisms: sayings; clichés

cowl: monk's hood

Canto XII

(Doctors of the Church, The Second Garland of Souls: Bonaventure, Praise of St. Dominic, Degeneracy of Franciscans)
1. What does Dante say about the Church indirectly?
    He says that the faithful leaders and followers were few, but out of the few, God raised up champions who would reunify and teach the believers.
2. What is the land to which the West wind returns each Spring?
    That land is Spain.
3. Who was it that before he was born his mother saw his future in her dream?
    It was Dominic.

Note:
Dominic's mother had dreamed that she gave birth to a black and white dog with a torch in its mouth. Dominican can be broken down to mean *Domini cane*, or Dog of the Lord. The members of his Order wore black and white.

4. What was Dante saying about the Papacy?
    He was saying that it was good before, but it had become degenerate—not of itself but because of the man who presently occupied it.
5. What did Dominic ask the pope?
    He wanted permission to teach the people the Faith and to combat heresy, not to gain material wealth.

Note:
He was fighting the Albigensian heresy which was anti-Church and denied the Resurrection.

6. Who is it that speaks about Dominic?
    Bonaventure speaks about him. (Bonaventure was a Franciscan).

Note:
Bonaventure speaks about the split among the Franciscans. There were some who kept to the rule of absolute poverty, even against the wishes of the pope. This poverty inspired people to give gifts to them, resulting in the necessity for administrators to manage the gifts. St. Bonaventure taught that the gifts were the property of the Church but could be used by the monks in their work. Other Franciscans were lax in their practice of the *Rule*. Both ways, being too strict and too lax, caused a split.

Words to Know:

sempiternal: everlasting

paladin: medieval champion of a cause

Canto XIII

(The Intellect of the Faith: Theologians and Doctors of the Church: Aquinas)
1. How does Dante generally describe the appearance of these spirits?
    He describes them as two wreaths of stars, one inside the other, and turning in opposite directions.
2. What do these spirits sing about?
    They sing about the Trinitarian God.
3. Who is the "lamp from which the glorious life of God's beloved pauper had been spoken?"
    That is St. Thomas Aquinas.
4. Who is "God's beloved pauper?"
    He is St. Francis of Assisi.
5. Who does Dante speak about in lines 37-39 "…from which was carved the rib that went to form the lovely cheek for whose bad palate all mankind was starved?"
    He speaks about Adam and Eve.
6. Who was the one who asked God for wisdom in the governance of his people?
    That was Solomon.
7. Why are earthly things imperfect?
    They are imperfect because they are worked upon by nature.
8. Who is exempt from comparison with Solomon for earthly wisdom?
    Adam and Christ, who were created directly by God, are exempt.
9. What advise does Aquinas give Dante?
    He advises him to be slow and careful in making judgments.

Question for Further Thought

Why is Aquinas' advice to Dante relevant for all of us?
   It is relevant because we can easily be misled by arguments, which though they may be convincing, might not necessarily be valid. Also, we can form opinions about others based on external things without really knowing their hearts and true intentions.

Canto XIV

The Fourth Sphere: The Sun, Ascent to Mars, The Fifth Sphere: Mars

(The Two Circles of Souls: Philosophers and Theologians, Solomon; The Third Circle of Souls: Warriors of God, The Vision of Christ on the Cross)
1. What question does Dante have before he even realizes it?
    He wants to know if after the resurrection of the bodies and the reuniting of the bodies with the souls, if the souls' radiance will be as bright and if so, how will the eyes be able to endure it?
2. Who is "that One and Two and Three?"
    That is the Blessed Trinity—the Father, the Son and the Holy Spirit.
3. How does Solomon answer Dante's question?
    He says that we will be given new eyes which will be able to see God's radiance.
4. Do all souls have the same intensity of the vision?
    No, they do not. Dante says "Each robe reflects love's ardor shining forth."

Unit 1: Poetry

5. To where have Dante and Beatrice ascended, and how do you know?
    They have ascended to Mars which is the "red star."
6. What does Dante offer to God?
    He offers his immortal soul as a holocaust (burnt offering).
7. What does Dante see here?
    He sees Christ's cross formed from intense light upon which flash many smaller dancing lights singing a hymn.
8. Does Dante turn away from the vision of Christ on the Cross to Beatrice?
    No, he stays enraptured by the vision.
9. What does he say about Beatrice's beauty?
    He says it increases the higher up in Heaven they go.

Canto XV
The Fifth Sphere: Mars

(The Warriors of God, Cacciaguida)
1. Why does the music stop?
    It stops to allow Dante to speak.
2. Where does the light of the spirit which speaks to Dante come from?
    It comes from a star, moving from the right hand of Christ down to the foot of the cross.
3. What does the spirit of Cacciaguida ask Dante?
    The spirit asks him if there was ever anyone else to whom the gate of Heaven was opened twice.
4. What does Dante ask?
    He asks the spirit's name.
5. How does the spirit answer?
    The spirit says "I was your root."
6. If the spirit's son was the father of Dante's grandfather, who is the spirit?
    The spirit is Dante's great-great grandfather.
7. What does the spirit say of the one who gave Dante his name?
    He is in Purgatory on the first ledge where the proud are purified, and Dante should offer good works for him.
8. How does Cacciaguida describe Florence?
    He says it was a place of virtue but no longer is.
9. What is the significance of his following the emperor Conrad?
    He was a Christian and went on a Crusade.
10. How did he die?
    He was martyred by the Moslems.

Questions for Further Thought

A. What is the meaning of *O sanguis meus*?
    It means "Oh, blood of mine."
B. What is Dante's surname?
    His surname is Alighieri.
C. Who are the sinning shepherds about whom Cacciaguida speaks?
    They are the popes.

Words to Know:

diadem: crown, or bright star

Ilium: Troy

Canto XVI

1. In what does Dante show pride, even in Heaven?
    He shows pride in his lineage.
2. How does Dante address Cacciaguida?
    He uses the "voi" form of you, which is a sign of deference.
3. What does Beatrice seem to do when she hears Dante use the voi?
    She seems to admonish him against its use through her smile.
4. What is St. John's sheepfold?
    It is Florence, whose patron saint was St. John the Baptist.
5. What does Cacciaguida say about the people of Florence today?
    He says they are "mongrelized," meaning that they have intermarried with outside families.
6. What does he say is an evil to the city-states?
    He says that "confusion of blood" has been that evil.
7. What does he say about human institutions?
    He says they all disappear eventually.
8. To what does Cacciaguida attribute the undoing of the prominent families?
    He attributes their undoing to their pride.

Question for Further Thought

What was the significance of flying the flag with the lily upside down?
    To fly a flag upside down was to show that the people of that flag had been defeated in war. In this passage, Cacciaguida is saying that Florence had never been defeated in war, though she had seen the corruption of her leading families.

Canto XVII

1. What does Beatrice urge Dante to do, and why?
    She urges him to ask his question so that he will learn to express what he learns to others.
2. What concerns Dante?
    He is concerned about future troubles which have been prophesied for him.

Note:
Contingency refers to what could or could not exist. It is dependant on what necessarily exists—that is certain, infinite and primary. (See notes for line 16)

3. What does Cacciaguida tell Dante?
    He tells him that he will leave Florence and his friends and family, and that his exile is being planned by the pope.
4. Is the future completely bleak for Dante?
    No, it is not. Cacciaguida tells him that truth will win out.

Unit 1: Poetry

5. What will be his biggest burden?
    His biggest burden will be the people he will encounter.
6. What will Dante enjoy?
    He will enjoy fame and the patronage of the great Lombard of the Scaligeri family and another warrior.
7. What does Cacciaguida tell Dante to do with what he has learned about his patron?
    He tells him to keep his knowledge to himself.
8. How does Cacciaguida advise Dante to treat those who harm him?
    He admonishes him not to hate his neighbors, because his reward will last longer than they will.
9. If Dante were to speak what he knows, who would be offended?
    Those with shame on their consciences would be offended.

Questions for Further Thought

A. Just guessing from the previous canticles, which pope do you suppose Dante is referring to who is plotting his exile?
    He is referring to Boniface VIII.
B. What party did Dante belong to?
    He belonged to the Whites, but Cacciaguida predicts that he will be a party of one in the future.

Words to Know:

punctilious: meticulous, conscientious

abjure: renounce, reject

Canto XVIII
The Fifth Sphere: Mars, Ascent to Jupiter

(*The Courageous: Cacciaguida, Great Warriors of God; The Just and Temperate Rulers, The Vision of the Flashing Lights and of the Eagle*)

1. Who is "that holy mirror" in the first line?
    That is Cacciaguida, with whom Dante has been speaking.
2. What does Beatrice tell Dante to do?
    She tells him to put aside his unhappy thoughts about his future, because she who dwells close to God will be with him.
3. Where does Dante see the lights of the spirits here?
    He sees them on the cross.
4. Who are some of the spirits (the Warriors of God) he sees?
    He sees Joshua, Maccabeus, Charlemagne, Roland and William of Orange.
5. What does Dante notice about Beatrice?
    He notices that the higher they go, the more beautiful and radiant she becomes.
6. What does Dante suddenly realize?
    He realizes that he has left the Sphere of Mars and entered the sixth Sphere of Jupiter.
7. How does Dante describe Jupiter?
    He describes it as the Temperate Star.
8. What do the lights form before Dante's eyes?
    They form letters into the words *Diligite iustitiam. Qui iudicatis terram.* ("Love righteousness, ye that are judges of the earth").
9. Whom does he invoke for help in describing what he sees?
    He invokes Pegasean, the nine Muses.

10. What becomes of the *m* in terram?
    It becomes an eagle.
11. What does the eagle represent?
    The eagle represents the Roman Empire.
12. Dante launches a diatribe against what?
    He launches a diatribe against the Church which has gone astray.
13. What abuse is prevalent?
    The abuse of excommunication is prevalent.
14. What does his reference to "the saint who lived alone and who was forced to give his head in forfeit" mean?
    It means that the pope lusts after the florin (Florentine gold coin) which bears the image of John the Baptist.

Canto XIX
The Sixth Sphere: Jupiter

(The Just and Temperate Rulers; The Eagle)
1. What is it that forms the eagle?
    It is the radiance of each of the bright souls in this sphere, the Just and Temperate Rulers.
2. How does each soul appear?
    Each soul appears as a ruby.
3. Why do the spirits speak with "I" and "my?"
    They speak that way because together they speak for Justice.
4. What does the eagle say about man's ability to see justice?
    He says that man cannot penetrate its depth.
5. To what does he liken man's understanding?
    He likens it to the eye's inability to see the bottom of the ocean—he can only see the surface and the bottom only near the shore, but he cannot see the depth.
6. What puzzles Dante?
    He wants to know what becomes of a good Indian who never learns about Christ.
7. How does the eagle respond?
    The eagle says that none come to Heaven who did not believe in Christ, but many non-Christians will be closer to Him than many who claim to know Him.
8. The eagle proceeds to list a number of people who will not reach Heaven. Generally, who are they?
    They are renegade rulers who are guilty of a variety of crimes.

Question for Further Thought

In speaking of the "cripple of Jerusalem," the eagle says his good deeds will be marked with an *I* and his villanies with an *M*. What does he mean?
    He means that the number of his evil deeds will number a thousand (M is the Roman numeral for 1000) and the number of good deeds will be so insignificant as to be marked with an I (I is the Roman numeral for one).

Words to Know:

Halcyon: peaceful, heavenly, quiet

empery: absolute dominion, sovereignty

Canto XX

1. What comparison does Dante make between day and night?
   He says that during the day the world is lit by one sun, while at night, the sky is lit by many lights which take their light from the sun.
2. What comprises the eagle's eye?
   The brightest spirits in the sphere comprise his eye.
3. Who is in the center of the eye?
   In the center of the eye is "the sweet Psalmist of the Holy Ghost," King David.
4. Who consoled the widow who lost her son? (See *Purgatorio*, Canto X: 70-90).
   Emperor Trajan consoled her.
5. Who by true penitence delayed death? (See *II Kings*, XX: 1-11)
   King Hezekiah delayed death.
6. Who moved to Greece in order to give the Shepherd sovereignty?
   Constantine the Great moved to Greece and left the Western part of his empire to the Church.
7. What lesson did he learn?
   He learned that even though his good intentions resulted in bad fruit, his soul was not harmed as a result.
8. Who is the fifth light in the eagle's eye?
   The fifth light is William II of Sicily.
9. Who is the sixth light?
   The sixth light is Ripheus the Trojan, mentioned in the *Aeneid*, as the most just man among the Trojans.
10. Why does Dante marvel?
    He marvels because Trajan and Ripheus the Trojan were pagans yet they are here.
11. How did Trajan come here?
    He came back to life from Hell by virtue of the prayers of another (Pope Gregory the Great), and he believed in Christ.
12. How did Ripheus come here?
    Ripheus had always believed, having foreseen our redemption a thousand years before Christ died, and he was baptized by the three ladies (Faith, Hope and Charity) after he died.
13. What does the eagle admonish?
    He admonishes men not to judge, because we do not know God's will.

Canto XXI

Ascent to Saturn, the Seventh Sphere: Saturn

(The Contemplative: Peter Damiano)
1. How does the Canto begin?
   It begins with Dante realizing again the growing beauty of Beatrice and ascending to the Seventh Sphere, which is the Sphere of Saturn.
2. What does Dante see?
   He sees a golden ladder with many lights descending along its rungs.
3. What does Dante ask the brightest spirit?
   He asks why there is no music in this sphere.
4. What is the answer?
   The answer is that his mortal ears cannot tolerate the beauty.
5. Why doesn't Beatrice smile?
   She doesn't smile because she would be too radiant for Dante's mortal senses.
6. What else does Dante want to know?
   He wants to know why this spirit was predestined to speak to him.

7. How does the spirit respond?
   The spirit says that he beholds God through the ray of His (God's) light shining on him, but even the soul who is closest to God (the Seraph) cannot comprehend God's ways; therefore Dante should not try to understand destiny.
8. Who is the spirit that speaks?
   He is Peter Damiano, a cloistered monk in the eleventh century, who is a Doctor of the Church.
9. What does Peter Damiano say about the cloister?
   He says that at one time it produced many saints, but now it has been corrupted.
10. What is the hat which seems to always pass from bad to worse?
    It is the hat of a Cardinal of the Church.
11. What does he say about modern pastors?
    He says they are fat and wealthy.

Questions for Further Thought

A. What concept has been introduced in this Canto, and what is it?
   The concept which has been introduced is that of predestination. In the *Inferno* and *Purgatorio*, the souls exercised free will, and the consequences of the exercise of free will were graphically described. The souls that get to Heaven, however, are so perfectly aligned with the will of God, that there is no question of deviating from that perfect will, because the love which surrounds them is enough.
B. How would you describe the spirit of Peter Damiano?
   The spirit is in a trance while enjoying the vision of God, and it is spinning.
C. By the presence here of Peter Damiano, a cloistered monk, what other people would you expect to find in this sphere?
   You would expect to find monks, nuns and other contemplative souls.

Canto XXII
The Seventh Sphere: Saturn, Ascent to the Sphere of the Fixed Stars, The Eighth Sphere: The Fixed Stars

(The Contemplative: St. Benedict; Dante Looks Back at the Universe Below)
1. Why does Dante reel?
   He hears a thunderous burst of voices.
2. How does Beatrice reassure him?
   She tells him that it was a prayer of righteous anger (perhaps at mention of the corrupt Church).
3. How is Heaven's retribution perceived by those who wait for it?
   It is perceived as coming too soon.
4. How is Heaven's reward perceived by those who wait for it?
   It is perceived as coming too late.
5. Who is in the largest glowing globe which approaches Dante?
   St. Benedict is there.
6. Who carried the name of Christ to the mountain near Cassino?
   St. Benedict carried His name there.
7. What does the emboldened Dante request of Benedict?
   He asks to see his physical image.
8. How does Benedict respond?
   He says that Dante shall see him in the last sphere.
9. What does Benedict say about his *Rule*?
   He says that it has been neglected, and the monastery is full of corrupt men involved in usury.

Unit 1: Poetry

10. What is the "fruit whose poison fills the hearts of monks with madness?"
    That fruit is greed.
11. Why does Beatrice have Dante look down on the world?
    She wants him to have a more joyous heart as he enters the Triumphant Court.
12. What does he note as he looks "down" on the world?
    He notes how small the Earth is compared with the other planets.
13. What does Dante say about worldly things?
    He says they are of little account.

Question for Further Thought

What is the sign that follows Taurus in the Zodiac?
    The sign (constellation) that follows Taurus is Gemini.

Words to Know:

diffidence: shyness, reserve

usury: lending of money at extremely high rates

purlieu: an outlying or neighboring area

Canto XXIII
The Eighth Sphere: The Fixed Stars

(The Triumph of Christ; The Virgin Mary; The Apostles; The Angel Gabriel; St. Peter)
1. To what does Dante liken Beatrice in waiting?
    He likens her to a bird, protecting her nestlings while eager to leave them for food.
2. What comprises the militia of Christ's triumph?
    The militia of Christ's triumph is made up of the countless souls which have been saved.
3. What does Dante experience?
    He experiences Christ's radiance.
4. What happens to Dante?
    He swoons again.
5. What is he able to do when Beatrice tells him to open his eyes?
    He is able to see her radiant smile.
6. To whom does Beatrice direct Dante's vision?
    She directs his vision to the Rose, the Virgin Mary.
7. Who are next to her?
    Next to her are the lilies, the Apostles.
8. What happens to Christ's radiance?
    It withdraws so that Dante can see the rest of the vision.
9. What is the brightest ray which Dante then sees?
    The brightest ray is the Virgin Mary.
10. What does Dante say about music in Heaven?
    He says that it makes the sweetest earthly music sound like thunder.
11. Whom do the lamps of light surround?
    They surround the Virgin Mary.

12. What are the New and Old Consistories?
    They are the *Old* and *New Testaments*.
13. Who is the soul that holds the great keys?
    The soul that holds the great keys is St. Peter.

Questions for Further Thought

A. What is the meaning of *Regina Caeli*?
    It is a title of Mary meaning "Queen of Heaven."
B. What might the author be referring to when he speaks of the tears of the Babylonian exile?
    He may be speaking of the time all of us spend on Earth, waiting for Heaven.

Canto XXIV

(The Triumph of Christ; St. Peter: The Examination of Faith)
1. What are the spirits here called to?
    They are called to the supper of the Lamb.
2. What does Beatrice request of the spirits?
    She requests that Dante be allowed a crumb from the table.
3. Who responds to Beatrice?
    St. Peter responds.
4. What does Beatrice ask St. Peter to do?
    She asks him to test Dante regarding his faith.
5. How does Dante respond to St. Peter's question about faith?
    He uses St. Paul's words "faith is the substance of what we hope to see and the argument for what we have not seen. This is its quiddity, as it seems to me."
6. How do we know Dante's answer pleases St. Peter?
    St. Peter says "You have assayed this coinage…accurately."
7. To what does Dante attribute his faith?
    He attributes it to the Holy Spirit working through the Scriptures.
8. What specifically in the Scriptures helped Dante's faith?
    His faith was specifically helped by the accounts of the miracles.
9. What is the proof of miracles if one does not take the word of Scripture as truth?
    The proof is the conversion of the world to Christianity.
10. What is Dante referring to when he says that St. Peter had sowed a good plant which is now a thorn?
    He is referring to the fact that Peter had established the Church in Rome but that Church is now corrupt (another swipe at the pope).
11. What last thing must Dante explain to St. Peter?
    He must explain what specifically he believes and what the source is of his beliefs.
12. What does Dante declare?
    He declares his beliefs as stated in the *Credo*.
13. How does St. Peter respond?
    His spirit dances three times around Dante singing praise.

Questions for Further Thought

A. Dante prepared to answer Peter's questions "as a bachelor arms himself for disquisition in silence till the master sets the terms for defending, not deciding, the proposition." What does that mean?
    When a student presents himself for a Bachelor's Degree, he often has to have written a thesis in which he sets

Unit 1: Poetry

forth some proposition which he attempts to prove. Once presented, he has to defend his work in the face of questions from people who have higher degrees (Masters or PhDs). Dante did not have a choice in the questions he would be asked.
B. What is the irony of St. Peter being the inquisitor about Dante's faith?
The irony is that St. Peter had significant moments in dealing with his own faith (ie. his faith wavered when Christ told him to walk on the water, and he denied Christ when put to the test in the courtyard).

Words to Know:

disquisition: a formal discourse in which a subject is examined and discussed

quiddity: the essential nature of something

sophist: one skilled in devious argumentation

Canto XXV

(St. James, the Examination of Hope; St. John the Apostle)
1. What hope does Dante express in the opening lines of this Canto?
        He expresses the hope that this poem will be the vehicle with which he will return from exile to Florence.
2. Where would he want to receive the poet's crown?
        He would want to receive it in the baptistery where he received the Faith which Peter has just confirmed.
3. Who is the Baron of whom Beatrice speaks?
        He is St. James the Apostle, who went to Compostela in Spain.
4. What virtue does James represent?
        He represents the Theological Virtue of Hope.
5. Who are the mountains to whom Dante raises his eyes?
        They are Peter and James.
6. How does Dante respond to the question of what Hope is?
        He says it "is the certain expectation of future glory. It is the blessed fruit of grace divine and the good a man has done."
7. What does St. James mean when he says that he followed that grace even to the palm?
        He means that he lived the virtue of Hope even unto his martyrdom.
8. What does St. James ask next?
        He asks Dante what Hope promises.
9. How does Dante respond?
        He says that Hope promises the life of Heaven, and he learned of it in the writings of Isaiah and St. John.
10. What symbol of Christ is seen next as Dante has correctly responded to the questions about Hope?
        Christ is seen as the Pelican.
11. Who is "he who lies upon the breast of Our Pelican?"
        "He who lies upon the breast of Our Pelican" is St. John.
12. What does Dante strain to see?
        He strains to see St. John's body, but he becomes blinded.
13. What does St. John say to him?
        He says that he should not try to see what is not here because his body is on earth, waiting for the resurrection of all the dead. The only two with bodies here are Jesus and Mary.
14. Why is Dante distressed?
        He cannot see Beatrice even though she is near.

QUESTIONS FOR FURTHER THOUGHT

A. What is the Church Militant?
   The Church Militant is the Church on Earth. The Church Suffering is comprised of the Holy Souls in Purgatory, and the Church Triumphant is comprised of the Holy Souls in Heaven.
B. When Dante speaks of Egypt and Jerusalem together, what do the two symbolize?
   Egypt is earthly life or bondage, Jerusalem is Heavenly life or freedom.

WORDS TO KNOW:

luminescence: light occurring due to a chemical change at low temperature

incandescence: emission of visible light due to an increase in temperature

CANTO XXVI

(Examination of Love (Caritas); Adam)
1. What does St. John assure Dante about?
   He assures him that his loss of sight is not permanent and that Beatrice will heal him.
2. What does the spirit of St. John ask Dante?
   The spirit asks what made him seek Heaven.
3. How does he answer?
   He says his love for God was kindled by philosophic arguments and the Scriptures.
4. Where does truth lead to, according to Dante?
   Truth leads to God.
5. What has maintained Dante's love for God?
   His own existence and that of the world and the crucifixion have maintained Dante's love for God.
6. Whom does Dante love in addition to God?
   He loves other people (the leaves that green the Eternal Garden's grove…)
7. What happens to Dante after he declares his love for God and man?
   He regains his sight and it is clearer than before.
8. After his vision clears, whom does Dante see?
   He sees Adam "…the first and only fruit earth ever saw spring forth full ripe…"
9. Why was Adam exiled from Paradise?
   He was exiled for violating God's decree.
10. How long was he exiled from Paradise?
    He was exiled 4302 years in Limbo.
11. How long did Adam live on earth?
    He lived 930 years.
12. What language did he speak?
    He spoke an ancient tongue which had disappeared before the Tower of Babel was built.
13. Why do languages die out?
    They die out because they are made by men.
14. How long was Adam in the Garden of Eden?
    He was only there six hours.

Canto XXVII
The Eighth Sphere: The Fixed Stars; Ascent to the Primum Mobile

(Denunciation of Papal Corruption)
1. Who are the four great torches of whom Dante speaks? (They have all spoken).
    They are Peter, James, John and Adam.
2. Who outshines them all and now speaks?
    St. Peter speaks.
3. What does St. Peter say?
    He says that the present pope (Boniface VIII) should not be pope and that the Papacy has been totally corrupted with blood and filth.
4. What happens to St. Peter's spirit?
    It turns red, as in a sunset, because of his righteous indignation.
5. Who were Linus and Cletus?
    They were the popes who followed St. Peter.
6. What does he say about the Church, the bride of Christ?
    He says it was not nurtured on his blood and that of the first popes to come to this point of corruption and division.
7. What does Peter tell Dante to do?
    He tells him not be silent about what he has just said when he returns to Earth.
8. What does Beatrice tell Dante to look at?
    She tells him to look back at the Earth (the threshing floor).
9. Where are Dante and Beatrice?
    They are in the place where all motion and time begin.
10. What powers everything?
    God's love powers everything. (Cunctitenant is God, the all-containing).
11. What does Beatrice lament?
    She laments the fact that greed has overtaken mankind.
12. What do children quickly lose?
    They lose faith and innocence.
13. Who is the fair daughter of the Sun?
    The fair daughter is the Church.
14. What does Beatrice predict?
    She predicts that things will change for the better on Earth.

Question for Further Thought

What is the significance of Scipio?
    Scipio overthrew Hannibal; thus preserving Rome.

Canto XXVIII
The Ninth Sphere: The Primum Mobile

(The Angel Hierarchy)
1. What does Dante see reflected in Beatrice's eyes?
    He sees a bright point within the circling sphere where each circle moves more slowly the further it gets from the center.

2. How many spinning rings of fire does he see?
    He sees nine spinning rings of fire.
3. How does Beatrice explain why the circle closest to the center moves most swiftly?
    It is spurred by burning love, being closest to the origin of love.
4. How do things move in a circle on earth?
    Those on the periphery spin faster than the center (observe a blender or food processor in action).
5. Of what are the rings comprised?
    They are comprised of the hierarchy of Angels.
6. What is the order of the hierarchy?
    The order of the hierarchy is as follows:
    - Seraphim
    - Cherubim
    - Thrones
    - Dominations
    - Virtues
    - Powers
    - Principalities
    - Archangels
    - Angels
7. On what is the most blessed condition in Heaven based?
    It is based on seeing rather than on love, and each one sees in relation to his worthiness.
8. Who gave us this ranking of the Angelic Hierarchy?
    Dionysius the Areopagite who was converted by St. Paul, named the Hierarchy. (*Acts*: 17: 34)
9. Why do the angels face up and down?
    They are all drawn to God and draw others (from Earth) toward Heaven.

QUESTIONS FOR FURTHER THOUGHT

A. What is the function of the different choirs of Angels?
    - Seraphim: Angels having six wings, two covering their faces, two covering their feet and two for flying, in attendance before God's throne,
    - Cherubim: Manlike in appearance and double-winged, they guard the glory of Yahweh
    - Thrones: Carriers of the throne of God
    - Dominations: Angels which control the lower ranking Powers and Virtues in the intermediate hierarchy
    - Virtues: Oversee groups of people; they inspire living things to many things such as art or science
    - Powers: Brightly colored, oversee groups of people
    - Principalities: Ruling class of Angels, wear crown and carry a scepter, and are the guardians of nations and countries
    - Archangels: Ruling Angels, mentioned often in Scripture, often serving as messengers from God; the three Archangels mentioned often are Michael, Gabriel, Raphael
    - Angels: Spiritual beings who carry out whatever missions God assigns them on behalf of men
B. What does Pope Gregory have to learn when he reaches Heaven?
    He has to learn that his arrangement of the Angels in Heaven was incorrect, while that of Dionysius the Areopagite was correct.

CANTO XXIX

1. What question of Dante's does Beatrice discern without his asking?
    His question is where and when the angels were created.

Unit 1: Poetry

2. How does she answer?
   She says that God created the angels as a reflection of His splendor at the same time that form and matter were created.
3. What was intrinsic to every essence of creation?
   Order was intrinsic in everything.
4. What did God place at the top of His creation?
   He placed the angels which influence mankind.
5. What did he place at the bottom of His creation?
   He placed mankind (pure potential) which can be influenced, but cannot influence.
6. What was in the middle?
   In the middle are the Heavens ("potential and act were tied together that never more shall be unbound") which can influence mankind and can also be influenced by the angels above.
7. What error did Hieronymus (Jerome) make, according to Beatrice?
   He said that the angels pre-existed mankind.
8. What do the angels do?
   They circle and reflect God.
9. What was the origin of the Fall?
   Its origin was Satan's pride.
10. What does Beatrice say about grace?
    She says it is received in proportion to one's affection and openness to it.
11. What confusion does Beatrice dispel?
    She says the angels have no need of memory because by having their sight on God, nothing is concealed from them.
12. What does she say about preachers?
    She says they waste time discoursing on invented truths instead of on the Gospels.

Questions for Further Thought

A. Who are the children of Latona (lines 1-6)?
   The children of Latona are Apollo and Diana, the Sun and Moon.
B. What is Dante's discussion about in lines 115-126?
   He is speaking about friars who sold false indulgences to the gullible. Tippets were the points of the hoods they wore, and they would carry religious goods and fake documents in them. The money never minted refers to the false promises (the unauthorized indulgences) which they sold.

Canto XXX
Ascent to the Empyrean, The Empyrean

(Praise of Beatrice's Beauty; The River of Light; The Mystic Rose; The Throne of Henry VII; Denunciation of Evil Popes)
1. What time of day is it?
   It is dawn.
2. What does Dante say about Beatrice's beauty?
   He says that everything he has said so far does not add up to the reality, and he does not have the words to adequately express it.
3. What is this part of Heaven?
   It is the point of pure light, pure love.
4. What blinds Dante?
   Dante is blinded by the pure light.

5. What must Dante do in order to see this place?
    He must drink from the river of light with his eyes.
6. What is the form of the sea around God?
    It is the form of a rose.
7. Does Dante see the form directly?
    No, he sees its reflection.
8. What does Beatrice point out about the rows of thrones around God?
    She points out that they are almost full and few are wanting here.
9. Who will sit on the empty throne?
    Henry the Great will sit there.
10. What else does she say about Henry?
    He will try to bring order to Italy and will die before Dante.
11. Who will oppose Henry?
    The "prefect of the holy court," Pope Clement V will oppose him.
12. Where will the pope end up?
    He will end up in Hell with Simon Magus (See *Inferno* XIX).

Words to Know:

aureole: halo, corona

nimbus: cloud of light around a deity, halo

Canto XXXI
The Empyrean

(The Mystic Rose; the Angel Host; Beatrice Leaves Dante; St. Bernard)
1. Who comprises the host of the sacred soldiery espoused by Christ?
    Those of the sacred soldiery espoused by Christ are the souls of the Earthly mortals.
2. Who comprises the other host?
    The other host is made up of the angels who never left Heaven.
3. What does Dante see?
    He sees above the center of the rose the angels who "swarm like bees" as sparks of light, flying to those in the rows around God imparting His peace and love.
4. What happens when Dante turns to question Beatrice?
    Beatrice is no longer by his side. St. Bernard now speaks to him.
5. Where is she?
    She is in the third circle from the highest rank, sitting on "the throne her merit has assigned her."
6. What does Beatrice do when Dante looks up and speaks to her?
    She smiles and then turns her gaze back to God.
7. Who will give Dante the grace to gaze upon God?
    Mary, the Queen of Heaven, will do so.

Questions for Further Thought

A. Who was St. Bernard?
    St. Bernard was the Abbot of Clairvaux, a famous Cistercian monastery, and he lived from 1090 until 1153. He was a contemplative and particularly devoted to the Virgin Mary.

Unit 1: Poetry

B. What role might St. Bernard have?
   He is an intercessor to Mary.
C. The notes at the end of this Canto regarding St. Bernard state that he is identified with the worship of the Virgin Mary. Is that accurate?
   It is not. He did not worship her (worship is due only to God), but he had a special devotion (love) for her.
D. Does the diagram of the Empyrean match your imagination of it? Why, or why not?
   Answers will vary

Words to Know:

oriflamme: source of inspiration

delectation: enjoyment, appreciation

intercessor: one who asks another for something; in religious terms, one who prays to God for the needs of another (as St. Bernard would pray to Mary who would intercede with Christ, her Son)

contemplation: concentration of the mind on achieving unity with God

Canto XXXII

(St. Bernard; The Virgin Mary; The Thrones of the Blessed)

1. What does St. Bernard do?
   He explains the arrangement of Mary and the Saints in the Mystical Rose.
2. Who is the one who dealt and deepened the wound which Mary healed?
   That is Eve.
3. Who are seated together in the third tier?
   Rachel and Beatrice are seated together.
4. Who forms the wall dividing those who believed in Christ to come from those who believed in Christ descended?
   Beginning with the Virgin Mary, then Eve, the Hebrew women of the *Old Testament* (Rachel, Sarah, Rebekah, Judith, Ruth, etc.) form that wall.
5. Who sits on the side where the flower is in full bloom?
   The *Old Testament* believers sit there.
6. On which side are there many empty seats?
   There are many empty seats on the side where those who believed in Christ descended sit.
7. Who sits opposite the Virgin Mary on the top tier?
   John the Baptist sits there.
8. Who follows in the line of John the Baptist, forming another wall?
   Following John are Francis, Benedict, Augustine and others.
9. Who are here because of the merits of others?
   Here, due to the merits of others (the faith of their parents), are children who died before they could declare their faith.
10. What was required for Hebrew boys to reach Heaven before Christ died?
    Circumcision was required.
11. What was required for children to reach Heaven after Christ came?
    Baptism was required.
12. Who is the angel who looks into Mary's eyes?
    The angel is Gabriel.

13. Who is the man whose appetite left bitterness for man?
    That was Adam.
14. To whom did Christ give the twin keys?
    He gave them to Peter.
15. Who foretold the evil days of the Sweet Bride?
    John the Evangelist foretold those days in the *Book of Revelation*.
16. Who was the leader of the rebellious clan to whom manna fell?
    Moses was the leader.
17. What had Lucy done?
    She had urged Beatrice to go to Dante when he was in danger of losing his soul. (See *Inferno* II)
18. What must happen for Dante to finally see God?
    St. Bernard must pray that the Virgin Mary will help him to have the grace necessary.

Questions for Further Thought

A. What is the wound dealt by Eve?
    It is the wound of Original Sin.
B. From the *Inferno* II, line 102, we learned that Rachel had sent her prayers with Beatrice for Dante. Do you recall what Rachel represents?
    Rachel represents the contemplative life, and is thus seated with Beatrice.
C. Why does Dante say John the Baptist bore Hell's distress?
    He says John bore Hell's distress because John died before Jesus died to open the gates of Heaven and spent time in Limbo before the Resurrection.
D. Who were the twins who fought in their mother's womb?
    They were Jacob and Esau. *Genesis* XXV:21.
E. What does *Ave Maria, gratia plena* mean?
    It means Hail Mary, full of Grace, and was said by the Angel Gabriel when he announced to her that she would be the Mother of God.

Canto XXXIII

(St. Bernard, Prayer to the Virgin; The Vision of God)
1. How does St. Bernard's prayer begin?
    His prayer begins with praise for Mary.
2. What does Bernard say about those who seek grace?
    He says they seek in vain if they do not first seek Mary.
3. What does Bernard ask for Dante?
    He asks that Mary will grant him the grace to see God and that he will be able to remember his vision.
4. How does Mary respond?
    She responds with pleasure and looks toward God.
5. How does Dante feel?
    He feels calm.
6. What does Dante say about the vision?
    He says he was consumed in it but cannot remember it all. He recalls the feeling it generated in him. His speech is not adequate to describe it.
7. What little does he remember?
    He saw a light within which were three circles of different colors, reflecting each other, and within one was man's image.

Unit 1: Poetry

8. What revelation does Dante have?
    He realizes that his will and desire are in perfect conformity with God's love, and therefore, he could see God.

WORDS TO KNOW:

benignity: gentle disposition, kindness

subsume: to include into something larger

geometer: one who specializes in geometry

QUESTIONS FOR FURTHER THOUGHT

A. Were you surprised by Dante's graphic placement of the souls in Heaven? Why or why not?
    Answers will vary.
B. How does your own idea of Heaven differ from that of Dante?
    Answers will vary.
C. How did the language used by Dante change in the course of the *Divine Comedy*?
    As Dante descended further into Hell, his language became coarser. He was more gentle in his descriptions in the *Purgatorio*. By the time he reached Heaven, his language was very refined and had a reverent tone.
D. How did Dante's focus change throughout the *Divine Comedy*?
    When he began his journey, his gaze was upon the souls he encountered and upon their suffering and punishment. The closer he got to Heaven, however, his gaze was directed toward God. He needed a guide throughout, and the guides provided helped him to focus on what he needed to see so that he would reach the perfection needed for the culmination of the journey—his vision of God.

Paradise Lost

by John Milton
Penguin Books

About the Author

John Milton was born in 1608 in London. He studied languages at Christ's College, Cambridge University and composed and translated poetry. He traveled to Italy and came to know and love Italian culture. With his education and experience of culture, he felt compelled to write a great work on the level of Homer and Virgil.

Though Anglican by birth and training, Milton saw much corruption in the Anglican Church, and he began writing political pamphlets which exposed the corruption. He believed the church and the monarch were too closely connected (as Dante had). His sympathies lay more with the Presbyterians, but eventually he parted company with them when they refused to try or execute their king.

The persistent theme in his writing was individual liberty, i.e. liberty to obtain a civil divorce, liberty to publish without previous censorship and liberty of the press. He also wrote of Parliament's right to execute bad monarchs after Charles I was beheaded, an act which put him temporarily in danger when the monarchy was restored with King Charles II. He went blind in 1652, and his condition was attributed to his concentrated work on the political pamphlets, a sacrifice which he considered worthy. He was a diplomatic correspondent in the Commonwealth established by Oliver Cromwell.

Milton was not fortunate in his private life, having lost two wives and two children to early death. His children by his first wife did not get along with his third wife, so they were estranged.

Milton wrote *Paradise Regained* in 1671. He died in 1674, having seen his work accepted. *Paradise Lost* is considered the greatest English-language epic.

Paradise Lost

Paradise Lost is an epic which was written to justify God's

ways to men and to bring glory to England, the English language and to Puritanical beliefs. It was completed by 1665 and published in 1667.

John Milton's language is referred to as the "grand style" and it combines English with forms and meanings from the many languages he had studied. Because he was blind when he wrote the work, Milton dictated it to a scribe. As a result, *Paradise Lost* has the qualities of an oral poem. Unlike his predecessors, Homer and Virgil, Milton rejected war as a central subject. Instead, his theme is man's disobedience and the resulting loss of Paradise. Satan is the cause.

As to structure, the work is composed of twelve books. Before each book is an "argument" or summary of the book to follow. The author made ample use of the soliloquy, beginning with Satan's soliloquy to the sun in the first book. A soliloquy is a speech made while alone, which conveys the speaker's thoughts to his audience. He also used simile, which is a comparison, often preceded with "as" or "like."

Thither winged with speed a numerous brigade hastened. As when bands of pioneers with spade and pickaxe armed forerun the royal camp…(*Paradise Lost*, Book I, lines 674-677).

Note the references to light and darkness as you read.

Unit 1: Poetry

THE VERSE

1. What does the author say about the use of rhyme in his work?
    He says he will not use it, as it is an inferior form of expression which limits the ability to say what one wants to say.

BOOK I

(1-26)
1. What is the subject of the first book?
    The subject is man's disobedience and the resulting loss of Paradise; the prime cause of which is Satan.
2. After stating his subject, what does Milton do?
    He invokes the Muse.
3. What does Milton propose?
    He proposes to justify the ways of God to men.

(27-248)
4. Who were the grand parents?
    They were Adam and Eve.
5. What caused the fall of Eve?
    Satan's pride and subsequent fall led to his warring on God and his creation.
6. What did God do to Satan?
    He cast him out of Heaven because he rebelled.
7. Who was Satan's companion?
    His companion was Beelzebub.
8. Satan said that even though he and the other fallen angels were in Hell, all was not lost. What remained?
    The unconquerable will, the study of revenge, immortal hate, courage not to submit and a desire to wage eternal war on God remained.
9. What did Satan say they would do?
    They would never do good, only ill, acting contrary to God's will and perverting that same will.
10. Satan had been chained in the burning lake, but then he could fly. Why?
    God freed him.
11. What was to be result of his evil?
    He would continually damn himself while at the same time God would show forth His grace and mercy on those who were seduced by Satan.

(249-678)
12. What did Satan say about the mind?
    He said it was without time or place and could make of Heaven a hell, or of Hell a heaven.
13. What choice did Satan make?
    He chose to reign supreme in Hell rather than to serve in Heaven.
14. Who was Moloch?
    He was an ancient pagan god who demanded human sacrifice.
15. Who were Chemos, Peor, Baalim, Ashtaroth, Osiris, Belial, etc?
    They were pagan gods who are now in Hell.
16. Who else did Milton place in Hell?
    He placed the Greek gods.
17. How did Satan appear as he stood before his legions?
    He was eminent in shape and gesture; he still had some of his original brightness; his face was scarred by thunderbolts, his brows showed courage, and his eyes were cruel.

18. What did Satan say of God's power?
    He said that God's powerful force was unmatched, and they, therefore, would have to work by fraud to overcome Him. They would never submit to God.

(679-798)
19. What did Milton say about Mammon?
    He said that Mammon always had his eyes on the riches of Heaven when there, not on the beatific vision, and he led the fallen angels to seek gold in the bowels of Hell.
20. What was the name of Satan's capital?
    His capital was Pandemonium.
21. What was to be held in Pandemonium?
    A council was to be held, with all the fallen angels present.

QUESTIONS FOR FURTHER THOUGHT

A. What was Milton referring to when he wrote of brute images adorned with gay religions…and devils to adore for deities?"
   He was referring to the pagan gods who were believed to be fallen angels.
B. Why is Pandemonium a fitting name for Satan's capital?
   It is fitting because it reflects the very opposite of what God created: for God created Order, and Pandemonium is chaos.

WORDS TO KNOW:

adamantine: impenetrably hard mythological substance

obdurate: obstinate, stubborn

guile: cunning, slyness, deviousness

apostate: traitor, one who completely renounces his faith

perfidy: treachery, betrayal

puissant: powerful

reprobate: degenerate, rascal

BOOK II

(1-49)
1. How did Satan come to be the leader in Hell?
   He came to that position by the fixed laws of Heaven, and through the use of his own free will he merited it.
2. Was Satan envied his position? Why?
   He was not envied because he had the greatest share of endless pain.
3. What counsel did he seek?
   He sought counsel about whether he and the other fallen angels should wage open war on Heaven or use covert guile.

Unit 1: Poetry

4. What gave the demons strength?
    Despair gave them strength.

(50-284)
5. What did Moloc counsel?
    He counseled open war.
6. Why was war worth the risk?
    War was worth the risk because Hell was so terrible—what could be worse?
7. Being immortal, what could they do?
    They could seek vengeance on Heaven.
8. What did Belial counsel?
    He said that revenge was futile because Heaven is heavily guarded; rather than risk bringing even worse suffering upon themselves, they should wait things out and maybe God would lessen their suffering. He counseled "ignoble ease and perfect sloth, not peace."
9. What did Mammon say about Heaven in the event God would relent and welcome them back?
    He said it would be wearisome to stand in the presence of God, praising him in submission.
10. What did Mammon counsel?
    He counseled that they should live for themselves, accountable to no one and without war.

(285-509)
11. After hearing the others, what did Beëlzebub say?
    He said that God was in control over them even in Hell; they should forget about attacking Heaven and look for something easier. He had heard about a new world where Man would be created about this time, and they should turn their attention in that direction.
12. What was resolved?
    They resolved to seduce the new creation and mingle Earth with Hell.
13. What remained to be decided?
    It remained to be decided who would go to seek out Earth.
14. Who volunteered?
    Satan volunteered.
15. How did the demons respond?
    They honored him as a god, praising him.

(510-794)
16. What surrounded Satan?
    He was surrounded by a ring of fiery Seraphs.
17. What did the demons do when Satan left?
    Some competed in games, some sang with harps, some sat apart thinking, and others explored Hell.
18. What did the four rivers that disgorged into the burning lake bring?
    The Styx brought hate, Acheron brought sorrow, Cocytus brought regret, and Phlegethon brought rage.
19. What was Lethe?
    Lethe was the river of forgetfulness.
20. Who guarded Lethe to prevent the damned from drinking?
    Medusa guarded it.
21. What or who guarded the gate of Hell?
    The gate of Hell was guarded by two creatures. One was a half woman, half serpent, and her middle was surrounded by barking hounds which crawled in and out of her womb. The other was a formless figure which appeared to wear a king's crown. Both were fierce creatures.

22. How many angels were cast out of Hell with Satan?
    One-third of the total rebelled and were cast out with him.
23. What did the woman/serpent reveal to Satan?
    She was in Heaven with him and her name was Sin. She became pregnant by him, carrying the beast who guarded Hell's gates with her.
24. Who was her son?
    Her son was Death.

(795-1055)
25. Who were the offspring of Death and Sin?
    The hounds were the offspring.
26. What did Satan promise Sin?
    He promised that they would have freedom to prey on the men on Earth.
27. What happened to the gates of Hell?
    They remained open after Satan left because she could not close them.
28. What was outside the gate of Hell?
    Outside the gate of Hell was Chaos.
29. Who was there?
    In Chaos were Night, Rumor, Chance, Tumult, Confusion, and Discord.
30. Did Satan drop or climb toward Earth?
    He dropped.
31. How was the Earth held up?
    It was held up by a golden chain.
32. Who followed Satan from Hell?
    Sin and Death followed him.
33. What did Satan see as he approached Earth?
    He saw the light of dawn.

Questions for Further Thought

A. If the demons were mortal, what could happen to them in their war against Heaven?
    If they were mortal they could be destroyed and killed and thus relieved of their suffering.
B. What was ironic about the demons reverencing Satan after he volunteered to seek out Earth?
    They did not want to reverence God in Heaven, but they were willing to reverence Satan out of fear.
C. What was the perverted parallel between Satan and the Blessed Trinity?
    Satan was the one who thought of the first sin and then committed it by rebelling against God, conceiving Sin in the form of the woman/serpent. Then he conceived with her (his daughter) Death in the form of the hounds who entered and left her womb at will.
D. What did Satan see when he reached the border between Chaos and Nature?
    He saw the Earth and Empyreal Heaven.

Words to Know:

timorous: nervous, frightened

egress: way out, exit

portcullis: heavy gate which is suspended from chains and is raised and lowered

alacrity: enthusiasm, speed

amain: with full force and speed

BOOK III

(1-134)
1. What or whom did Milton invoke?
    He invoked the Holy Light of God.
2. What did he ask of the Holy Light?
    He asked that he be able to "see" "things invisible to mortal sight."
3. Where was God?
    He was on His throne looking down on creation.
4. Who sat at God's right?
    His only Son sat at His right.
5. What did God see as He gazed at creation?
    He saw the blissfully happy Adam and Eve in the Garden; he saw Hell and the great abyss of chaos; and He saw Satan right outside the world.
6. What did God tell His Son?
    He told His Son that Satan would succeed in perverting man.
7. Whose fault would it be and why?
    It would be man's fault that he would be perverted because he would choose through the use of his own reason and will.
8. Why did God give man and the spirits free will and the ability to reason?
    He gave them those gifts because he didn't want obedience and reverence out of servitude. He said there would be no pleasure in coerced obedience which, at any rate, would serve necessity rather than Him.
9. What did God say about predestination?
    He said that his foreknowledge was not the cause of what happened. It did not overrule man's will.

(135-294)
10. What was the difference between the fall of the angels and the fall of man?
    The angels tempted themselves while man was deceived by the fallen angels.
11. Why could mankind be saved but the fallen angels could not?
    The fallen angels, because they had tempted themselves, would find no mercy from God. God would exercise justice and mercy on mankind who had been tempted by one of the angels.
12. How did God say mankind would be saved?
    He would be saved through the grace freely given by Himself.
13. Would all men receive grace in equal measure?
    No, some would be elect over the others according to God's will.
14. What about the others?
    God would call to them all and warn them of their sins.
15. What would help them to receive that grace?
    Prayer, repentance and obedience would help.
16. What did God call the "voice" they would hear?
    He called it His "umpire conscience."
17. Did God exclude anybody from His mercy?
    No, He did not.
18. For all this to happen, what was necessary?
    Somebody would have to die for mankind.

19. Who volunteered?
    God's Son volunteered.

(295-415)
20. What did God mean when He said "So man, as is most just, shall satisfy for man, be judged and die, and dying rise…"
    He meant that His Son would become a man in order to satisfy for the sins of man through Adam.
21. What would the Son once returned to Heaven do?
    He would sit incarnate, reign as both God and man as the universal King with power over all the angels, and He would judge all men and angels.
22. What would become of the world?
    It would burn, and from the ashes would spring a new Heaven and Earth where the just will dwell.

(416-644)
23. Meanwhile, where was Satan?
    He walked upon the Earth, hidden by darkness.
24. Where did Satan light?
    He lit in China (Sericana), a "windy sea of land."
25. Along with the builders of the Tower of Babel and pagan gods, what specific group of people did Milton place in the Paradise of Fools? (Note his reference to Dominic and Francis, relics, beads, bulls, etc).
    He placed Catholics there.
26. As he continued on his exploration of the world, what did Satan see?
    He saw a ladder embellished with precious gems leading up to Heaven.
27. What else did he see?
    He saw a passage to Earth which allowed him to view it in its entirety.
28. Who used the passage?
    The angels descending from Heaven to help mankind used the passage.
29. Where did Satan land?
    He landed on the Sun.
30. How did Milton describe the Sun?
    He described it as consisting of molten metals.

(645-742)
31. Whom did Satan see?
    He saw the Archangel Uriel who is one of the seven ever in God's presence. (*Revelation* 19:17)
32. How did Satan disguise himself?
    He disguised himself as a stripling Cherub.
33. How did Satan deceive Uriel?
    He asked him where man was so that he could see him and praise God for His creation.
34. What did Milton say about hypocrisy?
    He said that neither man nor angel could discern it. It was the only evil that was invisible to all but God.
35. What had Uriel witnessed?
    He had witnessed God's creation of the material world.
36. Where was Paradise?
    It was near Mt. Niphates (a mountain between Armenia and Assyria).

QUESTIONS FOR FURTHER THOUGHT

A. What did Milton mean when he said of the light that "thou revisit'st not these eyes, that roll in vain to find thy piercing ray, and find no dawn…"
    He could not see the light because he was blind as he wrote this.

Unit 1: Poetry

B. What motivated the Son to offer to die for the salvation of mankind?
   His motivation was pure love.
C. How do Protestant and Catholic beliefs about salvation differ?
   Protestants believe Faith alone saves. Catholics believe man must have faith, but must back up his faith with good works and prayer (James 1:26, 2:14-26). Also St. Paul says "work out your salvation with fear and trembling (Philippians 2:12). Protestants, as shown by Milton's words, thus saw Catholic religious practices as futile and superstitious.
D. Do you think Milton's characterization of Catholics was fair? Why?
   Answers may vary. He was not fair. He saw problems in the religious orders and applied them to everybody who followed the Faith.

WORDS TO KNOW:

ingrate: somebody who shows no gratitude

enthrall: captivate, beguile

vouchsafe: to allow or promise

sufferance: patient endurance

omnipotent: all-powerful, supreme

BOOK IV

(1-194)
1. Who was the warning voice who saw the Apocalypse?
   The warning voice was John the Evangelist.
2. What did Satan feel as he saw Eden?
   He felt horror, doubt and despair.
3. Where did the author say Hell is?
   Hell is wherever Satan is, he cannot escape it.
4. What brought Satan down?
   His own pride and ambition, a desire to be above God, brought Satan down.
5. Why could Satan not be forgiven?
   He would not be forgiven because he refused to submit to God and feared shame before those he had seduced.
6. As Satan renounced Hope, Fear and Remorse, what did he embrace?
   He embraced Evil with the words "Evil be thou my Good."
7. How did Uriel know Satan was an evil spirit?
   Uriel noticed how Satan's form became disfigured and his gestures became fierce.
8. How did Satan enter the garden?
   He leapt over the wall.
9. To what did Milton liken Satan's entrance into Paradise?
   He likened it to the priests who were paid in the Church--"lewd hirelings."
10. Where did he land?
    He landed on the Tree of Life.

(195-449)

11. How was he disguised?

    He was disguised as a cormorant—a large bird.

12. What did Satan notice first about Adam and Eve?

    He noticed that they stood erect and naked, the image of God.

13. Milton said they were not equal. What attributes did he give to each?

    He said that Adam was created for contemplation and valor, for God only, and for absolute rule. He said that Eve was created for softness and sweet attributes, grace, for God in Adam and subject to Adam.

14. What characterized Adam and Eve?

    They were characterized by simplicity and spotless innocence.

15. How did Satan get close to Adam and Eve?

    He changed his form to the different animals so that he could approach them.

16. What did Satan hear?

    He heard Adam and Eve talking about their work in Paradise and the command not to eat of the Tree of Knowledge. He also heard them praising God.

(450-775)

17. What had Eve done when she first awoke after being created by God?

    She had gone to a stream where she saw her own reflection and desired it, till a voice told her it was herself and led her to Adam.

18. Did she prefer Adam to her reflection.

    No, at first she did not.

19. Who guarded the gates of Paradise?

    Gabriel guarded the gates.

20. Who warned Gabriel about Satan's arrival in Paradise?

    Uriel warned him.

21. What did Gabriel say about Satan's ability to enter unseen?

    Satan could enter because spirits are not contained by earthly (physical) barricades.

22. What did Milton say occurred at night?

    The stars and other heavenly bodies shed their light on nations yet unborn, and spiritual creatures walked the earth singing praise to God.

(776-1015)

23. While Adam and Eve slept, what did Gabriel do?

    He sent his guards to search for Satan.

24. Where did they find him?

    They found him squatting near Eve's ear, filling her dreams with rebellion.

25. Why did the guards not recognize Satan?

    They did not recognize him because his form was so ugly.

26. Why, according to Satan, did he break loose from Hell?

    He broke loose to escape pain.

27. What did the angel ask Satan?

    The angel asked if he had come alone, because he was less hardy than the other condemned spirits.

28. What was Satan's response?

    He said he was a faithful leader who took the risk alone before subjecting the others to it.

29. What did the angel say about Satan?

    He said Satan was a liar.

30. What did Satan do?

    He fled.

Unit 1: Poetry

Questions for Further Thought

A. Why was it so difficult for Satan to find an entrance into Paradise?
   Paradise was on a hill, protected all around with an undergrowth of shrubs and vegetation, trees and a wall, so Satan could not find a ready entrance.
B. Satan's long discourse at the beginning of Book IV is known as a soliloquy. What is a soliloquy?
   A soliloquy is a long speech spoken by one who is alone and is addressed to the audience or reader.
C. Eve's story of admiring herself in the stream is reminiscent of a story from classical mythology. Do you remember it, and if so, how do the stories differ?
   In the story of Narcissus and Echo, Narcissus refuses the advances of Echo because he is so enamored of himself. He is turned into a golden flower known today as the Narcissus. In this story, Eve is called by God to leave her own image, and she finds Adam whose wisdom is more important than her beauty.

Words to Know:

sylvan: wooded, full of trees

bane: blight, curse

BOOK V

(1-129)
1. Upon awakening, why was Eve troubled?
   She had heard a voice in her sleep which sounded like Adam's, inviting her to get up and go to the Tree of Knowledge.
2. What form had Satan assumed?
   He had assumed the form of an angel.
3. What did Satan do in her dream?
   He plucked a fruit from the tree, sampled it and gave it to Eve saying she would be happier than she was because she would be a goddess.
4. What argument did Satan make to Eve about the Good?
   He said that the more good is communicated, the more abundant it becomes and gives more honor to the One who created it.
5. How did Adam respond to her telling him of the dream?
   He responded with fear and sadness, and he explained that the soul has faculties besides reason—among them fancy, which produces images in the mind.
6. What did Adam say about temptation: "Evil into the mind of God or Man?"
   He said it could come and go unapproved, leaving no blame.

(130-313)
7. To what did Adam attribute Eve's tears?
   He attributed them to "sweet remorse and pious awe, that feared to have offended."
8. Who was Raphael?
   He was the archangel who accompanied Tobias in search of a wife. Milton refers to him as the "sociable Sprit."
9. Who sent Raphael to Paradise?
   God sent him, feeling pity on Adam and Eve.
10. What did God want Raphael to do?
    He wanted him to speak with Adam and remind him of his free will and the danger that was near.

11. Would Satan use violence to make Adam and Eve sin?
    No, he would use deceit and lies.
12. What kind of angel did Raphael appear to be?
    He appeared to be a Seraph, one with six wings.

(314-503)
13. What did Adam tell Eve to do when he saw Raphael approaching?
    He told her to prepare an abundant meal for him.
14. How did Raphael greet Eve?
    He greeted her as the mother of mankind.
15. Did Raphael eat?
    Yes, he did eat.
16. What did Adam ask Raphael?
    He asked him how the earthly food compared to the heavenly food.
17. What did Raphael tell Adam?
    He told him that what man had was perfect for his needs, and that eventually man would work up to becoming a spirit and in the presence of God, "if ye be found obedient." At that point his need for earthly food would end.

(504-802)
18. What puzzled Adam?
    Raphael had said "if ye be found obedient," and Adam didn't understand that he could be anything but obedient.
19. What did Raphael relate to Adam?
    He related how God the Father gathered all the angelic spirits around Himself and decreed that His Son was His anointed, and all were required to confess that the Son was Lord. Most of the angels were inclined to do so, but Satan was full of envy and would not do so.
20. What did God tell his Son about Satan?
    He told His Son about the planned rebellion, and said they should be on their guard, lest they lose their high place.

(803-907)
21. When Satan had gathered a third of the Heavenly angels around him and established his own throne, who rose up against him?
    Abdiel, who at first agreed to follow him, rose up against him.
22. What did Satan deny?
    He denied that he was created by God, saying "we know no time when we were not as now."

Questions for Further Thought

A. In her dream, did Eve eat the fruit?
    No, she did not.
B. What did Raphael mean in saying that God had created Adam perfect, not immutable?
    Immutable means unchangeable, or incapable of being corrupted. God had created Adam as a perfect being, free from sin and corruption. However, God gave Adam (and mankind) the gift of free will by which mankind was free to choose what he would do. Not being immutable, he could become corrupted.
C. Does Milton's statement about obedience and free will parallel the Catholic belief about salvation or the Protestant belief in "faith alone?" ((515-545)
    The statement more closely parallels Catholic belief about salvation, because freely choosing to obey God implies action. It implies behaving in such a way that God is not offended. By the very word obedience, action (deed) is required.

Unit 1: Poetry

D. Milton has God say "This day I have begot whom I declare My only Son…" Does that statement reflect traditional Christian belief about Jesus?
   No, it does not. Jesus was incarnated at a certain point in time, meaning that He became Man for a time on earth. However, being God, He had no beginning or end, so He could not have been begotten in Heaven "this day…"
E. Did Milton tell us what Satan's heavenly name was?
   Yes, he did. It was Lucifer.
F. Milton's statement through God that they must be vigilant lest they lose their high place seems to put doubt of His omnipotent power in God's mind. Does that seem like a realistic response on God's part?
   It does not. Satan may have been powerful, but God was the creator of all, including Satan, and His power could not be vanquished by any creature.
G. What virtues did Abdiel demonstrate?
   He demonstrated many virtues, among them repentance (he had followed Satan and then changed his mind), fortitude, loyalty, obedience and love.

Words to Know:

interdicted: banned by law

orisons: prayers

mutable: changeable

progenitor: ancestor, originator

obloquy: disgrace, humiliation

perfidy: treachery, betrayal

Book VI

(1-99)
1. What resides in the cave within the Mount of God?
   Light and darkness reside there.
2. How was Abdiel received after he left Satan?
   He was received with joy.
3. What did God say was worse to bear than violence?
   He said universal reproach was worse to bear.
4. How did God refer to His Son?
   He called Him King Messiah.
5. Whom did God send to fight Satan and with what orders?
   He sent Michael and Gabriel to fight Satan with an army that was the same size as Satan's, with orders to drive them into the Chaos of Tartarus.

(100-255)
6. When the two sides met, where was Satan?
   He was in a chariot surrounded by fiery Cherubim.

7. What did Abdiel say to Satan?
   He told him he was a fool to think he could defeat God and His armies, and that he was right to dissent from Satan, while thousands erred.
8. How did Satan compare his state and that of Abdiel?
   He said that he was free while the angels opposing him were slaves.
9. How did Abdiel respond?
   He said it was not servitude to serve one who was worthy; rather, it was servitude to serve the unwise one who had rebelled against the worthier one. Satan was now in servitude to himself.
10. What did Abdiel do after he spoke?
    He struck Satan with his sword.
11. What limited the might of the angels?
    God limited their might.

(256-354)
12. After much fighting, whom did Satan encounter?
    He encountered Michael.
13. What happened as Satan and Michael fought?
    Michael cut into Satan's side, but as his was a spiritual body, the wound quickly healed, though he felt excruciating pain.
14. What did Satan's legions do?
    They carried him back to his chariot.
15. Can angels be killed?
    No, they cannot, because they are pure spirit.

(355-550)
16. Meanwhile, with whom was Gabriel engaged in fighting?
    He was fighting Moloch.
17. What was the doom of the damned, in addition to Hell?
    They were doomed to eternal infamy and namelessness.
18. Why was there a truce?
    There was a truce because night fell.
19. What did Satan propose to his council?
    He proposed that they make better weapons to fight God's legions.
20. What were Satan's legions enduring that God's legions did not?
    They were suffering "physical" pain as well as defeat.
21. What kind of weapon did Satan describe?
    He described cannons.
22. How did they pass the night?
    They mined Heaven to make their ammunition for the next day's battle.

(551-674)
23. How did Satan attempt to deceive the heavenly army?
    He approached with the cannons hidden by the ranks of rebels.
24. How did Satan further try to deceive the heavenly army?
    He proposed a false peace and while they were talking, his army ambushed the angels.
25. What happened to the angels who were hit by the cannon balls?
    They were knocked off their feet.
26. What encumbered them?
    They were encumbered by their armor.

Unit 1: Poetry

27. How did God's army respond to the mocking by Satan's army?
    They shed their arms and flew to the hills. Once there they uprooted the mountains and threw them down at the rebels.

(675-912)
28. Why did God allow this war?
    He allowed it so that His Son would be avenged on his enemies and thus honored.
29. Why would there otherwise not have been a victor in the war?
    There would have been no victor because both sides were equally matched.
30. Why did Messiah have to be the one to vanquish Satan?
    Satan's wrath was directed at Messiah, so Messiah had to do what the angels could not.
31. Did Messiah intend to destroy the rebels?
    No, he intended to exile them from Heaven.
32. What happened to Satan and his army?
    A wall of Heaven opened and they threw themselves into Hell, falling for nine days before they arrived there.
33. What did Raphael warn Adam about?
    Raphael told Adam that Satan was plotting his ruin, and he should not listen to his temptations.

QUESTIONS FOR FURTHER THOUGHT

A. Does Milton's account of the battle in Heaven follow traditional belief? Why or why not?
    No, it does not. In the *Book of Revelation*, Satan is driven out of Heaven by Michael. (*Revelation* 12:7-9)
B. What symbols from pagan literature were used in the description of Christ going into battle against Satan?
    Some pagan symbols were the chariot, lightning, thunder, and the single-handed ability to vanquish a powerful, almost numberless enemy.
C. Milton wrote this work in the 1600s. Did warfare in that era employ swords as we saw in the first battle?
    By the 1600s, warfare employed crossbows, longbows and firearms, along with pikes, which were used by tightly packed infantrymen. The sword was the main weapon of the middle ages and while still used, it was no longer the primary weapon.
D. By choosing to have the demons manufacture the gunpowder and cannons, do you think Milton was making a judgment about the weapons?
    Answers may vary.
E. Why had Raphael related the story in such graphic detail to Adam?
    He had related it in that way to impress upon him the serious consequences of disobedience to God.

WORDS TO KNOW:

obsequious: submissive

surcease: a temporary stoppage of an action (like a truce)

ignominious: humiliating, shameful

truce: temporary cessation of fighting

BOOK VII

(1-242)
1. Whom did Milton call upon to help him continue his story?
    He called upon the Muse Urania.
2. What did Adam want to know?
    He wanted to know how, why and when Heaven and Earth were created.
3. How did God decide to repopulate Heaven?
    He decided to create Earth and place mankind there; through merit, man would rise to Heaven.
4. How did God create the earth?
    He sent His Son into Chaos to create it.
5. What did the Son use to circumscribe the universe?
    He used a compass.
6. What was the first thing (after Heaven and the angels) created by God?
    The first thing created was light.

(243-570)
7. What was the order of creation after light?
    The order of creation was as follows:
    - The firmament
    - Dry land
    - The seas
    - The plants
    - Sun and Moon (The two great lights), and then the stars
    - Life in the waters and the air (fish and fowl, whales, etc.)
    - Land creatures
    - Man in the image of God

(571-640)
8. What would the angels do for man?
    They would serve as God's messengers.
9. What good did the apostasy of Satan and his followers promote?
    It provided the impetus for God to manifest His might through creation.
10. What did God do on the seventh day?
    He rested.

BOOK VIII

(1-129)
1. What had Adam thirsted for?
    He had thirsted for knowledge.
2. What misconception did Adam have about the earth?
    He thought it was sedentary and that the heavenly bodies rotated around it.
3. What did Eve do when the conversation about the heavenly bodies continued and why?
    She went to tend the garden because she preferred to have Adam tell her about their conversation than hear it from Raphael.
4. How did Raphael refer to Heaven?
    He referred to Heaven as the Book of God.

Unit 1: Poetry

5. For what did the Sun, Moon and stars shine?
   They shone for mankind, not the Earth.
6. What are the six to which Milton refers in line 128?
   He was referring to the planets Mercury, Venus, Mars, Jupiter, Saturn and the Moon.
7. Which planet did Raphael add to the above?
   He added Earth.

(130-334)
8. What did Raphael advise Adam to do?
   He advised him to leave thoughts of the heavenly motions to God, to praise God for His creation, and think more about what concerned him.
9. How did Adam seek to detain Raphael?
   He proposed to tell Raphael his own story.
10. Where was Raphael when God created Earth?
    He was on a heavenly mission to insure that a spy did not leave Hell while God was creating.
11. What did Adam do after he first woke from his own creation and walked about?
    He named everything he saw.
12. What did Adam ask all the creatures?
    He asked how he himself came to be.
13. When he received no answer, what did Adam do?
    He lay down and slept.
14. What did Adam's dream reveal?
    His dream revealed to him what to eat and what not to eat—the fruit of the Tree of Knowledge—and the dire consequences if he should choose to disobey.

(335-499)
15. How were the animals named?
    They came to him in pairs to be named.
16. What troubled Adam?
    He was alone without another rational being like himself.
17. How did God respond?
    He told Adam that He, too, was alone, without equal, but He was not displeased.
18. How did Adam respond?
    He told God that he, as man, was not perfect as God was, and he needed someone to make up for what he lacked and to cooperate in the propagation of his species.
19. Why had God allowed Adam to be alone for awhile?
    He had allowed it to test his knowledge of himself.
20. After Adam and God had spoken, what did Adam do?
    He fell asleep again.
21. Why was Adam able to "see" what was happening as he slept?
    He was dreaming.
22. How was Eve created?
    While Adam slept, God took one of his ribs and fashioned her from it.
23. What virtues did Eve possess?
    She possessed innocence, modesty and a sense of her own worth.

(500-654)
24. According to Adam, why did Eve turn away from him when they first met?
    She turned away because it was his place to woo her.

25. What did Adam "understand" about Eve?

    He "understood" that she was inferior intellectually and was less like God than he was. She was also not able to reason as well as he could.

26. How did Raphael admonish Adam?

    He told him not to dismiss Eve's wisdom in favor of her physical appearance and to honor her as his equal, not his subject.

27. What would Eve do in return?

    She would honor him as her head.

28. What did Raphael say about passion?

    He said that passion was not where true love was to be found.

29. According to Raphael, what did Adam need to do?

    He needed to guard against seeking only carnal pleasure with Eve.

30. What did Adam ask Raphael about the heavenly spirits?

    He asked how they showed love.

31. What was Raphael's answer?

    He said that they experience pure love without hindrance of a body.

32. What was Raphael's final admonition to Adam?

    His final admonition to Adam was that he not be carried away by passion and fall into temptation which could lead him into disobedience.

Questions for Further Thought

A. Adam uses certain words that describe his desire to know more about creation, as well as his desire to detain Raphael. What are some of those words?

    He uses words that have to do with the sense of taste: hunger, satiate, sweetness, thirst, etc.

B. Why does it seem a bit unusual for Adam to say "Woman is her name, of man extracted; for this cause he shall forgo father and mother, and to his wife adhere;…"

    It is unusual because he knew nothing of mothers and fathers; he was the first father (after God, of course).

C. How did Milton handle the question of the position and movement of the heavenly bodies?

    He had Raphael indicate that the question was not important for man to explore and that kind of knowledge was best left to God.

D. How did Eve's account of their first meeting (Book IV) differ from Adam's?

    Eve said she saw her reflection and desired herself more than Adam until she was led to him, while Adam said she saw him and turned from him so that he would woo her.

Words to Know:

abstruse: obscure, mysterious

propitious: favorable, encouraging

colloquy: dialogue

diffident: hesitant, insecure

abashed: embarrassed, ashamed

Unit 1: Poetry

BOOK IX

(1-120)
1. What scenario does Milton set up at the very beginning of Book IX?
    He lets us know that the innocence of Adam and Eve is about to end with their revolt, and punishment is inevitable.
2. What does Milton say about the story he is about to tell?
    He says it is more heroic than the stories of the *Iliad* and the *Aeneid*, and will deal with "the better fortitude of patience and heroic martyrdom" which are not sung about.
3. What does he ask the Muse to do?
    He asks the Muse to visit him while he sleeps and inspire him then.
4. How will the story change?
    It will become tragic.
5. Where had Satan been?
    He had been circling Earth, devising how to bring mankind down.
6. How did he enter the Earth?
    He entered the coast at night at the Tigris River, in the guise of mist.

(121-334)
7. How did Satan feel about the beauty of Earth?
    He felt tormented by the beauty because he could not participate in it.
8. Who would glorify Satan for destroying mankind?
    The other condemned demons would glorify him.
9. Whom did Satan fear in the garden?
    He feared the angelic guards.
10. What did Satan say about revenge?
    He said at first it was sweet, but it soon lost its sweetness.
11. Where did Satan enter the serpent?
    He entered through the serpent's mouth.
12. Why did Eve propose that they separate to do their work?
    There was much work to be done, and she thought they could accomplish it better working apart and not being distracted by each other.
13. How did Adam respond to her proposal?
    He was doubtful and fearful, knowing that Satan was lurking about to destroy them as he had been warned by Gabriel.
14. What did Eve think Adam doubted?
    She thought he doubted her strength to resist the foe.
15. What did Adam say about his virtue?
    He said that it was magnified when he was in her presence.

(335-494)
16. What did she mean in asking what faith, love and virtue unassayed were?
    She questioned what they were without being put to the test, and said that Eden was no paradise if each one of them was insecure without the other.
17. Did God create man imperfect?
    No, He created man perfect, but He gave him free will and Adam was afraid that reason could be deceived.
18. Why did Eve doubt the deceiver would choose her?
    She doubted that the deceiver would choose her because she was the weaker of the two, and it would be a bigger rebuff to be repulsed by her.

19. Why did Satan avoid Adam?
    He avoided Adam because he considered him more intellectual, stronger and more courageous than Eve.

(495-699)
20. How did the serpent approach Eve?
    He moved upright rather than crawling on the ground.
21. What did Satan do to ingratiate himself to Eve?
    He flattered her.
22. What amazed her?
    She was amazed that the serpent could speak.
23. Why was the serpent able to speak?
    He had eaten of the Tree of Knowledge.
24. Other than being able to speak, what did the serpent "gain" from eating the fruit?
    He was able to reason and contemplate creation.
25. How did Satan counter Eve's explanation that the tree would bring about her death?
    He said that, on the contrary, it had enhanced his life, giving him powers normally reserved for man, so it would do even more for her.

(700-814)
26. How did Satan explain God's prohibition?
    He said God wanted to keep her low and ignorant.
27. What would she and Adam know about if they ate the fruit?
    They would know about good and evil.
28. What "reasoning" did Eve use to convince herself to eat the fruit?
    She reasoned that the serpent had eaten and lived, spoke, reasoned and discerned after eating the fruit. If he had not died, why would man? It made no sense to her that death would come when the serpent had only received gifts from the same tree.
29. What happened when she ate the fruit?
    The entire Earth reacted with sadness.
30. What did the serpent do?
    He slunk away.
31. What did Eve do?
    She gorged herself with the fruit and then worshipped the tree.

(815-989)
32. How did she refer to God?
    She referred to Him as the "great Forbidder."
33. What did she ponder?
    She pondered whether or not she should tell Adam.
34. Why did she decide to tell Adam?
    She could not endure the idea of him having another woman, and decided they should die together.
35. What did she tell him to convince him to eat the fruit?
    She told him that her eyes had been opened, and if he did not eat it, they would be unequal.
36. How did Adam react?
    He was horrified at what she had done and could not speak.
37. Why did he eat the fruit?
    He did not think he could live without her.

Unit 1: Poetry

(990-1189)
38. Why was Eve happy?
    She was happy because Adam loved her more than he feared death.
39. How did Earth respond when Adam ate the fruit?
    For the second time Earth trembled and groaned, and there was thunder and rain.
40. How did Milton refer to this sin of Adam?
    He called it "the mortal sin Original."
41. What was the immediate result of their eating the fruit?
    They were intoxicated and overcome with lust for each other.
42. After they sealed their guilt, how did they sleep?
    They slept without rest, having unsettling dreams.
43. What did they feel in the morning?
    They felt shame and realized they were naked, lacking in honor, faith, innocence and purity.
44. What did Adam say they should do?
    He said they should cover their bodies.
45. To what did Milton liken the covering they made out of the fig leaves?
    He likened it to the covering worn by the natives whom Columbus had recently discovered.
46. What began to happen to Adam and Eve?
    Their passions were aroused and they felt anger, hate, discord, sorrow and suspicion.
47. How did he reproach her?
    He said that if she had listened to him that morning and stayed with him, this would never have happened.
48. How did she respond?
    She asked him why he had not commanded her to stay since he was her head.
49. At the end of this book, what did Milton say?
    He said they spent the time endlessly blaming each other, but each failed to acknowledge his own part in the fall.

Questions for Further Thought

A. What did Milton mean when he said the snake led her "from succour far."
    He meant that Satan led her far enough away from Adam that he could be no help to her.
B. What means did Satan use to convince Eve to eat the fruit?
    He used deceit and flattery.
C. Did Eve use the same means to convince Adam to eat the fruit?
    No, she did not. He was not deceived and he chose to disobey God's command because he could not endure the thought of losing Eve.
D. After Eve ate from the tree and pondered whether or not to tell Adam, she said "for inferior who is free?" Who else had said that and what was the result? What does this portend for Eve?
    Satan had said that while still in Heaven, and he decided he would not live inferior to God and His Son. As a result, he went to war and was driven out of Heaven. Because of her decision, she and Adam would be driven out of Paradise.
E. Adam "reasoned" that the serpent had gained human powers by eating the fruit, and, therefore, man could only rise to a new level as well. He thought that God, though He had threatened, would not really destroy mankind and give the victory to Satan. What do people say today about Hell and the likelihood of man being punished there?
    Many people say that God, who is all merciful, would not allow anybody to go to Hell. They are deceived as Adam and Eve were, and fail to see that it is not God who sends people to Hell; it is the logical consequence of the bad use of free will.
F. What was the climax of the story?
    The climax was the fall of Adam and Eve.

G. Was Satan a character for whom you could have any sympathy? Why or why not?
    Answers will vary.
H. What knowledge did Adam and Eve gain?
    The knowledge they gained was how much good they had lost and how much evil they had brought upon themselves.

Words to Know:

sedulous: doing something with great care and concentration

carbuncle: a red gemstone, garnet

pernicious: destructive, harmful

concupiscence: tendency toward lust

Book X

(1-94)
1. According to Milton, why did Adam and Eve deserve to fall?
    They deserved to fall because they had been forewarned of the temptation to eat of the forbidden fruit.
2. How did the angels in Heaven respond when the guardian angels returned with news of the fall?
    Though they were sad and felt pity, their bliss was not disturbed.
3. What did God reassure the angels about?
    He reassured them that what happened was not their fault—they could not have prevented Satan from entering Paradise.
4. What had God foretold?
    He had foretold that Satan would seduce man.
5. Whom did God decide to send to judge Adam and Eve?
    He sent His Son whom he referred to as "Vicegerent Son."
6. What did the Son say to His Father?
    He said that He would go to judge them, and would temper justice with mercy, as well as appease His Father.

(95-196)
7. What did Adam and Eve do when they heard God approaching?
    They hid.
8. How did Adam and Eve appear?
    They appeared guilty, shamed, and full of despair, anger, obstinacy, hate and guile.
9. How did Adam explain their hiding?
    He said they hid because they were afraid due to their nakedness.
10. What was Adam's dilemma?
    He didn't know whether to accept all the guilt and blame for the sin or to implicate Eve.
11. What did he tell God?
    He told God that the woman gave him the fruit.
12. What did God ask Adam?
    He asked him if Eve had been placed by him as his guide or as his God that she could cause him to surrender his manhood.
13. What was Eve's excuse for eating the fruit?
    The devil (serpent) made her do it.

Unit 1: Poetry

14. Whom did God curse?
    He cursed the serpent to crawl on his belly, eating dust. Included in the curse was that there would be enmity between the serpent and the seed of the woman, and her seed would bruise his head.
15. How was the woman to be punished?
    She would bear children in sorrow and be ruled by her husband.

(197-318)
16. How was the man to be punished?
    The ground would be cursed, and with great toil would he have to work it to bring forth food.
17. What merciful act did God perform for Adam and Eve?
    He clothed them with the skins of beasts and with His robe of righteousness.
18. What did Sin propose?
    Sin proposed that She and Death forge a path from Hell to Earth.
19. What did Death sense?
    He sensed a change in the smell of Earth—the smell of death.
20. To what did Milton liken the bridge from Hell to Earth?
    He likened it to the bridge of ships constructed by Xerxes to the Hellespont over which his army could march to invade Greece. The sea destroyed the bridge.

(319-572)
21. What had Satan gained for Sin and Death?
    He gained their liberty from Hell, and they were now free to roam the Earth as his substitutes.
22. What did Satan report to his legions when he returned to Hell?
    He told them about his daring adventure to Paradise and the success he had there.
23. What response did he get after telling his story?
    He only received hisses, because he and all of the other fallen angels were transformed into serpents and could not speak.
24. What happened when the serpents ate the fruit of the trees?
    The fruit was filled with cinder and soot, so their thirst and hunger weren't slaked.

(573-705)
25. What was to happen annually?
    The fallen angels would resume their previous shape, only to return again to being ugly serpents.
26. How did Death answer Sin's question of what he thought of their new empire?
    He said that it made no difference whether he were in Hell, Paradise or Heaven, because no amount of plunder or prey (ravin) could satisfy him.
27. What did God do next?
    He called forth the angels to alter the seasons and the earth on its axis.

(706-864)
28. What caused the beasts of the earth to war and prey on each other?
    Discord, Daughter of Sin introduced antipathy among them.
29. What did Adam say as he saw Paradise being destroyed?
    He said he was cursed and mankind for all time would blame him.
30. What did he say about his own creation?
    He said that since he did not ask to be created, he should be returned to dust because he had failed in his mission.
31. What would he do if he could?
    He would take all the punishment in order to spare his offspring the same.

32. What did Adam admit?
    He admitted his own guilt.

(865-1104)
33. When Eve approached, how did Adam rebuff her?
    He told her to leave his sight, "thou serpent."
34. Against whom did Adam and Eve sin?
    Adam sinned against God, Eve sinned against Adam and God.
35. What did Eve acknowledge?
    She acknowledged her sin and guilt.
36. What did Adam finally agree to?
    He agreed to stop blaming her and live with her, sharing her burdens, and she his.
37. What did Eve propose?
    She proposed that they not have children and that they kill themselves.
38. Why did Adam disagree with her proposal?
    He disagreed because to do so would mean Satan would escape the punishment he was due by having her seed bruise his head. Also, they could not possibly escape God's judgment on them.
39. What further hope did Adam give Eve?
    He said that God would have pity on them and instruct them in what they needed to know to survive.
40. What did Adam and Eve then do?
    They went to the place where God had judged them and fell down, begging His pardon and confessing their sins.

QUESTIONS FOR FURTHER THOUGHT

A. Could God have prevented the Fall?
   Yes, He could have because He is omnipotent. However, if He had intervened, He would have trampled on the freedom He had given to Adam and Eve.
B. What did Milton mean that Mary was the Second Eve?
   He meant that through Mary, the mother of the Son, the redemption of man would be accomplished. It would be her seed that would bruise Satan's head (do battle with Satan).
C. What did God mean when He told His Son that Sin and Death would be hurled into Hell forever with "one sling of thy victorious arm, well-pleasing Son."
   He meant that Sin and Death would remain on Earth until Judgment Day when they would finally and forever be thrust back into Hell.
D. The term suppliant was often seen in the literature of Ancient Greece. Milton uses it in the same way in line 917. What does it mean?
   It means to approach one on your knees and to wrap your arms around his knees in a gesture of pleading. That is how Eve approached Adam.

WORDS TO KNOW:

loquacious: talkative

vitiate: to make something defective

thrall: somebody who is completely dominated by another

ravin: plunder or prey

Unit 1: Poetry

antipathy: hostility, ill-feeling

sinister: evil, ominous; (from the left side)

suppliant: humbly entreating

contumacy: defiance of authority

BOOK XI

(1-161)
1. How did the Son take the prayers of Adam and Eve to His Father?
   He took them in a golden censer mixed with incense.
2. What did the Son say about the offering He brought?
   He said it was more pleasing than the fruits sown by Adam's own hand because they came from a contrite heart.
3. What did the Son ask?
   He asked the Father to allow Him to pay with His death for the sin of Adam and Eve.
4. What did God answer?
   He said He would accept the Son's offering, but Adam and Eve had to be expelled from the garden.
5. What were the two gifts God had given mankind?
   He had given them happiness and immortality.
6. How would man be refined?
   He would be refined by faith and faithful works.
7. Whom did God send to remove Adam and Eve from the garden?
   He sent Michael.
8. How was Michael to send them out of the garden?
   He was to send them out in peace, reminding them of God's covenant with the woman's offspring.
9. What "title" did Adam give Eve?
   He called her the "Mother of Mankind."

(162-292)
10. How did Eve respond to Adam's saying she was the mother of mankind?
    She said she was unworthy of such a title, because she had become Adam's snare; it would be better to reproach her.
11. What did they observe in the early morning?
    They observed the bird of Jove hunting, an eclipse and a predator hunting a deer.
12. How did Michael appear to Adam?
    He appeared as a man, solemn and sublime, rather than as an angel.
13. What did Adam tell Eve to do as Michael approached?
    He told her to retire.
14. Why did Michael go to the garden?
    He went to send Adam and Eve out from it.
15. How did Adam respond?
    He felt deep sorrow.
16. What would be Eve's native soil?
    Wherever Adam was to be would be her native soil.

(293-529)
17. What did Adam say he would miss?
    He would miss most his encounters with God.

18. How did Michael comfort him?
    He told him that God is everywhere and cares for him.
19. What would Michael show Adam?
    He would show him what would come in the future.
20. What were some of the things which Adam saw?
    He saw Cain slay Abel and he saw disease in many forms.

(530-699)
21. After seeing death in so many ways, what did Adam want to know?
    He wanted to know if there was any other way that man would die.
22. What did Michael answer?
    He said that those who lived with temperance in food and drink would live to old age in which they would lose their youth, strength and beauty.
23. When Adam said he would rather have a short life, what did Michael advise?
    He advised him to live well for however long Heaven permitted.
24. What else did Michael show Adam?
    He showed him men at work and then women singing and dancing.
25. How did Michael rebuke Adam when he saw the women with pleasure?
    He told him not to judge what was best by pleasure.
26. Why were the women at Cain's tents?
    They were there to lead the men to sin.
27. Did Michael hold the women responsible for corrupting the men?
    No, he said the men were weak and didn't use their superior gifts to resist.
28. What did Michael show Adam next?
    He showed him war and violence.
29. Who were the people Adam saw?
    They were his descendants.

(700-901)
30. Adam saw a just man. Who was he?
    He was Enoch, the seventh from Adam who tried to prevent the wars. (*Genesis*. 5:1-22)
31. Who was the man who testified against the ways of man?
    That man was Noah.
32. How did Adam respond to the vision of his descendants being destroyed by the flood?
    He grieved, knowing not only his own unhappiness, but also that of the future generations.
33. Why did Adam rejoice?
    He rejoiced because he had a vision of Noah surviving the flood, which meant mankind would survive.
34. What did the rainbow signify?
    It signified the covenant made by God that He would never again destroy the earth by flood.

QUESTIONS FOR FURTHER THOUGHT

A. Why do you think Milton had Michael show Adam the future?
   Perhaps he had Michael show the future in order to demonstrate man's disobedience throughout the centuries and his need for repentance.
B. On what were Milton's descriptions focused?
   His descriptions were focused on the sins of mankind, such as gluttony, lust, sloth and greed.
C. Noah, as the only righteous man of his time could be compared to whom?
   He could be compared to Christ. In biblical study, Noah is a type of Christ: one who points the way to Christ by his example.

Unit 1: Poetry

D. Why did Noah and Enoch stand out?
   They were men of virtue, even when they were ridiculed for it, and they never wavered from what they knew to be God's will.
E. How would you summarize Michael's mission to Adam?
   His mission was to send him forth from the garden but also to give him hope for the future of his race, despite the sin and death into which he had now entered.

Words to Know:

propitiation: the winning of another's favor

synod: a church council to discuss religious issues

peccant: guilty of sin; sinner

Book XII

(1-62)
1. What is the "second source" of men?
   The "second source" of men are the offspring of Noah.
2. What would keep Noah's offspring living in peace?
   The memory of the recent chastisement would keep them in peace.
3. Who would eventually make war on others?
   Nimrod would do so.
4. By what name do we know the tower Milton speaks about in line 44?
   We know it as the Tower of Babel.
5. What did God do when he saw the tower?
   He confused the language of the people so they couldn't understand each other.

(63-167)
6. What did Adam say about the authority God gave to man?
   He said that man's authority was only over beasts, not over other men.
7. What did Michael tell Adam about liberty?
   He told him that true liberty was lost with his sin, and that true liberty always dwells with right reason. Man's passions now ruled his reason and reduced him to servitude.
8. Why was God's judgment just?
   It was just because man was no longer in control of his reason, and he was instead, ruled by unworthy powers.
9. Who was the irreverent son of Noah and how did Noah curse him?
   Noah's irreverent son was Ham, who saw his father naked and didn't cover him. Noah cursed him to be a slave to his brothers. (*Genesis* 9: 20-27)
10. From whom would God raise a mighty nation?
    He would raise a mighty nation from Abraham from Ur of Chaldea.
11. Who would be Abraham's grandson?
    His grandson would be Jacob, and he would have twelve sons.
12. Who was the son who was second to Pharaoh in Egypt?
    Second to Pharaoh in Egypt was Joseph.
13. Who were the "inmate guests too numerous?"
    They were the Hebrew people who became slaves in Egypt.

(168-332)
14. Who led the slaves out of Egypt?
    Moses led them out of Egypt.
15. How was access to God to be gained?
    It was to be gained by a mediator.
16. What did Adam ask Michael?
    He asked why so many laws were needed among the people with whom God would dwell.
17. How did Michael answer?
    He said that because of sin, they would need laws to control themselves.
18. What did Michael say about sacrifices?
    He said that the sacrifices of bulls and goats would not be enough; in order to be justified toward God, a greater sacrifice would be needed. (That would be the sacrifice of Christ).
19. Who would be the final mediator between man and God?
    Jesus would be the mediator.
20. From whose stock would Jesus come?
    He would come from the stock of David.
21. Who was the son "for wealth and wisdom famed?"
    He was Solomon.

(333-465)
22. Who fought among themselves, bringing strife upon the temple?
    The priests fought among themselves.
23. What was the result of the priests' fighting?
    They lost authority, and Israel came under the domination of a foreign power.
24. What did Adam finally come to understand about the Messiah?
    He came to understand that the Messiah was the "Seed of Woman" who would vanquish Satan.
25. How would the Messiah redeem mankind?
    He would do it not by overcoming Satan in hand-to-hand combat, but by being obedient to the will of His Father in Heaven and overcoming man's death with His own.
26. How would mankind benefit from the Messiah's death?
    Mankind would benefit by faith in the merit of His death, not in works.
27. How would Satan's head be crushed?
    His head would be crushed by the defeat of Sin and Death through Christ's death.

(466-749)
28. When Adam saw the good that would come through the Messiah, what did he do?
    He rejoiced and wondered whether he should repent of his sin or be happy that his sin led to the good of man's redemption.
29. Who would guide the remainder of the Deliverer's flock after He ascended back to Heaven?
    The Apostles, under the guidance of the Holy Spirit, would guide his flock.
30. What did Michael tell Adam would happen after the deaths of the apostles?
    False teachers would arise who would taint the written Word with superstition and traditions.
31. Whom was Milton attacking?
    He was attacking the pope and leaders of the Catholic Church.
32. What lesson did Adam learn?
    He learned that to obey is best, that he must walk with fear in God, and that suffering for truth was the highest victory.
33. What did Michael tell Adam to do?
    He told him to be content with the wisdom he had gained, to "hope no higher," and to add deeds, faith, virtue, patience, temperance and love. In that way, he would possess Paradise within himself and be happy.

Unit 1: Poetry

34. Why was Eve disposed to leave Eden?
    While she slept, Michael had given her dreams which comforted her.

Questions for Further Thought

A. What has been the general pattern of human behavior from the time of Adam to the present when he has not had to work hard to survive?
    Adam had everything he needed in the garden, yet he fell into sin. When mankind is prosperous and life is easy, history has shown that he becomes lax in his self-discipline, slothful in the pursuit of virtue, and soft in general. The ancient military generals understood how important it was to keep the soldiers training, even when they were not fighting, because to allow them to be idle would compromise their readiness for war.
B. What do you think Milton's story of Nimrod reflected?
    It may have reflected his own mistrust of governments and the control that governments have over individuals.
C. Is it realistic to believe that man can live without being governed?
    It is not realistic, and Milton himself illustrated that through the visions he showed Adam. The good were always tempted and ended up warring or sinning. Without some kind of imposed order, there would always be chaos. Men would give in to their lusts and other vices, and the innocent would need protection. Though man had the faculty of reason, it was not enough to guarantee that he would always use it correctly.
D. Do you agree that the fall of Adam was actually a good thing? Explain.
    The fall itself was not a good thing, because it brought sin, corruption and death into a perfect world. From the standpoint of redemption, however, good came from the fall and allowed God to show His mercy on mankind.
E. What knowledge did Adam and Eve take from the garden?
    They took the knowledge that they had sinned and lost paradise, but they also knew that God was merciful in giving them a second chance. They had to live in obedience and work out their salvation in a new way, remembering the lessons they had been taught by Michael.
F. Who was the tragic hero of this story? Why?
    Adam was the tragic hero, because by definition, he brought about his own downfall due to a fatal flaw within himself. He failed to be firm in his resolve not to eat the fruit because he feared losing the company of Eve.
G. Did the book end on a happy or a sad note? Why?
    Answers will vary.
H. Did Milton give any hints of his attitude toward Catholicism? Explain.
    He seemed to hold Catholicism in contempt. He referred to the Scriptures being tainted with superstitions and traditions and sarcastically referred to infallibility. Many people, not only from his time but even today, view Catholic practices as superstitious.
I. Did Milton stand apart from his work or did he interject anything of himself in it?
    He interjected himself in it. For instance, he referred to his blindness and age. He asked the Muse to help him where he might fail on his own resources. And surely, there were his own religious and political beliefs expressed in the look into the future which Adam witnessed.
J. Did Milton accomplish his purpose "to explain the ways of God to men?"
    Yes. He laid out the conditions of the fall of Adam and Eve, and he wove a story which explained why man suffers and how he will be redeemed. He showed God's justice and also His mercy in dealing with mankind.

Word to Know:

sequent: following

Beowulf

Translation: Burton Raffel
Mentor Books

The origin of Beowulf is unknown. A single manuscript from about 1100 is all that remains, and it is incomplete. Some scholars believe the poem was composed in England 400 years before the Norman Conquest of 1066, while others place it in the 1100s. Even though the poem is English, it glorifies war and fame and pays scant attention to the mundane lives of the majority of the people among the Danes, not the English. Slaves have no names, but swords do. There are Christian elements intermingled with the paganism of the Swedes and Danes. Reflected in the poem are the behaviors and ideals of the day. It is a poem about heroic warriors who exemplify virtue as they understand it.

Beowulf is a narrative poem about the kings and heroes of the Danes and Geats, of whom Beowulf is the greatest. It was originally composed in Old English.

Because the names are foreign to most modern readers, I have listed below some of the more frequently used terms and names from the work:

- Scyldings — Danes
- Weder people — People of Southern Sweden known as the Geats
- Hrothgar — King of Denmark
- Thane — A follower or attendant
- Beowulf — Geat hero of the poem
- Grendel — Danish monster which Beowulf kills
- Scylfings — Swedes
- Herot — Mead Hall which was the center of social activities
- Mead — fermented drink made from honey
- Scop — Entertainer in a royal court, a storyteller

Unit 1: Poetry

Prologue

(1-50)
1. How did Danish kings earn glory?
    They won glory by winning many lands.
2. Who founded Danish royalty?
    Shild, an abandoned child, sailed to Denmark alone from an unknown place and established himself as the first king over the people who had no ruler.
3. Who was Beo?
    He was the son of Shild.
4. How had Shild bound the warriors to his son?
    He had bound them with his treasure.
5. How was Shild "buried?"
    He was put on a ship filled with treasure and was cast off.

Questions for Further Thought

A. From the introduction, what do we learn about Danish nobles?
    We learn that their primary activity was warring on others; that courage in battle was highly valued as well as generosity with the spoils of war.
B. Does the author sound like a pagan? Why or why not?
    He does not sound like a pagan because he attributes their good fortune to the benevolence of the "Lord of all life," and to Shild being "called to the Lord's hands." Those are clearly Christian references to God.

(51-114)
1. How did Beo rule?
    He ruled as his father had done and was loved by the people.
2. Who was his son and what was his virtue?
    His son was Healfdane, and he was fierce in battle.
3. Who were his children?
    His children were Hergar, Hrothgar, Halga the Good, and Yrs, his only daughter who married Onela, the king of the Swedes.
4. When Hrothgar was king, what did he plan?
    He planned to build a great towering hall for his warriors in which he would divide the spoils.
5. What did he call the hall?
    He called it Herot.
6. What does the poet foretell?
    He foretells a feud and the destruction of Herot by fire.
7. What disturbed the happiness of Herot?
    Grendel, the sulking monster, disturbed its happiness.
8. To whom is Grendel linked?
    He is linked to Cain, who murdered his brother Abel.

Questions for Further Thought

A. What is the mood of the story at this point?
    The mood is one of joy tempered with a sense of doom by the presence of Grendel.
B. What are lines 91 through 114 about and what is their source?
    Lines 91 through 114 are about the creation of the world and are found in the *Old Testament, Book of Genesis*.

(115-257)
1. Why was Grendel able to enter the hall?
    He was able to enter it because the warriors were in a drunken sleep.
2. What did Grendel do?
    He killed 30 men and took their bodies away.
3. How did Hrothgar respond to the slaughter?
    He wept and mourned.
4. What did his warriors do?
    They fled.
5. What triumphed?
    Hate triumphed.
6. What became of Herot?
    It was deserted.
7. What alone did Grendel leave unmolested?
    He left Hrothgar's throne unmolested.
8. Why did he leave the throne alone?
    He knew it was protected by God who loved Hrothgar.
9. What did the Heathens hope for?
    They hoped that the Devil would help them drive Grendel away.
10. Who went to help Hrothgar?
    Beowulf and 14 of the bravest men of the Geats went.
11. Whom did they encounter when they landed?
    They encountered Hrothgar's lieutenant.
12. What did the lieutenant notice about Beowulf?
    He noticed his weapons and good looks and realized he was a great man.

QUESTIONS FOR FURTHER THOUGHT

A. What pagan elements have been introduced to the story?
    The warriors sacrificed to stone gods and made heathen vows, asking the help of the Devil in their battle against Grendel; and the omens were favorable for Beowulf to sail to Denmark.

(258-370)
1. Who was the Geat king?
    The Geat king was Higlac.
2. What did Beowulf offer?
    He offered to help Hrothgar find a way to overcome Grendel and his sorrow.
3. What could the men see as they marched into Denmark?
    They saw the glittering roofs of Herot.
4. What did Hrothgar's captain say about Beowulf and his men?
    He said that courage had brought them there.
5. Did Beowulf tell the captain the reason for his coming?
    No, he asked him to seek an audience for them with Hrothgar so he could speak with him directly.

(371-498)
6. What did Hrothgar say about Beowulf?
    He said that he knew him when he was a boy and related his lineage.
7. To what did Hrothgar attribute the arrival of Beowulf?
    He attributed it to the favor of God, as a sign of His grace.

Unit 1: Poetry

8. How were Beowulf and his men to present themselves to the king?
   They were to go in their armor and helmets, but without their battle-shields or spears.
9. Did they all go to the king?
   No. Beowulf left some to guard their weapons.
10. Why did the Geats send Beowulf to Denmark?
    He had been successful in war, in killing giants and in killing sea monsters and seemed to be able to take care of Grendel as well.
11. What did Beowulf request?
    He requested that only he and his men be allowed to hunt Grendel.
12. Why would Beowulf use no weapons?
    He would not want to shame himself before Higlac by using weapons.
13. What did he request if Grendel killed him?
    He requested that his armor be sent back to Higlac.
14. What would determine the outcome in the end?
    Fate would determine the outcome.
15. What did Hrothgar tell Beowulf about Edgetho, Beowulf's father?
    Edgetho had killed a Wulfing warrior and his father and people turned him away when he tried to return home. So he had gone to Denmark and was received by Hrothgar, who settled the problem with gifts sent to the Wulfings and a promise of future peace.
16. What did Hrothgar provide for Beowulf and his men?
    He provided a banquet with toasts, talk of victory and poetry sung by a scop.

(499-558)
17. Why was Unferth angry?
    He was jealous because somebody else had won more glory and fame than he had.
18. What did Unferth relate about Beowulf?
    He related the story of how he had competed against Brecca by swimming for seven nights in the icy waters off Norway, and Brecca won the contest. Unferth said Beowulf was driven by pride and recklessness.
19. How did Beowulf respond?
    He said that he had chosen to swim close to Brecca but after five nights they were swept apart by a flood. Beowulf was seized by a monster and was saved by the shining mail shirt he was wearing. He was able to kill the monster with his sword and thus, saved himself.

(559-709)
20. What else did Beowulf relate about the swimming match?
    He related how he killed nine monsters in all and finally surfaced on Finnish soil.
21. What did he say about Unferth?
    He said that he had not heard any tales of his bravery but knew that he had murdered his brothers and would, therefore, suffer in Hell.
22. What did Welthow, Hrothgar's wife, do?
    She toasted her husband, then his warriors and finally Beowulf, and thanked God for sending a savior.
23. Before leaving Herot, what did Hrothgar promise Beowulf?
    He left Herot in Beowulf's hands and promised ships full of treasure to return home.
24. How did Beowulf say he would meet Grendel?
    He would meet him with his hands empty.
25. What did he say about the victor in the coming fight?
    He said that God in His wisdom would reward whom He chose.
26. How did his warriors feel as they prepared to sleep?
    They felt sure they would never return home.

27. Does the poet indicate the outcome of the battle?
    Yes he does, in lines 696-701, he says that "God's dread loom was woven with defeat for the monster, good fortune for the Geats; help against Grendel was with them…"
28. Did Beowulf sleep?
    No. He lay in waiting.

(710-836)
29. How many men did Grendel kill before he came upon Beowulf?
    He killed only one.
30. How did Beowulf trap Grendel?
    He clutched his claws in his hands and cracked them.
31. Why were Beowulf's warriors unable to help him in his battle with Grendel?
    Grendel had bewitched all of the men's weapons.
32. What had Grendel discovered?
    He had discovered the futility of going up against God.
33. What proof did the Dane's have that Beowulf had killed Grendel?
    Grendel's arm and claw were hanging from the rafters.
34. Did Grendel die in the hall?
    No, he escaped and went to die in the marsh from whence he came.

Questions for Further Thought

A. What is unusual about the presence of Welthow in the hall?
    This poem is about men and manly business—the business of war. She is the first woman about whom anything of substance is mentioned. She is jeweled and gracious in a very feminine way. Her behavior is regal and she offers the cup of mead as a gesture of honor and friendship to her husband and then the warriors.
B. What descriptions does he give of Herot?
    He uses the following descriptions: gold-shining hall, iron fasteners, inlaid floor, sturdily built, beautiful walls, shaped and fastened with iron, artfully worked, gold-covered benches, built to withstand anything but fire, splendid with ivory, iron and wood. (Note that this is the second hint of how Herot will be destroyed).

(837-924)
1. There seems to be a digression in these lines, with a story about Siegmund. What was the story about?
    Siegmund was a brave warrior who also killed a dragon by himself. His bravery earned him a king's fortune.
2. What did the poet say about Hermod?
    Hermod was also a brave warrior who was undone by pride and betrayal. He refused to listen to others because his "heart had been hollowed by sin."

Question for Further Thought

What is the mood of the poem at this point?
    There is much rejoicing and retelling of the bravery of Beowulf. The women and the king are moving toward the great hall for a celebration. The story of Siegmund and Hermod, however, lends a hint of trouble to the story.

(925-1049)
1. Who was glorified by the birth of Beowulf according to Hrothgar?
    Beowulf's mother and God were glorified.

Unit 1: Poetry

2. What did Hrothgar offer Beowulf?
   He offered to make him his son and to love him.
3. How did Beowulf respond?
   He said that he had failed to kill Grendel because God's will was against him.
4. What person is mentioned as toasting with Hrothgar?
   His nephew Hrothulf toasted him.

(1050-1250)
5. In the story of Finn, what are some of the themes?
   The themes are betrayal, revenge, longing for one's country, and the suffering of a woman caught by marriage and blood between the two warring sides.
6. What does the queen do at the conclusion of the story?
   She once again offers the mead-cup and encourages her husband to be open-handed with gifts for Beowulf and his men.
7. According to the queen, who will take care of her sons once Hrothgar is dead?
   His nephew Hrothulf will take care of them because she and Hrothgar took care of him after his father died.
8. Earlier Welthow fulfilled her role as the queen and hostess. What role did she take on in this section?
   She was a mother, solicitous for the welfare of her sons. More than once she asked for Hrothulf and Beowulf to look after her sons and treat them well. There is almost a sense that something dreadful will happen.
9. This section closes out with an ominous prediction. What do we know?
   We know that a "savage fate" awaited them as they "lay down with death beside their beds."
10. How did Danish warriors sleep?
    They slept with their weapons at their sides, wearing their shirts of mail, always prepared to do their lord's bidding.

(1251-1472)
11. Who would avenge the death of Grendel?
    His mother would avenge his death.
12. Where was Beowulf when she went to Herot?
    He and his men were sleeping in a different hall.
13. Whom did she kill?
    She killed Hrothgar's closest friend and advisor.
14. Who had given Grendel his name?
    Hrothgar's people (peasants) had seen the beast and his mother and named him.
15. What did Hrothgar request of Beowulf?
    He asked him to slay Grendel's mother and again promised him vast treasure.
16. What did Beowulf respond?
    He said it was better to avenge friends rather than mourn them, and that fame after death was the noblest of goals.
17. What did Hrothgar, his men and Beowulf do?
    They followed the tracks of Grendel's mother to a bloody lake in a wood, where they saw hideous sea creatures and snakes. Beowulf resolved to go into the lake after the fiend. He put on his coat of mail, Hrothgar's helmet, and took a sword named Hrunting which Unferth lent him.

(1473-1650)
18. What did Beowulf ask of Hrothgar?
    He asked him to be a father to his comrades if he lost the battle with Grendel's mother and to send the treasure he had earned back to his king Higlac.
19. What failed Beowulf in his battle with the fiend?
    Hrothgar's helmet and the sword failed him.

20. What motivated Beowulf to continue?

    He was motivated by a longing for fame.
21. How did the poet express the fact that Beowulf escaped death at the hands of the she-wolf?

    He said "He'd have traveled to the bottom of the earth, Edgetho's son, and died there, if that shining woven metal had not helped—and Holy God, who sent him victory, gave judgment for truth and right, Ruler of the Heavens…"
22. After killing Grendel's mother, what did Beowulf do?

    He found a giant's jeweled sword and used it to cut off Grendel's head. Then, taking the hilt of the giant's sword and Grendel's head, he rose up out of the water.
23. What happened to the lake?

    It was transformed into a beautiful, peaceful, clean lake once the demons were killed.
24. How many men were required to carry Grendel's huge head?

    Four men were needed to carry his head.

Question for Further Thought

What illustrates the contrast between Beowulf and his comrades?

   It took four of his comrades to carry Grendel's head, while he had killed him single-handedly with his bare hands. He is truly a hero.

(1651-1816)
1. What did Beowulf tell Hrothgar?

    He related how he had found the sword and used it to kill Grendel's mother, how he had found the body of Grendel and cut off his head, how he had been helped by Almighty God, and then he assured him that all could sleep peacefully now.
2. What did Hrothgar do with the hilt which Beowulf gave him?

    He examined it and related the ancient history that was carved upon it.
3. What did Hrothgar advise Beowulf?

    He advised him to return home and be a wise protector of his people. He then related how Hermod had been a wicked king, not caring about his people, not sharing his wealth, and being bloodthirsty, and warned Beowulf not to be like that. He should learn what a king must be and not bring suffering to his people through sin.
4. What did Hrothgar say about prosperity?

    He said that prosperity always comes to an end, to be taken over by the next man.
5. What did he say about death?

    He said it comes to all, one way or another.
6. What did he say about pride?

    He said that pride grows in an unwary heart. It takes root and grows at the Devil's urging.
7. How did people sleep that night?

    They slept well.
8. What did Unferth do?

    He offered Hrunting to Beowulf as a gift.
9. How did Beowulf receive it?

    He accepted it, said he was proud to own it, and told Unferth he did not blame it for anything.

(1817-1887)
10. What did Beowulf tell Hrothgar as he was preparing to leave?

    He told him that he would always be ready to return to defend the Danes if needed and that Hrothgar's son would always be welcome in his country.

Unit 1: Poetry

11. How did Hrothgar respond?
    He said that he had never seen such wisdom in one so young, and hoped that Beowulf would be offered the Geat throne. Beowulf had cemented the friendship between the two people and they would hopefully always be friends.
12. What was the last gesture made by Beowulf before he boarded his ship?
    He gave the watchman a beautiful sword which brought the man honor.

(1888-2092)
13. What did the poet say about Higlac's wife?
    He said she was young, wise beyond her years and generous.
14. What evil behavior did Higlac's daughter Thrith exhibit?
    She would pretend to be insulted by any man who looked at her, forcing him to be killed.
15. Why had she supposedly changed?
    She had married Offa, the Angle king, who had tamed her, and she was known to be generous and noble.
16. What did Beowulf relate to Higlac?
    He told Higlac about his victory over Grendel and how he had been honored to sit with Hrothgar's son at the table; about how his queen served mead and distributed bracelets to Hrothgar's warriors; and about the impending marriage of Hrothgar's daughter Freaw to Ingeld, son of Froda the Heathobard, in hopes that the quarrel between the Heathobards and Danes could be mended.
17. What did Beowulf foresee?
    He foresaw that the marriage would not result in peace between the Heathobards and Danes because old grudges would surface as the men drank and talked at the marriage feast.

QUESTION FOR FURTHER THOUGHT

The rules of hospitality among the Greeks dictated that before a guest was questioned about his exploits or origins he was to be bathed, wined and dined. How was Higlac's reception of Beowulf different from that practice?
    The king Higlac was unable to wait to hear about Beowulf's experiences and he questioned him right away.

WORDS TO KNOW:

niggardly: stingy, miserly

imperious: domineering, arrogant, haughty

(2093-2220)
1. What did Beowulf say about the tales Hrothgar told in the hall?
    He said he told stories with unhappy truths about good and evil, about old age and previous victories.
2. What did Beowulf say about the armor he brought from Hrothgar to Higlac?
    He said it had belonged to Hrothgar's uncle Hergar who would not give them to his brave son.
3. What virtues did the poet say were necessary for a soldier to have glory?
    The soldier must not kill his comrades in a drunken rage, nor have a mean heart, and he must use his God-given strength bravely, and only in war.
4. How had Beowulf been treated by the Geats as a boy?
    He was perceived to be lazy and slow, and thus he was scorned.
5. How did Higlac reward Beowulf?
    He gave him his grandfather's sword plus land and houses.
6. After ruling as king for 50 years, what threat did Beowulf face?
    He faced the threat of a dragon which had been sleeping in a stone tower.

(2221-2390)
7. Why had the thief stolen a cup from the dragon?
    He stole it because he was needy; a slave who had been abused by his master.
8. How long had the dragon guarded the treasure?
    He had guarded it for hundreds of years.
9. What had the slave done with the cup he had stolen?
    He had taken it back to his master to buy his forgiveness.
10. How did the dragon take vengeance on the Geats for the theft?
    He burned down their houses, terrorized the people at night and burned down Beowulf's hall.
11. Whom did Beowulf blame for the dragon's wrath?
    He blamed himself.
12. How did Higlac die?
    He died of a sword wound in a war with the Frisians.
13. Why did Higlac's widow offer the crown to Beowulf instead of her own son?
    She did not think her son was strong enough to repel the foreigners.
14. Why did Beowulf refuse the crown?
    He did not think it right to accept it while the rightful heir lived.
15. What did Onela seek?
    He sought the death of Higlac's son Herdred, who had given protection to the men who rebelled against him.

Question for Further Thought

What vice did the dragon personify with his wrath at losing one cup amidst all the treasure which he hoarded and could not enjoy?
    He personified greed.

(2391-2459)
1. Who led Beowulf to the dragon?
    The slave who had stolen the cup led him.
2. Where did the cup end up?
    It ended up in Beowulf's hands.
3. As Beowulf was going to meet the dragon what did he realize?
    He realized that he was old and weak and would probably die.
4. What events from his life did he relate in a lengthy speech?
    He spoke about how Higlac had taken him in; how he had been victorious in all his battles; how Hrethel's son Herbald had died from the arrow of his brother Hathcyn who was subsequently hanged for the crime; and about the grief of his uncle over the death of his sons and his inability to take revenge.

(2460-2601)
5. What happened to Hrethel's third son, Hathcyn?
    He was killed in battle with the Swedes.
6. What did Beowulf say about the gifts he had been given by Higlac?
    He said that he had earned the gifts because his sword was always ready to serve Higlac, unlike others who had to be bribed with gifts.
7. What weapons would Beowulf need against the dragon?
    In addition to courage, he would need a sword, shield and armor.
8. What did he ask his friends to do?
    He asked them to stay and watch the battle to see how fate would decide the outcome.

9. What happened to Beowulf's shield?
    It melted from the heat of the dragon's flames.
10. What did the poet tell us about Beowulf and fate?
    He said this was the first time fate had not been with Beowulf as he fought.
11. What happened to Beowulf's sword?
    It broke as he plunged it into the dragon.
12. What did Beowulf's comrades do when they saw that the dragon would kill him?
    They fled.

Questions for Further Thought

A. What role change did we see for Beowulf as he went to face the dragon?
    When he faced Grendel and his mother, he had been the brave young warrior, invincible and working for the glory of himself and his king. Now he was the protector king of his people, weakened by old age, but still as courageous as he had ever been.
B. What tragedy do we witness in this section?
    We witness Beowulf, the guardian of his people, absolutely deserted by all but one of his hand-picked warriors. Beowulf who had been selfless in his courage and generosity is now left to his own fate.

(2602-2751)
1. Who alone stayed to help Beowulf?
    His loyal friend Wiglaf stayed behind.
2. What did Wiglaf do?
    He joined Beowulf in the fight and stabbed the dragon, extinguishing his flames.
3. Where was Beowulf mortally wounded?
    He was wounded in the neck.
4. Why could Beowulf die happy?
    He had a clear conscience—he had not sworn false oaths and he had never killed any members of his own family.
5. What did he instruct Wiglaf to do before he died?
    He instructed him to go retrieve the treasure and bring it to him.
6. What was the name of Beowulf's sword?
    His sword was Nagling.

Question for Further Thought

What motivated Wiglaf to help Beowulf?
    He was motivated by a number of things. First, he had a sense of gratitude for all that Beowulf had done for him and his family. Second, he was motivated by courage. Third, he honored the promise he had made to Beowulf to fight with him when needed, and fourth, he had a sense of duty as a young man helping his elderly king in a time of need.

(2752-2891)
1. What did Beowulf say and do with his final gasping breaths?
    He told Wiglaf to take the treasure to his people, to see that a tomb was built for him along the water, and then he gave him his necklace and armor.
2. When Beowulf's followers came out of the woods to see what had happened, what did Wiglaf tell them?
    He told them they were cowards who would not share in the wealth. They were a disgrace to their people.

Question for Further Thought

Would the death of the dragon bring peace to the people? Why or why not?
> The death of the dragon would not bring peace, and now the enemies of the Geats would dare to wage war upon them with their leader dead. So they were saved from the wrath of the dragon only to face the wrath of their enemies.

(2892-3182)
1. What did Wiglaf's messenger tell the people?
   > He told them that Beowulf was dead, and that they should now expect war with their enemies, the Franks and the Frisians, and he recounted the battles they had fought in the past with the Swedes.
2. What was to be done with Beowulf's body and the treasure?
   > The body was to be burned along with the treasure.
3. What did the poet say the dragon did by hiding the treasure in the tower?
   > He said it broke God's law to do so.
4. What did the poet attribute Beowulf's death to?
   > He attributed it to a spell placed on the treasure long before.
5. Who alone could break the spell?
   > God alone could break the spell.
6. Why did Wiglaf lead some of Beowulf's warriors into the tower?
   > He led them there so that they could retrieve the treasure to burn with Beowulf's body.
7. When they emerged, what did they do with the dragon's body?
   > They rolled the body over the cliff into the water.
8. What did the Geats do after burning Beowulf's body?
   > They built a tall tower as he had requested, and sealed up his ashes and all the treasure inside.
9. What was the final tribute paid to Beowulf?
   > Twelve of his bravest warriors circled the tower on horseback, telling of his brave deeds and expressing sorrow at his death.

Questions for Further Thought

A. What is an epic? Does the story of Beowulf qualify as one?
   > An epic is an extensive narrative poem which uses dignified language to relate the extraordinary deeds of a legendary or traditional hero. Beowulf does meet the criteria and is considered the oldest and one of the greatest epics of Anglo-Saxon literature.
B. What do Beowulf's single-handed slayings of Grendel and his mother represent in a broad sense?
   > They represent the battle between good and evil.
C. What two virtues were most admired among the Danes and Geats?
   > The virtues most admired were bravery and generosity.
D. How did the behaviors of Unferth and Beowulf toward each other change in the course of the story?
   > Unferth was jealous of Beowulf initially and Beowulf rebuked him by telling that he had killed his brother. As Beowulf proved himself, Unferth realized that he had earned respect and offered him his sword. After the sword failed Beowulf in his fight with Grendel's mother, he was gracious in not blaming the sword as he returned it to Unferth. In the end, Unferth gave it to Beowulf who graciously accepted it. Both of them matured in their treatment of each other.
E. What were some of the pagan elements in the story?
   > Some of the pagan elements were the dragon-like fiends which were overcome by brave warriors, the element of fate, the magic swords, the treasure guarded by the dragon, the constant feuds with enemies which required revenge and the funeral rituals.

Unit 1: Poetry

- F. What were some of the Christian elements in the story?
    Some of the Christian elements were the dependence on God, the emphasis on virtue, obedience to God's laws and trust in His interest in human affairs. Beowulf himself is a Christ-like figure in that he sacrifices himself to save his people.
- G. What was the role of women in the story?
    Women were more or less ornaments in the story. They served as hostesses in the great halls as the wives or daughters of the kings. They provided contrast to the very masculine theme, and except for a few of them, they were unnamed. The woman who mourned for Beowulf was anonymous and is the only one mentioned who is not described as the wife or mother of one of the characters.
- H. What was found in the narrative alongside the main actions of the poem such as Beowulf's encounters with Grendel, his mother and the dragon?
    Alongside the main actions were side stories—bits of history which explained various conflicts in the history of the Geats and Danes. These stories were related to the assembled warriors in the halls and at the funerals.

For Further Research:

Compare the character of Beowulf to one other epic hero, such as Achilles, Odysseus or Aeneas. Were they motivated by the same values? Were their deeds comparable? What was the cultural setting of each?

Research life in the 600s in England and Sweden. Does Beowulf present an accurate glimpse of the way life was? If so, in what ways does the poem reflect the society in which is it set? How was society structured?

Song of Roland

Translation: Frederick B. Luquiens
Collier Books

The *Song of Roland* is a Medieval French poem which portrays the high ideals of loyalty, courage, honor and strength. Its author and circumstances are unknown.

The *Song of Roland* may have begun as a narrative about Roland at Ronceval and through the centuries it acquired characters and events. It is part history and part poetry (Charlemagne withdrew from Spain in the late 700s), and it was put together by somebody at the end of the eleventh century. By the time the story was written down, much had changed in the world. The Moslems had taken the Holy Land and Pope Urban II had called for the First Crusade. The enemy in the song thus became the Saracens, and the story was told by troubadours who embellished it as they saw fit, using current events to appeal to their listeners. The song was lost for centuries and was rediscovered in the 1800s.

Roland, like Achilles and other epic heroes before him, demonstrates hubris, or excessive pride. The main French characters are related. Roland is Charlemagne's nephew and Ganelon is Roland's stepfather.

The story starts in the middle, *in medias res*, like most epics. Charlemagne's armies had gone to fight the Paynim Saracens 150 years before Omar, the Muslim Caliph, had captured Jerusalem and clashed with the Christians of Western Europe. By 732 the Muslims had overrun Spain and France but were stopped by Charles Martel. In Spain there were two Muslim dynasties, the Abbasides and the Omayyads. Charlemagne was acknowledged as King of all France in 771 and he further extended his realm. He was asked by the Abbaside Governor to help fight the Omayyads, so he marched into Spain. He was to remain north of the Ebro River and after beginning a siege on Saragossa, he had to leave Spain because trouble was brewing with the Saxons elsewhere.

Roland's story takes place during this retreat from Spain in the Basque province of Gascony. Charlemagne's army was ambushed by the Basques and his army was slain while the Basques escaped without a trace. Charlemagne has conquered Spain, and only Saragossa remains free…

Watch for hints of doom as you read, and jot them down.

Unit 1: Poetry

PROLOGUE

1. Which Spanish town remains to be conquered?
    Saragossa remains to be conquered.
2. Who holds the town?
    Marsila holds it.
3. What do we learn about him?
    He is a Muslim from Arabia.

THE COUNCIL OF MARSILA

(1-7)
1. What is the mood in Saragossa?
    The mood is one of fear.
2. What epithet does Blanchandrin give Charlemagne?
    He calls him "the arrogant," "the fierce."
3. What does he counsel?
    He counsels that Marsila make peace with Charlemagne and send gifts, pretend to receive the Christian Faith, and swear himself as a liegeman.
4. What is the goal?
    The goal is to save Spain for the Muslims.
5. At what price?
    They are to save Spain even to the death of their sons.
6. Whom does Marsila send to Charlemagne?
    He sends the ten most wicked of his wicked host.

THE EMBASSY

(8-10)
1. Why is Charles happy?
    He is happy because he has taken Cordova.
2. How is Charlemagne described?
    Charlemagne sits upon a golden throne, has a white beard and snow-white hair, and he has a noble face and form.
3. What does Blanchandrin say to Charlemagne?
    He promises gifts for all, asks Charlemagne to return to France, and he says Marsila's people will be his servants.
4. How does Charlemagne respond?
    He responds with caution and asks for a guarantee.
5. What does Blanchandrin promise?
    He promises 20 hostages, including his own son, and Marsila's baptism on St. Michael's feast.

ROLAND AND GANELON

(11-28)
1. Why does Charlemagne call a council?
    He calls a council to discuss Marsila's proposal.
2. Among the counselors, who is the traitor?
    Ganelon is the traitor.

3. What do the Franks say about the offer?
    They say it is a trap and warn him to take heed.
4. What does Roland do?
    He angrily counsels against this trap and reminds Charlemagne that Marsila has betrayed similar promises before.
5. What does Ganelon say?
    He says they should not listen to fools, should accept Marsila's offer and embrace peace.
6. After Naimon speaks, what is the consensus?
    The consensus is that Charlemagne should accept Marsila's offer, because Marsila is defeated and it is time to end the war.
7. Whom does Roland recommend to go to Marsila?
    He recommends that Ganelon go.
8. How does the man in Question 7 respond?
    He responds in anger and with a threat that if he returns he will bring Roland great unhappiness.
9. How does Roland respond?
    He laughs.
10. What does Ganelon predict?
    He predicts that he will not return, leaving the king's daughter a widow and his son without a father.
11. What does Ganelon threaten?
    He threatens the lives of Roland and his peers.
12. What "omen" occurs?
    The king drops his glove when handing it to Ganelon.
13. What do the weeping warriors predict?
    They predict that even the king will not save Roland.

THE TREACHERY

(29-52)
1. What does Blanchandrin say about the Franks?
    He says they don't love their king.
2. What does Ganelon say will destroy Roland?
    He says his pride will destroy him.
3. Why do the people love Roland?
    They love him because he gives them many gifts.
4. What did the two plot as they rode along?
    They plotted Roland's death.
5. What message does Ganelon deliver?
    He tells Marsila that Charles says that if he turns Christian, he will receive half of Spain in fief. If he doesn't become Christian, he will be taken forcefully to France to be killed.
6. What does Ganelon tell Marsila to do with regard to Charles?
    He tells him to send him rich gifts and promises. That will placate him and he will return to France, leaving only his rear guard with Roland, whom Ganelon will kill.
7. What does Ganelon swear before Marsila?
    He swears the death of Roland.

THE REAR GUARD

(53-67)
1. What does Ganelon give to Charles when he returns?
    He gives him the golden keys of Saragossa and the gifts from Marsila.
2. What tale does Ganelon tell about the Caliph of Carthage?
    He says he fled in fear and drowned when his ship sank in a tempest.
3. Why does Charles decide to return to France?
    Ganelon has told him that Marsila will be baptized, and so he sees no reason to continue toward Spain.
4. What did Charles dream that night?
    He dreamed that he was alone in the Pyrenees Mountains when Ganelon came and took his spear, which shivered and splintered.
5. The next day, whom does Ganelon recommend to guard the rear?
    He recommends that Roland do so.
6. Is Charles pleased?
    No, he is not pleased and he calls Ganelon a wretch, because he recalls his dream.
7. Does the king want to give Roland the rear guard?
    No, but he gives him the curving bow and offers men to accompany him.
8. Who accompanies Roland?
    The twelve Great Peers of France, Archbishop Turpin of Rheims and 20,000 men accompany him.
9. Why does the king weep on his way back to France?
    He realizes that Roland will be killed and that Ganelon is a traitor.

THE PAYNIM PEERS

(68-78)
1. What does Marsila's nephew Adalroth request?
    He requests the privilege of killing Roland.
2. What do Marsila's Peers vow to do?
    They all vow to kill Roland, his friend Oliver, and the Twelve Peers.

THE MADNESS OF ROLAND

(79-92)
1. What does Roland say about the stories that will be told in the future about the battle to come?
    He says that when songs are sung, there will be no scorn for the French.
2. What does each side fight for?
    The French fight for right, the Paynims for wrong.
3. How does Roland respond when Oliver tells him that Ganelon betrayed them?
    He says "Your words are madness, friend; it cannot be."
4. What does Oliver ask Roland to do?
    He asks him to sound the horn so that the king and his host will turn back and come to their aid.
5. Why does Roland refuse?
    He refuses because he would lose the praise of the French and bring indignity on his people.
6. How does the author contrast Roland and Oliver?
    He says that Roland is brave, while Oliver is brave and wise.
7. What does Archbishop Turpin tell the soldiers?
    He tells them that King Charles left them here to die for God and that their hour has come.

8. What does he do?
    He hears their confessions and absolves them of their sins, telling them that if they die they will be martyrs and win Paradise.
9. What penance does he give them?
    Their penance is to deal heavy blows on the enemy.
10. What does Roland finally acknowledge?
    He acknowledges that they have been betrayed.
11. What was the battle cry of the French king?
    The battle cry was "*Montjoy!*"*

* Montjoy was the hill which overlooked Jerusalem, so named because when pilgrims to the Holy Land came to it, they were joyful to see the city.

THE FIRST BATTLE

(93-110)
1. At the end of the first battle, how many Paynim peers remain?
    Only two remain.
2. Who encourages the knights with the battle cry throughout the fight?
    Archbishop Turpin encourages them, even as he too fights.
3. How many enemy soldiers were killed before they fled from the field?
    Tens of hundreds were killed.
4. How do we know that the Franks will perish even though the enemy has fled?
    We know because there is a violent storm throughout France, and the author tells us it is the earth sorrowing for Roland's death.

THE SECOND BATTLE

(111-127)
1. Who leads the next wave of Paynims?
    The King, Marsila, leads them.
2. Who leads the Franks?
    Archbishop Turpin leads them.
3. In the second battle we see many more French peers die. What drives the remainder on in battle?
    They seek vengeance on the ones who kill their friends.
4. How many battles have the Franks fought and won?
    To this point, they have fought and won four battles.
5. How many Franks remain?
    Only sixty remain.

THE HORN

(128-140)
1. What does Roland decide to do as he surveys the bodies of his dead comrades?
    He decides to sound the horn to call Charles back.
2. Why does Oliver discourage him from sounding the horn?
    He says that now that they are in battle it is too late, and it would bring everlasting shame on his lineage.
3. On whom does Oliver blame the situation?
    He blames it on Roland, who was arrogant and would not call the king when it would have done some good.

Unit 1: Poetry

4. Why does the Archbishop counsel them to call the king?
    He says the king and his men will come to avenge their deaths and return their bodies to France for burial.
5. Who tries to dissuade the king from returning?
    Ganelon tries, saying nobody would fight with Roland.

The Death of Oliver

(141-162)
1. What does Roland acknowledge as he speaks to his dead comrades?
    He acknowledges that his fearful pride is responsible for their deaths.
2. Who kills Marsila?
    Roland kills him.
3. How did the Carthaginian Caliph kill Oliver?
    He struck him from behind.
4. Who kills the Caliph?
    Oliver kills him.
5. What does Roland do as his friend dies?
    He swoons on his horse.
6. What does Oliver do?
    He strikes Roland, thinking he is a Paynim, because he can no longer see.
7. What is Oliver's final act?
    He dismounts and kneels; confesses his sins; and prays that he will enter Heaven, for Charles, for France, and for Roland.

The Archbishop

(163-167)
1. Who is left alive as Roland comes out of his second swoon?
    Only he and the Archbishop survive.
2. How had Roland been injured?
    He had broken his temples when he blew the horn with great force.
3. How does the king know Roland is dying?
    He hears the feebly blown horn.
4. How many Paynims charge Roland?
    Four hundred charge.
5. Do they kill him?
    No they do not, but they kill his horse and flee.
6. What does Roland do after he dresses the Archbishop's wounds?
    He brings the bodies of the Frankish Peers to him for a blessing.
7. Where does the Archbishop die?
    He dies in a field, on his way to get water for Roland.

The Death of Roland

(168-176)
1. For whom does Roland pray as he is dying?
    He prays for the French Peers and for himself.
2. What does he do next?
    He takes his sword and climbs a hill where there are four blocks of marble, then he swoons.

3. What does he do when the Paynim tries to kill him?
    He crushes his head with his ivory horn.
4. What does Roland try to do with his sword and why?
    He tries to shatter it on the marble, but it doesn't break. He doesn't want a Paynim or a coward to possess it.
5. How does he die?
    He dies praying for the forgiveness of his sins.

The Punishment of the Paynims

(177-184)
1. Why does Charles leave four knights and a thousand men at Ronceval while he goes to fight the Paynims?
    He leaves them there to guard the corpses of the fallen Franks.
2. Why does the daylight last longer than usual?
    God loves Charles and causes the sun to stand still until the Franks reach the Paynims in the Vale of Darkness.
3. What do the king and his soldiers do after they kill all of the enemy?
    They rest in the valley.

The Lament of the King

(185-267)
1. How does the king refer to Roland?
    He refers to him as nephew, friend, hero, and fairest of the fair young men of France.
2. Why does the king believe the Saxons and others will rise up against him?
    His bravest warrior of great reputation, Roland, is now dead, and there are no others with such courage.
3. What does the king desire?
    He desires his own death.
4. Where do they bury the men?
    They bury them in a common grave in the battlefield.
5. What do they do with Roland, Oliver and Archbishop Turpin?
    They remove their hearts, place them in silk and lay them in a shrine of marble. They then wrap their bodies in deerskin, anoint them with wine and spices and take them back to France for burial in the Church of Blaye.

Alda

(268-269)
1. Who is Alda?
    She is the woman whom Roland promised to marry.
2. What happens to her when the king tells her Roland is dead?
    She dies at his feet.

The Punishment of Ganelon

(270-end)
1. What defense does Ganelon offer for himself?
    He says that Roland had sent him to death in Saragossa.
2. What does Pinabel threaten?
    He threatens to kill anybody who judges Ganelon guilty.
3. Why does the council recommend leniency?
    The council is made up of cowards who are afraid of Pinabel.

4. Who alone calls for Ganelon's death before the king?
    Count Thierry calls for his death and pledges to serve the king.
5. What do Count Thierry and Pinabel do?
    They fight to the death.
6. Who wins?
    Count Thierry wins.
7. What becomes of the hostages Pinabel had pledged?
    They were hanged.
8. What became of Ganelon?
    He was quartered.

Epilogue

1. What happens as the king sleeps?
    The Angel Gabriel appears to him and tells him to march to a faraway place where the Paynims are harassing the Christians and the King of Imphe.
2. How does the king respond?
    He weeps and tears his beard, saying his life is very toilsome.

Questions for Further Thought

A. What elements of chivalry are evident in this story?
    The elements of chivalry seen in this story are the loyalty of the knights to their liege; the sense of honor; the sense of duty; the loyalty to fellow knights; the honor given to God; the love of the king.
B. Why is Roland a tragic figure?
    Roland is a tragic figure because he allows his pride to override his reason, and he is responsible for the deaths of all of his comrades as a result. He will not listen to others, and his hunger for glory proves disastrous for everybody.
C. How are the heroes Beowulf and Roland the same, and how do they differ?
    Beowulf and Roland are both superior warriors, completely loyal to their kings. They are men of honor and they know no fear. They differ in that Roland endangers great numbers of his followers as he goes out to face the enemy. Beowulf, on the other hand, fights his enemies almost single-handedly. He then lives to an old age and is the protector of his people at home, while Roland dies a young men due to his unrealistic assessment of the enemy far away from home.

Words to Know:

Paynim: Muslim

liege: a lord who deserves loyalty and service from his knights

hauberk: the chain-mail tunic of a knight

pennon: long narrow flag carried on a lance

succor: help, assistance

swart: dark and weathered complexion

gonfalon: identifying banner suspended from a crossbar

caitiff: coward

smite: slice, cut

league: a unit of distance, about 3 miles

palfrey: a woman's riding horse

swoon: faint, lose consciousness

fain: happily, eagerly

wain: wagon

treason: treachery, betrayal

calumny: slander, misrepresentation, lies

Unit 1: Poetry

Selections from Canterbury Tales

Translation: Nevill Coghil
Penguin Classics

About the Author

Chaucer was born in London in 1342. As a young man he served as a page in the home of a Duchess which provided the opportunity for him to meet the high and mighty, including the Duke of Lancaster, John of Guant, who would become his patron and protector. In the home of the Duchess he also learned good manners which were to serve him throughout his life. He could read many languages and was knowledgeable in the arts as well as the sciences. He held various offices under three different kings and traveled abroad on royal business. He was ransomed by King Edward III after he was captured while fighting in France, and he became a knight in 1385 and served as a Justice of the Peace.

Chaucer lived in Medieval England which shared much of the medieval culture of Europe. The crown of medieval life was feudalism.* The war in which he was involved was the Hundred Years War with France. According to the historian Trevelyan, "the Hundred Years War was the diplomatic and military aspect of the period of transition from the feudal to the national, from the Middle Ages to the Renaissance."

During the war, the bubonic plague hit England, reducing the population from 4,000,000 to 2.5 million. Because of this, those remaining laborers began to struggle for freedom. This struggle resulted in the Peasant's Revolt.

Chaucer was a poet without equal in England up to his time. His work reflects French influence, but also the influence of Dante and Boccaccio from Italy. He wrote when the language was in transition. Because of this, some of his meanings are lost. The Church played a large role in medieval life, and that is reflected in Chaucer's work. He was a Catholic, and some of his works reveal his piety. The

Canterbury Tales do not.

Chaucer died in 1400 and was buried in Westminster Abbey. He is known as the Father of English Poetry.

Chaucer's works, including *The Canterbury Tales*, were aimed at an educated sophisticated audience. He was tied to the Court and probably read his works to a courtly audience. That audience could relate to the classical references as well as his use of phrases from French and Latin. The work encompasses a number of literary types or genres, including courtly romance; short romantic poems known as *lays*; *fabliau*, which were short, often bawdy stories; *exempla*, which were the part of a sermon which illustrated the point; tragedies, sermons and beast fables.

The Canterbury Tales

The Canterbury Tales is a collection of stories told by thirty pilgrims on their way to and from Canterbury, the shrine of St. Thomas à Becket. They represent a cross-section of humanity, and thus, the variety in style. The tales give a picture of medieval life in the 1300s, and they also introduce the reader to the various offices in the Church which no longer exist. It appears that Chaucer intended for each pilgrim to tell a total of four tales, but he died before the work was completed. He retells in the words of

---

*Feudalism—the political and social system which existed in Medieval Europe, whereby vassals held land from lords in exchange for military service and legal protection. The vassal was obliged to show loyalty and homage to a feudal lord in return for being allowed to occupy land belonging to the lord and receiving his protection.

his pilgrims, stories which were told in other parts of the world, and they all have a kernel of wisdom, a lesson to be learned. This pilgrimage can be looked at as the journey of every pilgrim through life and toward eternal life.

This work begins with a Prologue in which Chaucer introduces all of the pilgrims. It is a graphic portrayal of the people who made up his world, and sets the tone for each to tell his tale. Chaucer's genius is seen in the Prologue, because he is able to paint a picture of humanity which everybody can recognize. In each portrait, Chaucer gives a physical description, reveals the social standing of the individual, and gives insight into the character of each man and woman.

The Canterbury Tales is a satire on social mores and clerical abuses. Chaucer wrote about what he saw going on in his world. He held to the truths of the Faith but satirized the humans who lived it. The Protestant Revolution was stirring and that is reflected in this work. He never finished the story.

Chaucer used allegory, but he also used direct speech to express his thoughts. In this way, his style is simple and direct, because he wanted to be understood. He was a moralist, using humor and irony to make his points.

Prologue

1. What time of year is it?
   It is springtime.
2. Where are the pilgrims going?
   They are going to Canterbury, shrine of St. Thomas a Becket.
3. How many pilgrims are there?
   There are 30, including Chaucer.
4. With what virtues does Chaucer credit the knight?
   The knight is truthful, openhanded, courteous, wise, meek, gentle, modest, and he had fought bravely in numerous battles in defense of the Faith in Prussia, Spain and Africa. In other words, he exemplifies the virtues of chivalry.
5. Why is the knight on pilgrimage?
   He is going to give thanks for his success in service.
6. How does Chaucer describe the squire?
   The squire, son of the knight, is about 20 years old, has curly hair and is of medium height; he is athletic and artistic; dresses elaborately; has proven himself in war, is lusty; serves well and with courtesy.
7. How does Chaucer describe the yeoman?
   The yeoman is dressed in green and carries his bow and arrow in careful fashion; his nutlike face is brown; he wears a St. Christopher medal and appears to be a competent forester.
8. How does Chaucer describe the nun?
   The nun is a Prioress (a superior in a religious order, below an abbess); known as Madame Eglantyne and speaks country French; well-mannered and clean in her eating habits; amiable; striving to be dignified in everything; sensitive to all, including animals; large ("by no means undergrown"); wears a rosary on her arm with green "gaudies;" wears a golden brooch with the words *amor vincit omnia* (love conquers all); accompanied by a nun and three priests.
9. How does Chaucer describe the monk?
   The monk is manly and loves to hunt, lax in religious practices; elegant in dress; fat and amiable. In a word, he does not live like a monk.
10. How does Chaucer describe the friar?
    The friar is merry and wanton; uses his role as a beggar priest to be bribed; spends time in bars and among the rich rather than among the poor and sick; wears quality clothing, he speaks with a lisp and his name is Hubert. Chaucer notes that he was the "finest beggar of his batch," meaning he made a profit from his activities.
11. How does Chaucer describe the merchant?
    The merchant has a forked beard and motley dress, with a beaver hat and buckled shoes; he rides a horse and is shrewd and in debt, though to hear him speak, one would never guess; and he is dishonest (you never new his name).
12. How does Chaucer describe the Oxford Cleric?
    The Oxford Cleric is a student whose only interest is studying; he is thin like his horse, threadbare and poor; he speaks only when necessary and his speech has a moral tone.
13. How does Chaucer describe the Serjeant at the Law?
    The Serjeant at the Law is a lawyer who is cunning and discreet; learned in the law; appears busier than he is and has made a fortune from his work.
14. How does Chaucer describe the franklin?
    The franklin accompanies the lawyer; is elderly and calm; lives for pleasure and enjoys rich food and practices hospitality toward many people.
15. Who are the guildmen and how does Chaucer describe them?
    The guildmen are the haberdasher, the dyer, a carpenter, a weaver and a carpet maker, and they are the finest of their lot, decked out in the proper attire as befits their professions.

Unit 1: Poetry

16. How does Chaucer describe the cook?
    He accompanies the guildmen, is skilled at his craft, but has an ulcer on his knee.
17. How does Chaucer describe the skipper?
    The skipper is skilled as a seaman but not as a horseman; enjoys too much wine, and is not bothered by his conscience.
18. How does Chaucer describe the doctor?
    The doctor is an astrologer who uses potions and magic in his cures; is crafty and rich in gold.
19. How does Chaucer describe the wife of Bath?
    The wife of Bath is deaf and an able weaver; has had five husbands plus lovers in her youth; has traveled on pilgrimage to numerous shrines; easily rides a horse; has large hips; likes to laugh and talk and knows many remedies for love's problems.
20. How does Chaucer describe the parson?
    The parson is faithful to the Gospel, kind, industrious, patient, tends his flock, wise and kind, holy and moderate.
21. How does Chaucer describe the plowman?
    The plowman is the brother of the parson; honest and hard-working, charitable and he lives the Gospel like his brother.
22. What does Chaucer say about the miller?
    The miller is a large, strong man, adept at wrestling rams; carries a sword and buckler, teller of crude stories; dishonest in his dealings; plays the bagpipes and leads the pilgrims out of town.
23. What does Chaucer say about the manciple?
    The manciple spends the money in his trust carefully in the buying of food for the law college and manages to put aside some for himself as a result.
24. What does Chaucer say about the reeve?
    The reeve is old and thin; he is astute in the management of his master's crops and animals; has enriched himself by close management of what has been entrusted to him; is from Norfolk and rides last in the line of pilgrims.
25. What does Chaucer say about the summoner?
    The summoner is frightening to behold with his scabby face and sores; he eats garlic and onions and drinks strong wine; is lecherous, easily bribed and abusive of his position; is not very bright.
26. What does Chaucer say about the pardoner?
    The pardoner accompanies the summoner with whom he has much in common; has long, stringy yellow hair and narrow shoulders; lacks masculine physical characteristics; abuses his position and thereby enriches himself at the expense of others.
27. What does Chaucer propose?
    He plans to present the stories to be told by the pilgrims exactly as they are told, without refinement of the language, so that they will be true to the storyteller.
28. What does Chaucer say about the host, and what does the host propose?
    The host is jolly and portly and proposes that each pilgrim tell four stories, two going and two returning, in order to make the journey go by quickly. The one who tells the best story will sup at the others' expense; he (the host) will be their guide and judge, and anyone who does not agree with his judgment will pay the expenses of the journey.
29. Who draws the lot to tell his tale first?
    The knight draws the lot.

Words to Know:

palmer: medieval pilgrim who carried palm leaves to prove he had been to the Holy Land

hostelry: inn

yeoman: a loyal servant

baldric: a sash worn over one shoulder to the opposite hip to support a sword

gaudies: the *paternoster* or "Our Father" beads on a rosary

wanton: reckless, willful

limiter: a begging friar assigned to a specific area so as to limit his activity

screed: lengthy piece of writing or speech

franklin: class of landowner, free by birth but not of noble blood

sanguine: cheerful, optimistic

apothecary: dispenser of drugs and medicines

stone: British unit of measure—one stone equals approximately 14 pounds

guile: cunning, craftiness

miller: one who operates a mill, grinding grain into flour

manciple: one who buys food and supplies for a college or monastery

reeve: steward or other minor estate official; the intermediary between a lord and his serfs

summoner: one who called sinners to trial in church court

victuals: food

THE KNIGHT'S TALE

(Part I)
1. Who was Theseus?
    Theseus was the ruler of Athens who was successful in war, having captured Scythia, land of the Amazons.
2. Whom did he take as his wife?
    He took the Amazon queen, Hippolyta.
3. Who accompanied Hippolyta and Theseus?
    Hippolyta's sister Emily accompanied them.
4. What did Theseus encounter as he approached home?
    He encountered a company of woman in mourning.
5. Why were the women weeping?
    Their husbands had all been killed during the siege of Thebes, and King Creon refused to allow their bodies to be returned or buried.
6. What did Theseus promise the women?
    He promised them he would take vengeance on Creon.

Unit 1: Poetry

7. What did Theseus do?
    He sent Hippolyta and Emily on to Athens and immediately left for Thebes.
8. What epithet did Chaucer give Emily?
    Her epithet was "the serene."
9. What happened when Theseus went to Thebes?
    He engaged Creon in battle and slew him, put his soldiers to flight, captured the city, and restored the remains of the men to their widows and families.
10. Whom did the soldiers find among the dead and wounded?
    They found two knights named Arcite and Palamon, princes of the House of Thebes.
11. What did Theseus do with the knights?
    He sent them as perpetual prisoners, without ransom, to Athens.
12. What did Palamon see from his prison window?
    He saw Emily in the garden.
13. What did Arcite see?
    He saw Emily as well.
14. What oath had the cousins made?
    They had bound themselves to each other till death and not to hinder each other in love.
15. What was the dilemma?
    They both fell in love with the same woman—Emily.
16. How did Arcite distinguish the love each had for Emily?
    He said that even though Palamon had seen her first, his love was mystical and holy, while he, Arcite, had loved her first with an earthly love.
17. What did Palamon say about the law as it related to love?
    He said the law could be broken for love, because in love, it was each man for himself.
18. How was Arcite freed?
    An old friend of Theseus, Perotheus, went to visit and pleaded for Arcite's release, which Theseus granted without a ransom.
19. What was the condition of his release?
    He was not to ever be found on any land belonging to Theseus, and if he was found, he would lose his head.
20. Was Arcite happy to be free?
    No, he was miserable, because he could no longer see Emily, and he felt as if he were in Hell.
21. What does Chaucer say about prayer?
    He says that man does not always understand what he prays for, because his prayers may be answered and bring him misery.
22. What did Palamon imagine?
    He imagined that Arcite in his freedom could raise an army to go and take Emily.
23. What did he say was the difference between man and beast?
    Once the beasts are dead, they feel no pain, but man continues to suffer.
24. What was killing Palamon?
    Jealousy was killing him.
25. What question did the knight ask of his listeners?
    He asked who suffered more, the one who could see his lady every day but could not be with her, or the one who wandered free but exiled from his lady.

Questions for Further Thought

A. Who do you think suffered more and why?
    Answers will vary.
B. To what did the mourning women attribute their situation?
    They attributed it to Fortune and her treacherous wheel.

C. To what did the cousins attribute their situation?
   They attributed it to Fortune.
D. To what did Arcite attribute Palamon's situation by which he was left in prison?
   He attributed it to Fortune.
E. What is fortune?
   In the sense that fortune is used in the above instances, it means chance, luck or destiny. The characters seemed to believe that they had no control over what happened to them, because their lot was either chosen by somebody else, the result of the position of the stars, or the result of chance.

Words to Know:

obsequies: funeral rites

descry: to discover something

(Part II)
1. How did Arcite fare back home in Thebes?
   He wasted away, was very sad, and he wept whenever he heard music. He was like "a maniac in melancholy madness."
2. Why did Arcite go back to Athens?
   He went back because Mercury had told him to do so.
3. In what guise did he go there?
   He went disguised as a poor laborer, in hopes that nobody would recognize him and that he might see "his" lady often.
4. What did he proffer?
   He proffered to do whatever menial work that was available at the Court.
5. What work did he get?
   He served as a page to Emily, using the name Philostrate.
6. Why was Arcite promoted?
   He was promoted because he served well and was a courteous gentleman.
7. How long did Arcite serve as a squire?
   He served for three years.
8. After seven years in prison, what did Palamon do?
   He escaped from prison with the help of a friend after drugging the jailer.
9. What did he intend to do?
   He intended to return to Thebes and raise up a small army of his friends to attack Theseus and thus win Emily as his wife.
10. What did Arcite lament within earshot of Palamon?
    He lamented his position as a servant to an enemy and his lowly state before Emily, going unacknowledged by her.
11. What did Palamon say to his cousin?
    He said they could not both love Emily, that only he (Palamon) could claim her, and he proposed to fight to the death for her love.
12. What was agreed upon?
    The two agreed that Arcite would bring the weapons and they would fight it out as knights in the same field where they now were.
13. To what did Chaucer attribute the fact that Theseus went hunting as the two men were fighting?
    He attributed it to Destiny.

Unit 1: Poetry

14. What did Palamon do when Theseus intervened in their fight?
    He confessed everything about the two of them and asked him to kill them both.
15. Why did Theseus forgive them?
    He forgave them because the women pleaded for mercy for the two men, and reason won out over anger. He had to take into account their humility.
16. What did Chaucer say about a noble heart?
    He said that pity runs swiftly in a noble heart.
17. With his pardon, what did Theseus demand of the men?
    He demanded that they promise never to war with him, but to be his friends.
18. What did Theseus propose to settle the question of who would get Emily?
    He proposed that they go away for one year and raise up 100 knights each to return and fight for her hand.

Words to Know:

proffer: to propose or offer something for consideration

chamberlain: manager of a royal or noble household

page: a youthful personal attendant

squire: apprentice to a knight

courser: a swift horse

(Part III)
1. What preparation did Theseus make for the coming duel?
    He built an exquisite amphitheater.
2. What temples did he build in his amphitheater?
    He built temples to Venus, Goddess of Love, Mars, God of War, and Diana, Goddess of the Hunt and Chastity.
3. What was painted on the walls in Venus' temple?
    Painted on the walls were portraits of love—love scorned, love desired, love realized, etc.
4. How was the temple of Mars decorated?
    It was painted with dark images of gnarled trees, earthquakes, and grisly scenes depicting treachery, violence and death.
5. How was the temple of Diana decorated?
    Her temple was decorated with paintings of hunting scenes and examples of violations of chastity.
6. Who came with Palamon from Thrace?
    Lycurgus, King of Thrace came, with a hundred nobles.
7. Who accompanied Arcite?
    In addition to the hundred knights, Arcite was accompanied by Emetrius, an Indian king, who was accompanied by a hundred lords.
8. What did Palamon do before daybreak of the day before he would fight?
    He went to pray to Venus and promised that if he should win Emily, he would worship the goddess forever. If he lost the battle, he prayed for death.
9. What did Emily do awhile later?
    She went to pray at the temple of Diana.
10. For what did she pray?
    She prayed that Arcite and Palamon would make peace with each other and that she would remain forever virgin and free. If that were not to be her destiny, she prayed that the one who loved her most would win.

11. What did Diana tell Emily?

    She told her that she was destined to marry one of the young men.
12. To whom did Arcite pray?

    He prayed to Mars that he would be victorious, and he promised the glory to Mars and his hair and beard as well.
13. What did Arcite hear after he concluded his prayer?

    He heard the word "victory."
14. What did Chaucer say about age and youth?

    He said that the aged have the advantage of wisdom, even though they lack the physical advantage of youth.
15. What did Saturn promise?

    He promised that Palamon would win the match.

Questions for Further Thought

A. What anachronisms do you observe in this tale?

   There are numerous anachronisms, such as reference to a Prussian shield, jousting knights in Ancient Greece, mead taken to the shrine, use of the word parliament by Theseus, etc.
B. Having heard the gods speak, do you know the end of the story?

   We do not know the end yet, but I suggest you write down your own conclusion and then compare it to Chaucer's!
C. By praying to the various gods, what did Emily, Arcite and Palamon acknowledge?

   They acknowledged that the gods are not almighty.

Words to Know:

chivalry: gallantry, courtliness, politeness, loyalty

anachronism: a thing or person belonging to a date or period other than the correct one (a medieval knight in Ancient Greece)

(Part IV)
1. What did Theseus decree?

    He decreed that since he wanted none to die, the use of cross-bow darts, poleaxes, knives, and stabbing-swords with pointed blades was forbidden; only one course with a spear was allowed each pair of combatants and they were to use them only in self-defense and on foot; the wounded would not be killed but would be taken to the stake for the remainder of the battle; and the men could fight with mace and long-sword at will.
2. Who wounded Palamon?

    King Emetrius wounded him and he was taken to the stake as King Theseus had decreed.
3. After Palamon was taken from the field, what did Theseus do?

    He declared Arcite the winner.
4. Why was Venus unhappy?

    She was unhappy because of Theseus' decision to award Emily to Arcite.
5. What did Chaucer say about women and Fortune?

    He said that women tended to follow Fortune's favors, meaning they went with whatever seemed in their best interests.
6. How did Pluto intervene?

    He frightened Arcite's horse and Arcite was thrown out of the saddle onto the ground.
7. What pleased the people?

    They were pleased that nobody was killed.

Unit 1: Poetry

8. After all the visitors left, what happened to Arcite?
   As he lay dying, he bequeathed Emily to Palamon, hoping to die with virtue.
9. Where did the soul of Arcite go?
   Chaucer did not say. He said "I am no divine. Souls are not mentioned in this tale of mine."
10. What did Aegeus tell Theseus about the world?
    He told him that the world was the road pilgrims walked through life toward death, and it was filled with woe.
11. How did Theseus honor Arcite?
    He held elaborate funeral rites for him.
12. What did Theseus say to Palamon and Emily?
    He said that the world was orderly because of the Creator who made it so. The Creator also intended that living things would generate in succession and that all things would come to an end.
13. Why should they no longer grieve for Arcite, according to Theseus?
    They should not grieve because he died with honor.
14. Why did Theseus call Palamon back from Thebes?
    He called him back so that he could end his grief and marry Emily.

WORDS TO KNOW:

panoply: full ceremonial dress, full armor

mace: club, scepter

transmutations: changes, transformations

eschew: avoid, give up

THE MAN OF LAW'S TALE

(Introduction)
1. What did the Host say about the time?
   He said it was getting late and time lost could not be regained.
2. What did the Man of Law say about the law?
   He said that the laws apply to everybody and those who make them for others must obey them as well.
3. What did the Man of Law say about Chaucer?
   He said that Chaucer had already told all of the tales in one or another of his books, so why should he tell them again?
4. When the Man of Law says he does not want to be compared to the Pierides, what does he mean?
   He does not want to fail by comparison to a better poet than himself (Chaucer), so he will leave the rhyming to Chaucer and speak in prose.

(prologue)
1. The Man of Law began by speaking about what topic?
   He spoke about poverty and the way one would feel who was reduced to it.
2. Where did the Man of Law hear the tale he was going to tell?
   He heard it from a merchant.

Question for Further Thought

Judging from the context, what did it mean in a game to throw "double-aces?"
    It meant you threw the dice with the least value.

Words to Know:

pithy: condensed, to the point

indigence: poverty, deprivation

enmity: hostility, antagonism

fête: honor, praise, celebrate

sagacious: wise, clever

(Part I)
1. Whom did the Syrian merchants hear about when they went to Rome?
    They heard about Constance, daughter of the Emperor.
2. What were her virtues?
    She was humble, temperate, courteous, holy, kind to all in distress and beautiful.
3. Whom did the merchants speak with when they returned to Syria?
    They spoke with the young Sultan and told him about Constance.
4. On hearing about Constance, what did the Sultan resolve to do?
    He resolved to have her as his wife, lest he die.
5. Why did his advisors hesitate about the match?
    They knew that the laws and customs of Christians and Moslems were very different, and it would be difficult to contract a marriage between a Christian princess and a Moslem man.
6. What did the Sultan decide to do?
    He decided to be baptized in order to marry Constance.
7. Are we led to believe this story will have a happy ending? Why or why not?
    The Man of Law says that on the day the couple left for Syria, "I say there came that day of fatal woe."
8. How did Constance feel about leaving?
    She was full of grief.
9. Whom did she invoke for strength to do what she must?
    She invoked Jesus Christ.
10. How did the Man of Law describe the Sultan's mother?
    He said she was a "well of vices."
11. Why did she object to the marriage?
    She objected because her son planned to convert to Christianity.
12. What was the ruse she planned?
    She planned that the members of the Sultan's court would pretend to be baptized.
13. Whom did the Man of Law say was Satan's instrument for bondage?
    Woman was his instrument (in this case, it was the Sultan's mother).

Words to Know:

thrall: one whose life is completely controlled by another

occident: the west

(Part II)
1. What is the near neighbor to worldly bliss?
    Sudden grief is the near neighbor.
2. What happened at the welcome feast?
    The Sultaness had her son and all the Christians slain and hacked to pieces, except for Constance.
3. What did they do with Constance?
    They put her in a boat and sent her off to Italy.
4. What did Constance pray for?
    She prayed that God would take her soul when she drowned at sea.
5. How long was Constance alone at sea?
    She was adrift for many years.
6. Who had prevented Constance from being slain?
    God had prevented it.
7. Who sustained her for three years?
    Christ sustained her.
8. Where did Constance finally land?
    She landed in Northumberland, in Northern England.
9. What did Constance ask the Constable-in-Chief to do?
    She asked him to kill her and put her out of her misery.
10. Why did Hermengild convert?
    She converted because of the example of Constance, as well as because of her prayers and weeping.
11. What happened to Hermengild?
    She was murdered as she slept by a young knight who lusted after Constance. Since Hermengild was sleeping with Constance, the knight left the knife that he had used and blamed Constance.
12. What did the poet say about fine hearts?
    He said they find pity quickly, and Alla, King of Northumberland, felt pity for Constance.
13. Why was the knight struck dead?
    He was struck dead because he swore on a Bible that Constance was guilty.
14. What was the result?
    Many people converted to Christianity, including King Alla.
15. Whom did Constance end up marrying?
    She married the king.
16. Who was unhappy about the marriage?
    Donegild, the king's mother was unhappy.
17. Where was the king when Constance bore their first child?
    He was away at war.
18. What happened when a messenger was sent with a letter from the constable with news of the birth?
    The messenger stopped by Donegild's home and offered to take a greeting from her to her son. She wined and dined him and while he was sleeping, she wrote a letter of her own, claiming that the queen had delivered a fiend, and switched her letter with the one the messenger was carrying.
19. How did the king respond to the letter?
    Though he was grieved, he asked God to bless and preserve his child and wife until he returned.
20. What vices did the messenger have which rendered him unsuitable for his job?
    He drank too much and talked too much.
21. When the messenger returned with the king's letter, he again stayed the night with Donegild. What did she write in

the letter which she switched with the king's letter?
   She wrote the constable that Constance was to be sent away from the kingdom with her son in the same boat in which she had arrived. He was to obey under pain of death.
22. How did the constable react when he received the letter?
   He asked God why the wicked should prosper and the innocent should suffer.
23. What was Constance's reaction to her sentence?
   She trusted in God and obediently went away.

Words to Know:

harridan: scolding, ill-tempered woman

alacrity: eager readiness

(Part III)
1. When Alla returned home and learned of the fate of his wife, how did he discover the truth?
   He had the messenger tortured until he confessed everything.
2. What did the king order?
   He ordered the death of his mother.
3. How long did Constance and her child drift at sea before they reached land?
   They drifted for five years.
4. How did Mary protect her soon after she landed?
   The apostate steward from the heathen castle where she landed was thrown overboard as he tried to assault her.
5. What did the poet say about lust?
   He said that even the will to behave with lust brings destruction, not only to the soul but to the body as well.
6. How did the Emperor (Constance's father) punish the Syrians when he received word about what had been done to his people?
   He sent a senator and a group of loyal men to take revenge and kill the Syrians.
7. Whom did the senator meet on the way back to Rome from Syria?
   He met Constance and her son on the little boat.
8. What did he do with her?
   He took her back to Rome to serve his wife.
9. Why did Alla head for Rome?
   He went to seek judgement and punishment from the pope for having had his mother killed.
10. Who unknowingly arranged for Alla and Constance to meet?
    The senator who had gone to Syria arranged it.
11. What did Constance ask Alla to do?
    She asked him to arrange for the Emperor to feast with them.
12. What became of Maurice?
    He became Emperor.
13. What became of Alla and Constance?
    They returned to England and he died within a year.
14. After his death, what did Constance do?
    She returned to Rome.

Questions for Further Thought

A. What does Constance symbolize in this tale?

Unit 1: Poetry

        She symbolizes perfection and universal goodness. In other words, she exemplifies virtue, because no matter what circumstances she is in, she behaves with dignity and honor.
B.   The male villains in the story exemplified which vice?
        They exemplified the vice of lust.
C.   Who were the villainesses and what did they exemplify?
        They were the mothers of Constance's husbands and exemplified the vices of jealousy, corruption and dishonesty.
D.   Does Chaucer express a specific religious belief through this tale?
        No. He expresses more the idea of Divine Providence; that is, the role of God in what happens in our lives. He does not abandon His people, even in awful circumstances. What at first may appear to be abandonment by God, actually is shown to work out as it should, precisely because He has intervened.
E.   Chaucer said that joy was always followed by sorrow. Do you agree, or was he being pessimistic?
        Answers will vary.

WORDS TO KNOW:

apostate: one who renounces his religious beliefs

vouchsafe: to promise something

HISTORY
Unit Two

Unit 1: Poetry

The Rule of St. Benedict

by St. Benedict
Translation: Meisel and Del Mastro
Image Books

St. Benedict was born at Nursia, c. 480 and died at Monte Cassino, 543. There is no complete biography of the saint available, and most of what we have are sketches of his life, primarily from St. Gregory's *Dialogues*.

He was the son of a Roman noble and the twin of Scholastica. He studied in Rome till the time came for him to leave to pursue his vocation, somewhere around the age of 20. He sought solitude rather than the life of a noble, and went to Enfide, about 40 miles from Rome, where he found other men who wanted to live a life of virtue and escape the evils of the city. He is said to have worked a miracle there which brought him notoriety, and since that was not what he desired, he fled to Subiaco. "For God's sake he deliberately chose the hardships of life and the weariness of labour" (St. Gregory, *Dialogues*)

On the way from Enfide, he met a monk named Romanus, whose monastery was on a mountain. After speaking with Benedict about his purpose there, Romanus gave him the habit of the monk, and for three years, Benedict lived alone and unknown to all but a few people in a nearby cave as a hermit, sustained by food brought to him by Romanus.

Though he lived in solitude, people came to know about him and his holiness, and when the abbot died, he was asked to take his place. Reluctantly, he did so, but his austerity didn't please the monks and they tried to poison him. Again, a miracle saved him from death. He returned to his cave, but people followed him. He eventually built twelve monasteries and established schools.

He became known as the Father of Western Monasticism and wrote his Rule which governed life in the monasteries. His influence has been felt down through the centuries, up to the present time.

About the Divine Office

It will be helpful to define a few terms which should help ease understanding of the monastic day. The terms are primarily those of the *Divine Office*. Today, the *Divine Office* is known as the *Liturgy of the Hours*. Monastic life was structured around the Hours of prayer and work.

The Hours of the *Divine Office* are:

Matins - the vigil prayer said around midnight. It consists of *Psalm 95*, a hymn, psalms, Scripture, commentaries on the Scripture, a reading for the day and a responsory.

Lauds - the second hour of prayer, at daybreak, so named because of the recitation of the psalms of praise 148-50, (Laudes).

Prime - literally the first hour (6:00 a.m.). It was the prayer said before the morning work and included a reading from the martyrology or saint of the day, a section from the *Rule* and a prayer for God's blessing on the day's work. Today, *Prime* is rarely said except in some monasteries.

Tierce - the third hour of the day, or 9:00 a.m.

Sext – the sixth hour of the day, 12 noon.

None - the ninth hour of the day, 3:00 p.m. The prayer for this hour was chanted at the middle of the 8th hour.

Vespers - was the seventh period of prayer and ended at sundown and the rising of the evening star.

Compline - the night prayer that is said at the end of the day before retiring for the night. During *Compline*, the monks thank God for the blessings of the day and beg His protection during the night.

INTRODUCTION

1. What is Monasticism?
    Monasticism is the seeking of God in community through prayer and penance apart from the world. This way of life affects not only the individual and community, but the world as well.
2. How long did monasticism flourish?
    It flourished for a thousand years.
3. What were some of the benefits to the world from the monasteries?
    Art and music were preserved in a time when they were being destroyed in the society. The study of architecture, science, history, theology and philosophy led to great contributions on the part of the monks. The Church grew during a time when it was under attack. The monks made great strides in agriculture and other practical arts.
4. What was the monastic ideal?
    The monastic ideal was to seek only the glory of God and perfect union with Him.
5. What was more important to the monk, the results of his work or the growth in virtue? Why?
    Growth in virtue was more important because it brought the monk closer to God and produced a serenity which was not troubled by the material world.
6. When was monasticism established as a separate entity?
    It was established at the end of the 4th century A.D.
7. What were three influences in the growth of monasticism?
    Three influences in the growth of monasticism were:
    - The official recognition and patronage of Christianity by Constantine which made it easier for people to be Christian and to live openly or as hermits if they chose
    - The teaching of Origen which said that man could have a part in his own sanctification (union with God) through a series of steps; these steps were accessed through the practice of asceticism
    - The decline of the Roman Empire which led people to realize that their material fortunes were in jeopardy from the invading barbarians
8. Which hermit had the greatest influence in the East?
    Antony the Great had the greatest influence.
9. What provided the impetus for cenobitic life?
    Men who fled to the deserts from the cities and the coming barbarians soon found other threats to their existence and quest for holiness. Among those threats were temptations, robbers, wild animals, etc. The solution was an enclosure, or wall around the huts of the hermits, which provided physical protection as well as the opportunity for spiritual instruction and community worship.
10. Who introduced the West to the life of Antony the Great?
    Athanasius, Bishop of Alexandria, introduced them through his book *The Life of Antony*.
11. Who were the primary transmitters of the ideals of asceticism and monasticism in the West?
    The three were Martin of Tours, Augustine of Hippo and John Cassian.
12. What were the three principles which Augustine established for monastic life?
    The three principles were communality or common good, obedience and authority.
13. What were the primary responsibilities of the superior?
    The primary responsibilities were the sanctification of the community as a whole and the salvation of the individual members.
14. What was the primary responsibility of the members of the community?
    Their primary responsibility was to obey.
15. Who is considered to have achieved the most "effective synthesis of Eastern and Western asceticism?"
    Benedict of Nursia was considered to have achieved this synthesis.
16. Who is the source of what we know about Benedict?
    Gregory the Great is our source, who wrote about him in the *Dialogues*, 2.

17. When was Benedict born?
    He was born c.480.
18. What led him to abandon his studies in Rome?
    He was frightened by the way his fellow students were being destroyed by vice.
19. What did Benedict do?
    He sought solitude, first in a church and then in a cave at Subiaco, where he was supplied with food by a monk named Romanus.
20. How did Benedict overcome the temptation of lust?
    He rolled naked in a patch of nettles.
21. What happened when a group of monks wanted Benedict to become their abbot?
    They could not tolerate the strict life of discipline which he insisted upon, and they tried to poison him.
22. What miracle is said to have taken place?
    When he blessed the pitcher containing the poison, it shattered and he was spared.
23. When people continued to come for guidance and counsel, what did Benedict do?
    He formed them into monasteries of twelve monks and an abbot each and spent his life directing them.
24. How did Benedict deal with disobedience and stealing within the community?
    He would confront the sinner with the details of his offence. When the sinner had repented of his offence, Benedict would forgive him, warn him and then restore the offender to the community.
25. When did Benedict die?
    He died in 547 and was buried next to his sister, Scholastica, in Monte Cassino.

The Rule of St. Benedict

1. What are seen as the greatest strengths of Benedict's *Rule*?
    Its strengths are its common sense and charity and care of the individuals who embraced it.
2. How did Benedict see the monastery?
    He saw it not only as a primary school in religious asceticism, but also as an acceptable end in itself. In other words, he did not view it as second-class to living in a hermitage.
3. Whose qualities was Benedict particularly concerned with?
    He was particularly concerned with the qualities of the abbot, who served as the father of the monastery.
4. What qualities did the abbot have to possess?
    He had to have wisdom and prudence, as well as be a man of virtue.
5. What obligation did the abbot have?
    He was obliged to love the monks as his own sons. Through this love he could effectively guide them on their quest for God and perfection.
6. What was Benedict's "master virtue?"
    That virtue was obedience, as practiced by the monks.
7. What was the chief work of the monks?
    Their chief work was the *opus Dei*, or the work of God.
8. Of what did the *opus Dei* consist?
    The *opus Dei* consisted of periods of prayer throughout the day and night.
9. Besides the *opus Dei*, what was another main component of monastic life?
    The other component was communal work which was vital to the support and functioning of the monastery.
10. A third component of monastic life consisted of what?
    The third component was intellectual pursuit which would help the monk achieve virtue and knowledge of God as well as himself, and enrich his life of prayer.
11. What was the vow of stability?
    The vow of stability was the promise made by the monk to stay with his particular community until his death.

Impact of the Rule

1. Why was the *Rule* of Benedict effective?
    The *Rule* exhibited common sense, compassion and coherence, and was therefore adopted by other communities.
2. What is the traditional belief about how the *Rule* was taken to England?
    Gregory wrote that he, as pope, sent monks from Rome to England, carrying the *Rule* with them.
3. Who was the leader of the monks in England?
    The leader (Abbot) was Augustine of Canterbury.
4. What usually happened when Benedict's *Rule* met other monastic traditions?
    The other monks tended to adopt his *Rule* and abandon the one they had followed.
5. When did England begin to send missionaries abroad?
    She began to send missionaries abroad in the eighth century.
6. Besides missionary work, what other activity did the monks pursue?
    They pursued education.
7. Who were notable educators among them?
    Bede and Alcuin were such men.
8. What was Bede's greatest contribution besides the education of many monks and boys?
    He wrote the *Ecclesiastical History of the English Nation*.
9. What influence did this work have on later histories?
    It set the standard for objective historical writing, because Bede only presented as fact what could be verified, and he noted what was not certain as interpretation.
10. What contributions did Alcuin make?
    He headed the group of scholars which Charlemagne gathered together in Aachen to teach his sons, those of his nobles and other talented children; he revised the *Gregorian Sacramentary* which insured liturgical uniformity and replaced the Gallic rites in the Empire; he helped revise the *Latin Vulgate Bible,* and he created a catechism.
11. What other activities flourished in the monasteries of the ninth century and on into the twelfth?
    The arts, music, liturgy, Scripture commentary, literature and architecture all flourished.
12. What condition facilitated this flourishing?
    The influence of Alcuin made him indispensable to the emperor and the fortunes of the monasteries followed the fortunes of the empire. Thus, the growth of one led to the growth of the other.
13. How was this link with the empire the source of the decline of the monasteries?
    The monks became too worldly and wealthy, and through that condition, the spirit of the monastic ideal was lost and the Rule was altered.
14. Was the *Rule* lost?
    No it was not. As men sought a return to the simplicity and life of the monastery, the *Rule* was revived.
15. Which copy of the *Rule* is considered the most accurate?
    The *Codex 914*, commissioned by Charlemagne, was made from a copy and is in the monastic library of St. Gall in Switzerland.

Words to Know:

hermit: recluse, one who lives alone

ascetic: austere, severe; one who practices self-denial and self-mortification

cenobite: monk; one who lives in a community

hagiographer: one who writes about the lives of the saints

Prologue

1. How does Benedict address his monks?
    He addresses them as sons and admonishes them to be obedient.
2. What does he admonish the monks to do?
    He admonishes them to pray, to be watchful and to practice good works.

CHAPTER 1

1. Benedict describes four kinds of monks. What are the first?
    The first are Cenobites, who live in a monastery headed by an abbot.
2. What are the second?
    The second type are Anchorites, who have been tested in the monastery and have gone to live as hermits.
3. What are the third?
    The third are Sarabaites, who have not lived by any rule and live in the world as they please with shaved heads, or tonsure.
4. What are the fourth?
    The fourth are Gyratory Monks, restless men who wander from one monastery to the next and who live wretched lives.
5. Which kind does Benedict consider the best?
    He considers the Cenobites the best.

CHAPTER 2

1. What is the meaning of Abba?
    Abba means father.
2. For what will God hold the abbot accountable?
    God will hold him accountable for his teaching and the goodness and obedience of the monks under his charge.
3. How is the abbot to rule?
    He is to rule by showing his charges what is good and holy through his deeds, and he is not to treat the monks differently based on their social condition.
4. How is the abbot to deal with the monks?
    He is to mix encouragement with reproof as a good father would and as the situation demands. Those who are stubborn, proud or disobedient should be punished with the whip.

CHAPTER 3

1. How are important matters to be decided?
    The abbot should call the community together and hear the opinions of the monks. After due consideration, he makes the decision as to the course of action.
2. What should happen to anyone who argues with the abbot?
    He should be punished as stated in the *Rule*.

CHAPTER 4

How could you sum up the "instruments of good works?"
    The "instruments of good works" are basically the commandments, the beatitudes, the virtues and obedience to the abbot.

Chapter 5

How should the monks respond to orders?
> They should respond promptly and cheerfully.

Chapter 6

What is the rule of silence in the monastery?
> The monks are to listen and learn and only speak with humility and submission. Silence is the rule and small talk is to be avoided.

Chapter 7

1. What is the path to Heaven compared to?
   > It is compared to a ladder which is climbed by the humbling of oneself, and each step is characterized by the achievement of a particular virtue.
2. What is the first step of humility?
   > It is the obeying of all of God's commandments.
3. What is the second step?
   > It is when one stops seeking to please himself.
4. What is the third step?
   > It is obedient submission to a superior for love of God.
5. What is the fourth step?
   > It is the forbearance of everything that is inflicted on a man.
6. What is the fifth step?
   > The fifth step is the confession of a monk to his abbot of all his evil thoughts or actions.
7. What is the sixth step?
   > The sixth step is the acceptance by the monk of his unworthiness.
8. What is the seventh step?
   > The seventh step is when the monk not only confesses, but believes in his heart that he is wretched.
9. What is the eighth step?
   > The eighth step is when the monk does only what the Rule or the example of his elders demands.
10. What is the ninth step?
    > The ninth step is where a monk only speaks when asked a question.
11. What is the tenth step?
    > The tenth step is where a monk refrains from laughter and frivolity.
12. What is the eleventh step?
    > The eleventh step is when a monk speaks gently, softly and with few words.
13. What is the twelfth and final step of humility?
    > The twelfth step is when the monk's humility of heart is manifested in his appearance and actions.
14. What is the goal of humility?
    > The goal of humility is that the monk will act for the love of Christ through the good habits he has cultivated, rather than act out of a fear of Hell.

Chapters 8 -20

What do these chapters speak about?
> These chapters speak about the way the *Divine Office* is to be celebrated.

Unit 2: History

Chapter 21

What is the function of the dean?
> The dean supervises his deanery (group of monks) according to the Commandments and the orders of the Abbot. He shares in many of the responsibilities of the abbot.

Chapter 22

How do the monks sleep?
> The monks sleep in one room, or at least in groups of 10s or 20s (depending on the size of the monastery), with their robes on and a candle burning.

Chapter 23

How is the monk to be disciplined?
> The monk is first admonished for his sins twice in private. If he doesn't repent, he is to be admonished in public. If he remains obstinate, he is subject to corporal punishment and excommunication.

Chapter 24

What form does excommunication take for minor faults?
> The brother is excluded from eating with the others, cannot intone a psalm or read in the oratory. He eats after the others and will be granted pardon after he has made atonement for his sin.

Chapter 25

How is a monk punished for grave faults?
> He is not only excluded from the common table and oratory, but nobody can speak to him and he must work alone. He is not to receive blessings.

Chapter 26

What happens to a monk who speaks with an excommunicated brother?
> He suffers the same penalty as the excommunicated brother.

Chapter 27

How should the abbot care for the excommunicated?
> The abbot should treat him with compassion and love and send an elder to console him and guide him.

Chapter 28

If the excommunicated monk does not repent, even after whipping and much prayer, what must the abbot do?
> The abbot must cast him out of the monastery so his sin does not infect the rest.

Chapter 29

Can a monk ever return to the monastery once he has left?
 Yes, he can return if he promises to amend his faults. He has three chances, after which, he may never re-enter.

Chapter 30

Are youths subject to the same punishments?
 If they do not understand the seriousness of excommunication, they are to be flogged or forced to fast.

Chapter 31

What is the duty of the cellarer?
 The cellarer manages the care of the goods inside the monastery and distributes them to the monks as required.

Chapter 32

Who takes care of the property and utensils?
 Brothers who exemplify virtue and reliability care for the clothes, tools and other property.

Chapter 33

What does the *Rule* say about private ownership by the monks?
 The monks are to own nothing, because private ownership is considered a vice. Everything the monk has is given to him at the order of the abbot.

Chapter 34

How are things to be distributed?
 They are to be distributed according to need.

Chapter 35

1. Who takes part in weekly kitchen service?
   All the monks are expected to spend time in this service of the others, except for the cellarer, the ill, and those whose duties do not permit.
2. Who washes the feet of the monks?
   The monk finishing his weekly service and the one starting his weekly service wash the feet of the other monks.

Chapter 36

What does the *Rule* say about the treatment of the sick?
 The sick are to be treated with compassion, not making unreasonable demands. However, those caring for them must be compassionate, even if they do make these demands. The sick are permitted baths as often as required and also to eat meat. Baths and meat are not part of the healthy monk's life.

Chapter 37

What is the rule for the treatment of the aged and children?
> Sympathy and kindness should direct their treatment and, due to their weakness, they should be allowed to eat before commons.

Chapter 38

1. What is to be done during meals?
   > A monk is to read during the meals and the others are to maintain perfect silence.
2. Why may the reader be allowed a draught of wine?
   > He may be allowed the wine because he will have fasted for Holy Communion and not have eaten. He will eat after the meal with those who have served and prepared the food.

Chapter 39

1. How many meals do the monks eat each day?
   > They may eat two cooked dishes at two meals, and sometimes a third dish when available.
2. How much bread is allotted to each monk daily?
   > Each monk is allotted a pound of bread.

Chapter 40

How much are the monks allowed to drink daily?
> The monks are generally permitted a quarter of a liter of wine daily and admonished to be temperate in their drink.

Chapter 41

When do the monks dine?
> The monks dine at the 6th and 9th hours, during appropriate seasons keeping the fast until the 9th hour. The evening meal must always be completed in daylight.

Chapter 42

What is prohibited after *Compline*?
> Talking is prohibited after *Compline*, but reading is permitted.

Chapter 43

1. What was required of the monk who was late for *Matins*?
   > He could not take his place in the choir but had to sit in a place where all could see him. Then he would do public penance.
2. What about the monk who was late for meals?
   > He would be given two corrections and if he did not reform, he would not be able to eat with the others and would be deprived of his wine.

Chapter 44

How does the excommunicated make satisfaction?
> He prostrates himself in front of the door to the oratory at the conclusion of the *Divine Office*. On entering the oratory he throws himself at the feet of the abbot and monks so that they may pray for him. He may not join in the chanting until given permission by the abbot.

Chapter 45

What happens if a monk makes a mistake while chanting or reading?
> He must humble himself publicly. Children should be whipped.

Chapter 46

How are other offences to be handled?
> The monk is to confess to the abbot and his brothers and offer to make satisfaction. If the cause is a sin, the monk should confess to the abbot or other priest.

Chapter 47

Who sounds the call to prayer?
> The abbot or one he designates shall do so.

Chapter 48

1. In what two principle ways did the monks spend their day?
   > They spent it in manual labor and holy reading.
2. Why are reading, prayer and work constant in the monastery?
   > They are constant because of the need to prevent idleness which can lead to sinful behavior.

Chapter 49

1. How is the life of a monk characterized?
   > It is characterized as a Lenten observance.
2. How is the monk's life different then, during Lent?
   > During Lent, private prayer, abstinence from food and drink, and more austerity are recommended. No monk should add anything to his practices without the abbot's blessing.

Chapter 50

What is required of monks who are too far away from the oratory to join in the *Divine Office*?
> They are to stop what they are doing and pray the *Office* kneeling.

Chapter 51

Can the brother who is away on an errand dine outside the monastery?
> He cannot dine outside the monastery without the permission of the abbot.

Chapter 52

What is the only function of the oratory?
    The only function of the oratory is as a place for prayer.

Chapter 53

1. How are guests to be receieved in the monastery?
    Guests are to be received as if they were Christ Himself.
2. Why does the abbot have a separate kitchen?
    He has a separate kitchen so that the monks will not be disturbed while preparations are made for the numerous guests who visit.
3. How do the monks conduct themselves with guests?
    They greet the guests with humility and ask a blessing, but they are not otherwise allowed to speak with them.

Chapter 54

What is to be done with letters or parcels received from the outside?
    All such goods are to be given to the abbot who decides what to do with them.

Chapter 55

What clothing provisions are made for the monks?
    The monks are provided with two tunics and cowls, a shift for labor and a pair of shoes.

Chapter 56

Where does the abbot eat?
    The abbot eats at his own table with any guests in the monastery. He may invite some of the brothers to eat at his table.

Chapter 57

Under what circumstances would a monk not be allowed to practice a craft in which he has skill?
    He would not be allowed to practice his craft if he became proud of his skill.

Chapter 58

1. What are the steps leading up to the admission of a new brother to the monastery?
    The steps leading up to the admission of a new brother are the following:
    - The newcomer must persist in petitioning admission over a period of time
    - After this period, he is admitted to a guest room
    - Then he moves to the novitiate where he meditates, eats and sleeps under the supervision of a senior monk
    - After two months the Rule is read to him and he is told that if he can observe it, he can enter; otherwise he is free to leave
    - If he can believes he can observe the *Rule*, he will return to the novitiate and be tested again with patience
    - After 6 months the Rule is read to him again and if he continues, it is read again after 4 months

- After the 4-month period, if he promises to follow the *Rule* and obey his superiors, he is admitted into the monastery
- At this point, he cannot leave
2. What happens upon his admission to the monastery?
   The newcomer promises God and the saints to be stable, obedient and to live as a monk, knowing he will be condemned if he does not. He writes out his promises. Then after reciting a psalm, he prostrates himself in front of each monk and asks for prayers. All his worldly possessions must be given away or to the monastery. He changes from his own clothes to those of a monk.
3. What happens if for some reason he should decide to leave?
   He would be stripped of his habit and expelled. His written promises would not be returned to him as they would be kept in the monastery records.

Chapter 59

Can children be admitted to the monastery?
   Yes they can. Their parents petition the monastery and present their sons. If they have means, they must promise not to give him anything.

Chapter 60

Can priests be admitted to the monastery?
   Yes, though permission is not immediately granted.

Chapter 61

How are pilgrim monks to be received?
   Pilgrim monks are to be received with welcome. Their ways are observed, and if they are found to be exemplary, they may remain. Otherwise they are to be sent away.

Chapter 62

Can a monk become a priest?
   Yes, if he is chosen by the abbot. He will be expected to keep to the *Rule* and obey the abbot in all things.

Chapter 63

How is rank determined and how does it affect life in the monastery?
   Rank is determined by the date of the monk's entrance into the monastery, by the merit of his life or by the abbot's order. The rank determines the order for receiving the kiss of peace, Communion, intoning the psalms and places in the oratory. Seniors call the junior monks Brother, and the junior monks call the senior monks Father. The abbot is called Abbot or My Lord. The junior monks ask the blessing of the senior monks and offer their seats to them.

Chapter 64

How is the abbot chosen?
   He is elected by the entire community based on his virtue and wisdom, regardless of his rank in the community.

Chapter 65

Who selects the deans and the provost and why?
> They are selected by the abbot to avoid the scandal of pride and dissension which could arise if the abbot and the others were selected by the community.

Chapter 66

Why should a wise old monk guard the gates of the monastery?
> He would know how to receive and answer questions and be old enough that he would not wander far from the door.

Chapter 67

What should brothers who leave on a journey do upon returning?
> They should prostrate themselves after each Hour of the *Divine Office*, asking for prayers for any sins they may have committed while being away.

Chapter 68

What should a brother do when asked to do something that is very difficult?
> He should accept the order with humility and if it is too difficult, he should tell his superior why in a spirit of humility and respect.

Chapter 69

Can one monk defend another?
> No, he cannot presume to do so because it might lead to scandal.

Chapter 70

Can the monks strike each other?
> They are not allowed to strike another unless the abbot has given the order and only at his discretion.

Chapter 71

Must the brothers obey one another?
> First they must obey the abbot and his superiors. Juniors are always to obey their seniors. When corrected, a monk must prostrate himself and make satisfaction, at which point he receives a blessing.

Chapter 72

What behaviors are made manifest by the monk full of zeal?
> The monk full of zeal avoids rivalry, lives for the others, accepts others, obeys others, lives in charity and chastity, loves his abbot, fears God and puts Christ above all else.

CHAPTER 73

What is the purpose of the *Rule*, restated?
> The purpose of the *Rule* is to guide those who follow it to virtue and the holy life. It is considered a little Rule for beginners.

QUESTION FOR FURTHER THOUGHT

Do you think any aspects of the *Rule of St. Benedict* could be applied to family life? If so, how? If not, why?

Unit 2: History

The Two Lives of Charlemagne

by Einhard the Frank
Translation: Lewis Thorpe
Penguin Classics

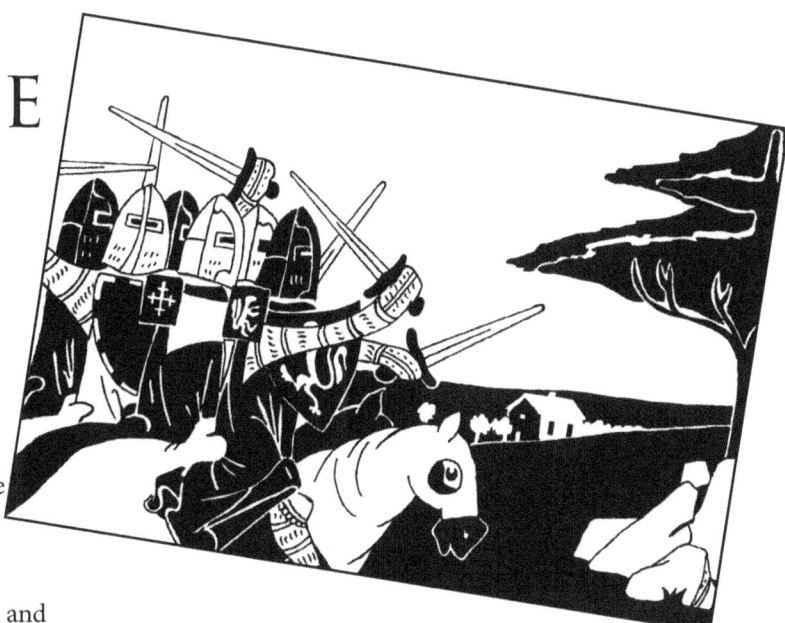

Charles the Great was the subject of numerous epic poems from France and Germany from the eleventh through the thirteenth centuries. He is a larger-than-life figure, much like the famous King Arthur, but much more is known about Charles than is known about Arthur. Charles the Great is known in literature as Charlemagne, and that is how we will refer to him in this work.

Charlemagne was born around 742 to Pepin the Short and Bertrada. He was illiterate, though he spoke Latin and understood Greek. He regarded education and the liberal arts highly, and he had an interest in the liturgy and music of the Church. As emperor, he is said to have insisted on the correct chanting of the Mass responses and the readings.

Pepin the Short was crowned King of the Franks by Pope Stephen II, and his sons Charlemagne and Carloman were appointed his joint heirs, establishing the Carolingian dynasty. When Pepin died, the sons inherited all of his territory which included the modern-day countries of Germany, Holland, Belgium, Switzerland and France. Charlemagne was 26 when his father died and Carloman was 17. Carloman died in 771, and all of his inheritance went to Charlemagne. Charlemagne sealed his alliance with Pope Hadrian I and proceeded to take on the Saxons in numerous wars. His reign was spent at war with his neighbors and people beyond his immediate neighbors. He made alliances with a variety of people such as Irene of Constantinople, the King of the Danes and the Emir of Cordova. Charlemagne had four memorable visits to Rome and during the final visit in 800 was crowned Emperor by Pope Leo III on Christmas day.

Under Charlemagne, the arts flourished through his Palace School in Aachen which was headed by Alcuin. Learning was centered on theology, and many of the students of his school became monks and then abbots. The school was responsible for restoring Latin as a literary language, and most of Latin poetry and prose was preserved by the scholar/copyists there. Charlemagne reigned as Emperor for 14 years, from 800 until 814.

Two Lives of Charlemagne

About the Author

Einhard spent twenty-three years serving Charlemagne. He wrote the *Vita Caroli* with gratitude to preserve his master's accomplishments in warfare, education, art, architecture and governance. His work is considered the more accurate of the two which are presented in *Two Lives of Charlemagne*, though the author omitted the more embarrassing facts about Charlemagne's personal life. He wrote of Charlemagne's achievements both at home and abroad, about his personal habits and interests, about the administration of his kingdom and of his death.

Einhard was a monk, distinguished for his decency, intelligence and wisdom. He taught at Charlemagne's Palace School in Aachen and became a close advisor and friend to Charlemagne. After Charlemagne died, Einhard served his successor, Lewis the Pious. Though a monk, he married, and he later died in 840.

The Life of Charlemagne was written between 829 and 836, after Einhard had left Aachen. Rather than injecting himself extensively into the work, he chose to remain anonymous and focus on the subject of his history. He used source-books and imperial archives for the history of Charlemagne dealing with his wars with the Saxons and diplomatic relations with foreign leaders. His style is based on the work of Suitonius, who wrote the *Lives of the Twelve Caesars*, in that it is short and to the point, and it follows a fixed structure.

Unit 2: History

Book I
The Early Carolingians

1. How was the Merovingian dynasty of the Franks brought to an end?
    King Childeric III was deposed by order of Pope Stephen II.
2. What had happened to the king's power?
    His power was in the hands of palace mayors and his was just a ceremonial role.
3. Who was the Mayor of the Palace when Childeric III was deposed?
    Pepin the Short, father of Charlemagne was the Mayor, having followed in the footsteps of his father, Charles Martel.
4. What happened to Carloman after he became king along with Charlemagne?
    He died within two years and his lands passed to Charlemagne. His wife and children fled to Italy.

Book II
The Wars and Political Affairs of Charlemagne

1. Why did Einhard decline to write about Charlemagne's birth and childhood?
    He said that nothing had been written about it and nobody then alive knew the facts, so he would not write about it.
2. What was the first war undertaken by Charlemagne and why?
    His first war was with Aquitaine, because his father had waged it but had not concluded it.
3. Did his brother help him in that war?
    No he did not.
4. Why did Charlemagne next go to battle with the Longobards?
    He went to battle because Pope Hadrian asked him to. This war, too, had been started by his father at the request of a different pope, and Charlemagne concluded it.
5. How did Einhard describe the Saxons?
    He said they were ferocious devil worshippers, hostile to Christianity.
6. Why did it take so long to conclude the war with the Saxons?
    They would surrender and then break their promises in defiance of the Franks.
7. What were the conditions imposed on and accepted by the Saxons at the end of the war?
    They gave up devil worship and converted to Christianity and were united with the Franks to form one people.
8. How long did the war with the Saxons last?
    It lasted for 33 years.

Question for Further Thought

What virtues does Einhard attribute to Charlemagne?
    He attributes him with the virtues of fortitude and courage.

9. What fierce people did Charlemagne's troops encounter on their return from victories in Spain?
    They encountered the Basques in the Pyrenees Mountains.
10. Why could Charlemagne not avenge the attack?
    It was night, and the Basques scattered and could not be found among the people.
11. What cowardly behavior did the Duke of Areghis exhibit in the face of Charlemagne's threat?
    He sent his two sons as hostages along with a large sum of money, and begged not to be forced to go himself.
12. Who encouraged Duke Tassilo in Bavaria to defy Charlemagne?
    The Duke's wife who was the daughter of King Desiderius encouraged him to defy Charlemagne.
13. What happened to the Duke?

He personally went to Charlemagne and after turning over his son and others as hostages, promised never to revolt against him again. He was not allowed to return home.
14. Who joined Charlemagne in his fight with the Slavs?
    The Saxons joined in, but their loyalty could not be counted upon.
15. What sea was Einhard referring to, around which lived the Danes and the Swedes?
    He was referring to the Baltic.
16. According to Einhard, what was Charlemagne's most important war outside of his war with the Saxons?
    The most important war was with the Huns, or Avars.
17. What were the results of that 8-year war?
    The area known as Pannonia was completely uninhabited, all of the Hun nobility died, all of their wealth was dispersed, the Franks were greatly enriched by the booty they took, and very few Franks died.
18. 18. What happened to the Danish king which prevented his arrival at Aachen?
    He was killed by his own followers.
19. 19. For how long did Charlemagne carry on at war?
    He carried on for 47 years.
20. Who were some of the monarchs who called themselves friends of Charlemagne?
    Some who were friends were Alfonso II of Spain, the Irish Kings, Harun-al-Rachid, King of the Persians, and the Emperors of Constantinople.
21. Who placed the Holy Sepulcher under Charlemagne's jurisdiction?
    The Persian King Harun placed it under his jurisdiction.
22. What was the Greek proverb which expressed the suspicion of Romans and Greeks toward the Franks?
    The proverb was "If a Frank is your friend, then he is clearly not your neighbor."
23. How did Charlemagne improve his kingdom outside of military activities?
    He built the church of the Holy Mother of God at Aachen, he built a 500-foot-long-bridge over the Rhine River at Mainz, and he began construction of two great palaces. He also ordered the restoration of sacred buildings throughout his kingdom.
24. What else did Charlemagne do to improve his kingdom?
    He had a large fleet built which could safeguard the rivers against the Northmen and the Moors.

Words to Know:

suzerainty: a nation which controls the international affairs of a dependent nation but allows it to control its own internal affairs

imperturbability: consistently calm

perfidy: deliberate treachery

Book III
The Emperor's Private Life

1. What kind of relationship did Carloman and Charlemagne have?
    Carloman was described as full of hatred and jealousy for his patient brother.
2. Why did Charlemagne marry the daughter of Desiderius, King of the Longobards?
    He married her because his mother wished him to do so.
3. What happened to his wife?
    She was dismissed after one year.
4. How many other wives did Charlemagne have?

Unit 2: History

      He had three other wives.
5. How many concubines did he have?
      He had five concubines.
6. In all, how many children did he have?
      He had 14 children.
7. How did Charlemagne treat his mother?
      He treated her with great respect.
8. What did Charlemagne provide for all his children?
      He provided them with an education in the liberal arts.
9. How did he handle the deaths of the three children who died before he did?
      He was very emotional and cried.
10. How did he handle the death of Pope Hadrian?
      He wept.
11. How did Charlemagne raise his children?
      He always ate with them and took them everywhere he went. He didn't give his daughters in marriage, and he ignored reports that they may have been involved in immoral conduct.
12. One son was not mentioned with the others. What does Einhard say about him?
      That son, Pepin, was a hunchback who conspired against his father. When he was caught, he was sent to a monastery.
13. On whom does Einhard place the blame for the German conspiracies?
      He blames it on his wife Fastrada who had a reputation for cruelty.
14. How did Charlemagne treat foreigners?
      He welcomed them and tolerated the strain they put on himself and the kingdom.
15. What was Charlemagne's appearance?
      He was strong, tall, had large eyes and a large nose, white hair, a happy expression, a short, thick neck and a belly. He had a firm step and was manly. He spoke distinctly, though he did not have a robust voice. He was in good health except for attacks of fever toward the end of his life.
16. How did he spend his time?
      He rode on horseback and hunted. He bathed in hot springs and exercised in the water by swimming.
17. How did he dress?
      He wore the Frankish national dress of linen underwear, long stockings, a silk-edged tunic, shoes and cloth wrapped around his legs. In the winter he wore a sleeveless jacket and a blue cloak, with his sword strapped to his side. His hilt and belt were made of silver or gold. On feast days and in the presence of foreign guests he carried a jeweled sword.
18. What virtue did Charlemagne exhibit with regard to food and drink?
      He exhibited the virtue of temperance by his controlled eating and drinking.
19. What did he like to listen to as he ate?
      He liked to listen to a reading from St. Augustine's *City of God*.
20. What did Charlemagne's formal education consist of?
      He learned to speak Latin as fluently as his Frankish tongue and he understood Greek. He studied rhetoric, dialectic, astrology and mathematics. He started too late to master writing.
21. How did Charlemagne practice his faith?
      He went to church twice a day and early morning Mass, prayed the Hours, insured that church liturgies were conducted with dignity, donated sacred vessels and vestments, and he reformed the chanting of the psalms and the reading of the lessons.
22. In what other important way did Charlemagne live his faith?
      He gave alms in his kingdom and in other lands, supported Christians wherever they needed help, and supported St. Peter's in Rome. He also financed other projects in Rome.
23. Why did Charlemagne go to Rome the last time, and what happened?

He went because the Romans had attacked Pope Leo III, blinding him and cutting off his tongue*, and he had been forced to plead for help from the Emperor. He went to aid the Pope and restore the Church. While he was there, the Pope crowned him Emperor and conferred on him the title Augustus.

*According to the notes, the Pope was attacked and an attempt was made to blind him and cut out his tongue, but the attackers did not accomplish this.

24. What was Charlemagne able to accomplish with regard to the laws?
    He had the laws of all the nations under his jurisdiction collected and written down.
25. What did he do regarding ancient poems?
    He had them written down as well, because up to that point they were transmitted orally.
26. What did he do for the Frankish language?
    He began to compile a grammar of the language and gave the months of the year Frankish names. He also named the 12 winds.

Words to Know:

tonsure: the shaved crown of a monk or priest, sometimes in the form of a cross

magnanimity: nobility, generosity

rhetoric: public speaking

dialectic: logical argumentation

Book IV
The Emperor's Last Years and Death

1. What did Charlemagne do when he was close to dying?
    He summoned a council of Frankish leaders and crowned his son Lewis as Emperor.
2. What was the last thing he did before he died?
    He received Holy Communion.
3. How old was he at his death?
    He was 72 and had reigned for 47 years.
4. When and where was he buried?
    He was buried on the day he died in the cathedral he had built in Aachen.
5. What signs were said to mark the coming end of Charlemagne?
    Marking the coming end of Charlemagne were eclipses; a black spot on the sun; the collapse of a portico and the burning of a bridge which had taken ten years to build; a meteor flash resulting in the spooking of his horse which fell and threw him; earthquakes, the lightning strike of the cathedral, and finally, the fading of the word princeps from an inscription in the cathedral.

Book V
Charlemagne's Last Will and Testament

1. Did Charlemagne finish his will?
    No, he died before it was finished.

Unit 2: History

2. He divided his estate into three parts. How were two-thirds to be handled?
    Two-thirds of the estate was divided into twenty-one parts. Each of the twenty-one parts was to go to one of the twenty-one cities of his kingdom to be used for charity.
3. How was the remaining third to be used?
    The remaining third was to be used for his maintenance as long as he lived. With any that remained after his death, it was to be divided into four parts. The first of the four parts would be divided among the twenty one parts mentioned above. The second part would be divided among his heirs (sons and daughters and their children). The third part was to be used for the poor, following Christian teaching. The fourth part would serve as a pension for the servants in the royal palace.
4. Were his wishes carried out after his death?
    Yes, they were.

Question for Further Thought

Based on this account of the life of Charlemagne, in what ways was he a good example as a Catholic Emperor? In what ways was he not a good example?
    Good: provided for the poor; virtuous traits of courage, fortitude, generosity and temperance; he provided for the needs of the Church and gave alms; treated his mother and children with respect

    Bad: dismissed his wife after one year and had three others, along with five concubines; ignored reports of immoral behavior on the part of his children which may have led to his not correcting their behavior

Word to Know:

pleurisy: inflammation of the lining of the lungs and chest which causes pain

Philosophy
Unit Three

Unit 3: Philosophy

The Prince

by Niccolò Machiavelli
Translation: George Bull
Penguin Books

About the Author

Niccolò Machiavelli was born in Florence in 1469. His education was normative for the time but not outstanding. Florence was an independent city-state and ruled by a republican government. Machiavelli wanted to preserve Florence's independence so that it wouldn't come under the rule of foreigners. He served as Chief Secretary of the Republic and head of the Second Chancery which managed the affairs of war and home. He traveled abroad and was in contact with notable heads of State and Church. He wrote political pamphlets which formulated his brand of political theory, gleaned from his experiences in other countries. He saw the need for law and order at whatever price, ommitting the moral implications of the actions of the key players who needed to retain power.

Italy, unlike other countries of Europe, was not unified, and she relied on mercenary soldiers to do her bidding. As a result, Italy could not prosper as an independent entity. Machiavelli tried to establish an Italian militia, but in the face of conflict, the militia gave up and the Republic of Florence collapsed. The Medicis returned to power and he was imprisoned for plotting against them. He proved his innocence but was forced into exile and retired to San Casciano to write. While in exile, he read the literature of Ancient Greece and Rome. During this period in history, Christianity was disintegrating into factions of Church and state in which the Roman Pontiff was seen as another temporal ruler.

Machiavelli broke with Classical and Christian thought regarding the behavior of heads of state. The Greeks believed that good leaders should be philosophers and men of virtue. The Christians also valued virtue in their leaders, even though there were many who did not exemplify it. These virtuous leaders would encourage virtue among the citizenry and create a state which was good for all. Machiavelli proposed an entirely different view of leadership.

He wrote a number of works, but *The Prince* is the one for which he is remembered.

The Prince

In his letter to the "Magnificent Lorenzo dé Medici," Niccolò Machiavelli says that men hoping to garner favor with powerful men usually give them gifts which speak of themselves or the recipient. Machiavelli states that his gift is the comprehension of the works of great men, about which he has learned through continuous study and personal familiarity with the present times. It is his hope that Lorenzo will benefit from the knowledge he has gained at the cost of much suffering.

I

1. What two types of states are there?
    There are republics and principalities.
2. What are the types of principalities?
    Principalities are either hereditary or new, which are won by a prince with arms and by luck or skill.

II

1. Why does Machiavelli not discuss republics?
    He says he discussed them in another piece.
2. Which type of principality is easier to rule?
    The hereditary principality is easier because people are used to the ruling family, and so long as the status quo is maintained and the people are not harmed, they are not likely to press for a change in ruler.

III

1. What is a new principality which is tied to an old state known as?
    It is a composite.
2. Why does this kind of principality bring problems?
    Men who agree to support this type expect to gain something for themselves, so they take up arms against their ruler, only to be deceived because things often get worse rather than better, or new factions appear. The prince cannot please everybody and yet he is dependent on their cooperation for survival.
3. What must happen for a new ruler to hang onto conquered people of the same language and culture?
    For him to hang onto them, he must destroy the family line of the former prince, leave the people to live according to their accustomed ways, and he must not impose new laws or taxes.
4. Why did the Turks succeed in securing Greece?
    They succeeded because their conqueror went to live there, thereby keeping watch for anything that would threaten his possession.
5. What else can a foreign prince do to secure his newly conquered lands?
    He can establish a few settlements, doing harm only to those who lose the land for the settlements. Those who keep their land keep quiet because they fear losing their land as well.
6. What happens when a prince sends in troops?
    Troops cost him a lot and the people resent their presence.
7. What should a foreign prince do about his smaller neighbors?
    He should strive to become their leader and protector and weaken those who are stronger.
8. Who would bring in a powerful foreign invader against a new prince?
    The people who are disaffected would support a new invader, as the Aetolians brought Rome into Greece.
9. Whom does Machiavelli hold up as the example of what he has so far proposed?
    He holds up the Romans and their treatment of Greece.
10. What is necessary to keep political problems from arising?
    Vigilance is necessary.
11. Problems left unchecked would benefit whom?
    Unchecked problems would benefit your enemies.
12. The Romans, instead of making the most of the present time, made the most of what?
    They made the most of their own ability and caution.

13. What fatal mistakes did Louis make in his effort to control Milan?
    He made six fatal mistakes:
    - He destroyed the weaker powers which could have been his allies
    - He increased the power of Pope Alexander who was already in Italy to occupy Romagna
    - He divided the kingdom of Naples between himself and the Spanish king
    - He had stayed away from Italy until he was forced to go there
    - He didn't establish settlements in Italy
    - He allowed the Venetians to lose their state by dividing it up

Note:
This section is about Louis XII who occupied Milan in 1499, but lost it within a year because the people rebelled and Ludovico the Moor was able to take it in 1500. Then Louis occupied it for a second time but lost it in 1512 when the *Lega Santa* (a coalition against France made up of Pope Julius II, Ferdinand of Spain and the Republic of Venice) intervened.

14. What do we learn about the Church during this time?
    The Church was involved in secular matters and in gaining worldly power, largely through the actions of Louis XII.
15. What rule does Machiavelli close this chapter with?
    The rule is that when one helps another to become powerful, he ruins himself.

IV

1. What was the situation in Asia after the death of Alexander?
    His successors ruled securely until the ministers within his government became ambitious to gain power.
2. In what two ways are all principalities governed, according to Machiavelli?
    They are either governed by a prince with ministers who help govern but who are all subservient to that prince, or they are governed by a prince and nobles whose rank is set by their lineage. In the second, the nobles have states and subjects of their own who show them allegiance and affection. The prince with ministers has greater power because all owe him alone their allegiance.
3. Who exemplifies the first way of governance?
    The Turks exemplify that with their empire ruled by one man and the empire divided up and administered by men chosen by him.
4. Who exemplifies the second way of governance?
    France exemplifies the second because its king is surrounded by many nobles.
5. Which type of government is easier to conquer?
    The second type, exemplified by King Louis XII, is easier because it can be easily divided.
6. Which kingdom stayed united after it was conquered by Alexander?
    The kingdom of Darius stayed united.

QUESTIONS FOR FURTHER THOUGHT

A. What is a government called which is ruled by an absolute ruler with unlimited power?
    That government is an autocracy and is what characterized the Turks and Darius.
B. What is a government called which is ruled by a prince with subject barons?
    It is a feudal government and is what characterized the government of France and other Europeans.

V

1. What are three ways of dealing with conquered states which have been living freely under their own laws?
   The three ways of dealing with them are:
   - Devastating them
   - Moving there to live
   - Allowing them to keep their own laws so long as they pay tribute and establishing an oligarchy to rule
2. Which way of dealing with the conquered states almost guarantees problems in the future?
   The third way almost guarantees problems.

Words to Know:

oligarchy: government in which power is held by a few people

tribute: tax

VI

1. What is more important for a new ruler; ability or fortune?
   Ability is more important.
2. To whom should one striving for power look for examples?
   He should look to people from history who have been successful, and then he should set his sights high.
3. Whom does he give as examples of rulers who succeeded because of their ability?
   He cites Moses, Cyrus, Romulus and Theseus.
4. What did fortune provide them?
   It provided them with opportunity.
5. Why are new principalities difficult to acquire?
   They are difficult to acquire because new laws and institutions have to be imposed on a resistant people.
6. Who are more likely to succeed, those who persuade or those who use force?
   Those who use force are more likely to succeed.

VII

1. What does Machiavelli say about men who gain power with little effort?
   He says that they have to exert themselves greatly to maintain that power.
2. Who is Machiavelli's example of a private citizen who became a prince through his own ability?
   Francesco Sforza became Duke of Milan through his own ability, and though it was a difficult struggle, once he succeeded, he held his kingdom.
3. Who is Machiavelli's example of a private citizen who became a prince through fortune?
   Césare Borgia, Duke of Valentinois, came to power through the fortune of his father, Pope Alexander VI, and lost it as soon as his father died.
4. What did Alexander do to acquire a state for his son?
   He destabilized the existing states and dissolved King Louis' marriage.
5. Why did Alexander not succeed in finally establishing his kingdom?
   His father died and he himself fell gravely ill when he was on the point of establishing himself, and he failed to manipulate the election of the new pope in his favor.
6. Why do men harm you, according to Machiavelli?
   They harm you because they hate you or they fear you.

7. In spite of his ultimate failure, why is Césare Borgia an example for others?

    He is an example of one who used fortune and arms to acquire power; he had great courage and good intentions; he was loved and feared by his subjects, he had the respect of his soldiers; he could be severe when necessary but had the love of others; he was generous; he was a good planner, and in general, had the virtues or traits of a ruler which Machiavelli thought were necessary to succeed.

Questions for Further Thought

A. What were some of the tactics employed by Césare Borgia in his quest for power?

    He seized opportunities as they presented themselves, he bribed people when necessary, he destroyed those who could harm him, he sought the welfare of Romagna, and he formed new allies as it was expedient to do so.

B. Do you think he was a virtuous man in the Classical sense?

    Answers will vary. In Ancient Greece and Rome, a virtuous man sought what was just and best for all, not just for himself. He showed mercy and didn't abuse his power. He was temperate in his behavior. Not all rulers could be called virtuous, because many became drunk with power, but some did stand out. In reading about Césare Borgia, he didn't seem to be concerned with personal virtue. His concern was the acquisition of power, by whatever means were necessary.

Words to Know:

satrap: governor of a province in ancient Persia

temporize: to delay acting in order to gain time

VIII

1. What did Machiavelli use Agathocles as an example of?

    He used him as an example of a man who became a prince through criminal methods.
2. What actions cannot be considered prowess?

    Actions such as the killing of citizens, the betrayal of friends, treachery, pitilessness, and lack of faith cannot be considered prowess, even if they are employed in the struggle for power.
3. What crimes preclude the inclusion of Agathocles from any list of great eminent men?

    He committed the crimes such as were mentioned in question 2 and was inhumane and cruel.
4. What crime did Oliverotto commit in his quest for power?

    He abused the hospitality of his uncle and killed him as well as all the guests at a banquet.
5. According to Machiavelli, how can cruelty be used for the good?

    It can be used when it is employed all at once and when one's safety depends on it. Once the crisis passes, it is let go.
6. According to Machiavelli, how is cruelty badly used?

    Cruelty is badly used when it continues to grow in intensity. When it does, power will be lost.

Words to Know:

nefarious: extremely wicked

audacity: boldness, daring, overconfidence

parricide: the murder of a parent or close relative

Unit 3: Philosophy

IX

1. What is a constitutional principality?
    It is one in which a private citizen becomes a ruler by the favor of his fellow citizens or by the nobles. This requires both luck and ability.
2. What two groups vie for power in this type of principality?
    The people and the nobles vie for power.
3. Why is a principality based on nobles rather than on the people harder to maintain?
    It is harder to maintain because the nobles consider themselves equal to the prince, while the people expect to obey their prince.
4. In what two ways does Machiavelli say the nobles behave?
    The nobles either become dependent on the prince or they retain their independence.
5. Those nobles who remain independent because of personal ambition are not to be trusted. Why?
    They will abandon the prince in times of adversity and work to ruin him.
6. How should a prince behave toward the people?
    He should grant them favors in order to oblige their allegiance to him.
7. In what situations is the allegiance of the people tenuous?
    When a prince rules through magistrates and adversity comes, the people are not likely to obey the prince because they have been used to taking their orders from the magistrates, not him.

Questions for Further Thought

A. What view of man does Machiavelli reveal in this chapter?
    He reveals the view that men are weak and untrustworthy, desiring only not to be oppressed. In good times they promise their allegiance and willingness to sacrifice for the prince and the state, but when times change, they turn and run.
B. What view of nobles does Machiavelli reveal in this chapter?
    He reveals the view that nobles desire the oppression of the people and generally seek their own interests.

Word to Know:

pusillanimous: timid, cowardly

X

1. What must a prince who doesn't have enough men or money to raise his own army do to protect himself from attack?
    A prince must fortify his city and provide for his people by laying in a year's worth of grain and other provisions, such as the items needed for the people to work and live. He must also maintain the friendship and loyalty of the people. Military exercises must be deemed important.
2. Which princes does Machiavelli use as examples of this kind of preparation?
    He uses the German princes as examples. They rule their territory and are completely independent of the others, even the emperor if they choose.
3. Why is this kind of city difficult for the enemy to take?
    It is difficult because an invader cannot maintain a siege for a year, and even though the people may lose their land and possessions outside the city walls, their fear of the enemy will keep them loyal to the prince who has provisions to see them through the difficulty.
4. What does Machiavelli say about the obligations between men and their prince?
    He says that people consider themselves obligated as much by the help they render as they do by the benefits they receive.

Words to Know:

circumspect: careful, guarded, vigilant

ignominy: humiliation, disgrace

XI

1. What maintains ecclesiastical principalities?
    They are maintained by powerful religious institutions.
2. How do ecclesiastical princes differ from other princes?
    They don't defend their territories nor do they govern their subjects.
3. What sustains these principalities?
    They are sustained by God.
4. Before Charles, the king of France invaded, who ruled Italy?
    Before Charles VIII, Italy was divided up between the pope, the Venetians, the king of Naples, the duke of Milan and the Florentines. The Venetians and the pope were the ones which had to be kept in check, so the others were allied against them.
5. Which pope strengthened his temporal power?
    Alexander VI did so with the help of his son, Duke Valentino (Césare Borgia).
6. What was Alexander VI's aim in acquiring territory?
    His aim was to further the interests of his son.
7. After Alexander VI died, what became of the holdings Duke Valentino had acquired?
    The Church inherited what he had won.
8. What were the goals of Pope Julius who succeeded Alexander VI?
    Pope Julius intended to enlarge the influence of the Church.
9. Who fomented feuds in the Church?
    The cardinals did so.

Question for Further Thought

Do you see a conflict of interests in having the pope be both a religious and a secular leader? Why or why not?
    Answers will vary. When a pope has temporal or secular power, he necessarily has to exclude some people from his spiritual care because they are seen as enemies in the temporal world. It is impossible for somebody who is warred upon by the pope to trust that the same pope will have his spiritual interests at heart. Also, the teaching of Christ precludes the kind of activities that popes engaged in, in pursuit of temporal power.

XII

1. What are the primary foundations of a state?
    The primary foundations of a state are good laws and a good military.
2. Which types of military are dangerous?
    Mercenaries and auxiliaries are dangerous to a state because they are disunited, power hungry, undisciplined, disloyal and lack fear of God.
3. On what does Machiavelli blame the destruction of Italy?
    He blames it on the use of mercenary troops.
4. What great ancient power relied on mercenaries to its own peril?
    Carthage relied on mercenaries. (Read about it in the *War with Hannibal* by Livy).

Unit 3: Philosophy

XIII

1. What are auxiliary troops?
   They are the troops of a powerful state which a prince might call upon for help. Machiavelli considers them worthless like mercenaries.
2. Why are auxiliary troops dangerous?
   They are united and led by their own leaders, so they pose the threat of holding what they were sent to help the prince acquire.
3. What example from the *Old Testament* does Machiavelli give to support his contention that a prince should not use foreign troops?
   He cites David, who declined to use Saul's weapons and armor because they were strange to him and would hinder him in his fight against Goliath. He was more effective with the weapon he was used to using--the sling.
4. In short, which is the best type of army?
   An army made up of citizens is best.
5. According to Machiavelli, what started the downfall of the Roman Empire?
   The downfall began when Rome started hiring Goths as mercenaries.

Question for Further Thought

From what you have read about Rome, do you agree with Machiavelli that the downfall of the Roman empire began with the hiring of Goths as mercenaries?
   Answers will vary. It is impossible to trace Rome's downfall to one cause. History has shown that corruption, intrigue, murder and licentiousness all played a part in demoralizing the people and rendering Rome incapable of continuing as it was. Yes, there were invaders from without, but Rome had lost the internal strength which might have saved her against the barbarians.

Word to Know:

enervate: weaken, debilitate

XIV

1. What should be the primary concern of a prince?
   His primary concern must be "war, its organization, and its discipline."
2. Why must a prince hunt?
   He must hunt to keep himself accustomed to hardship and knowledgeable about the geography of the land surrounding him.
3. What intellectual activity must a prince pursue?
   He must pursue the study of history, learning from the examples of men who have gone before him, and seeing why some were victorious and others not. In that way, he can emulate them.

Questions for Further Thought

A. Do you agree that war is the only thing a prince or ruler should be concerned about?
   Answers will vary.
B. What should be the primary concern of the president in a country like the United States?
   Answers will vary.

C. What is the primary purpose of the government as established in the United States as stated in the Preamble to the Constitution?

   The Preamble to the Constitution states that "We, the people of the United States, in order to form a more perfect Union, establish justice, insure domestic tranquility, provide for the common defense, promote the general welfare, and secure the blessings of liberty to ourselves and our posterity, do ordain and establish this Constitution for the United States of America."

XV

1. Why does Machiavelli say that a man who wants to act virtuously in everything naturally comes to grief?
   He comes to grief because so many around him are not virtuous, so he must be prepared not to act virtuously if necessary.
2. Which vices does Machiavelli say are less dangerous than others?
   Those vices which would not be sufficient to lose the state are less dangerous than others. He should not worry about those vices which are necessary for him to safeguard the state.

Question for Further Thought

How has Machiavelli separated himself from the philosophers of old in this chapter?
   He has dismissed the ideals that the philosophers held up for leaders in ideal states and presented human nature as it is. In Machiavelli's scheme, the interests of the state are more important than the interests of the individuals who inhabit it, and he allows for vice which is deemed necessary to maintain that state.

XVI

1. Why is a reputation for generosity not helpful for a prince?
   If the reputation reflects fact it will pass unnoticed and the prince will be reproached for the opposite of generosity, which is miserliness. To prove his generosity a prince would have to flaunt it, and in so doing, he would lose his fortune and have to tax the people, resulting in his own impoverishment and the ill-will of the people.
2. Why is miserliness a better way?
   If he is miserly the people will see that he lives within his means without burdening them, and he will be able to defend himself from outside attack.
3. What about the plunder a prince gains in war? How should the prince use that?
   He should share the plunder with his soldiers—that is the one area where he can afford to be generous because he is giving away what belongs to others, not himself or his people.

Words to Know:

parsimony: frugality, thriftiness, prudence

rapacious; greedy, grasping, gluttonous

ignominy: humiliation, disgrace

XVII

1. When is it alright for a prince to have a reputation for cruelty?
   A reputation for cruelty is alright if a prince keeps his subjects united and loyal. Cruelty can serve to make an example of those who would work against the prince, and therefore bring about order.

Unit 3: Philosophy

2. After he has established order, what virtues does a prince need?
    He needs prudence and kindness.
3. Which is better for a prince, to be loved or to be feared?
    According to Machiavelli, it is better for him to be feared.
4. What characteristics does he apply to man in general?
    He says man is ungrateful, fickle, he lies and deceives, he runs from danger and is greedy. He says when there is no danger, man is loyal, but when danger comes, he runs away.
5. Why, according to Machiavelli, is fear stronger than love?
    Fear is stronger than love because it is motivated by a dread of punishment.
6. What must a prince avoid, even though he is feared?
    He must avoid being hated, by keeping his hands away from his subjects and their property.
7. Why was Hannibal successful in commanding an army of aliens?
    He was successful because he was cruel.
8. Why did Scipio's troops mutiny against him?
    According to Machiavelli, they mutinied because he was excessively lenient and lax in military discipline.

Question for Further Thought

What did Hannibal and Scipio have to do with each other?
    Despite Machiavelli's assessment of both, Scipio (Africanus) defeated Hannibal at Zama in 202 B.C. and ended the second Punic War.

Words to Know:

rapine: plunder; use of force to take another's property

patrimony: inheritance

XVIII

1. What must a prince know in order to survive by fighting?
    He must know how to fight in the way both men and beasts fight. In other words, he must not only depend on brute force but also on his intellect.
2. What does Machiavelli say about a prince's word? Why?
    He says that he need not honor a commitment if it proves to be a disadvantage to him. He says this because he believes men are wretched and would not keep their promises either.
3. Even though a prince may lack the virtues of compassion, faithfulness, kindness, honesty, and devotion, what must he have?
    He must have the appearance of virtue.
4. Are those virtues good for a prince to have?
    They are good and desirable, so long as the prince is ready to dispense with them if it is to his advantage to do so.
5. How do men judge others?
    They judge by what they see, so it is important that a prince appear to be virtuous.

Word to Know:

gainsay: deny, contradict

XIX

1. What virtues are opposite the vices of fickleness, frivolity, cowardice, irresolution and effeminacy?
    The virtues opposed to those vices are grandeur, courage, sobriety, strength and constancy.
2. What is the prince's best safeguard against conspiracy?
    His best safeguard is the goodwill of the people he rules.
3. What should the prince do to keep the goodwill of the people?
    He should delegate to others, such as a parliament, the carrying-out of unpopular measures.
4. In addition to the ambitious nobles and insolent people, what third factor did the Roman emperors have to deal with?
    They had to deal with cruel and greedy soldiers.
5. Which group usually won the attention of the emperor, the soldiers or the populace?
    The soldiers won out.
6. Why was Marcus Aurelius successful, while other unadventurous emperors were not?
    He inherited the throne and had the esteem of both the soldiers and the people.
7. Why was Alexander, who was considered a righteous man and a successful emperor, killed by his army?
    He was thought to be effeminate and ruled by his mother.
8. Why was Pertinax despised?
    He tried to discipline the soldiers who had become licentious under Commodus, and he was old.
9. What did Commodus, Severus, Caracalla and Maximinus have in common?
    They were cruel and rapacious.
10. Why did the people despise Maximinus?
    They despised him because he was lowly-born (a shepherd) and he was fiercely cruel.
11. In what way does the Sultan's dominion differ from other principalities?
    It differs in that the ruler is elected by those with authority to do so, and the state institutions are old.

Question for Further Thought

What was the main point of the discussion about the Roman emperors?
    The main point was that the prince must avoid hatred and contempt or come to a violent end.

Word to Know:

indolence: laziness, idleness, inactivity

dissolute: degenerate, immoral

XX

1. Why is it expedient for a prince to arm his subjects?
    It is expedient for a prince to arm his subjects because it insures that he is armed through them. They become loyal subjects who will use their arms for him.
2. Why did the Venetians foster the dissenting factions of the Guelfs and Ghibellines in the cities that were subject to them?
    They fostered them so that the two sides would never rally together against them.
3. What condition should exist for a prince to build fortresses?
    The prince who fears his own people should build a fortress.

Unit 3: Philosophy

4. What is the best fortress?
    The best fortress is avoidance of the hatred of the people.

XXI

1. What brings a prince prestige?
    A prince gains prestige by mounting great military campaigns and demonstrating his own abilities.
2. What was King Ferdinand of Aragon's claim to fame?
    He was the first king of Christendom, and in the name of the Church, drove the Moors out of Spain and successfully campaigned in Africa, France and Italy.
3. Besides showing prowess in foreign war, how else can a prince gain prestige?
    He can gain prestige by governing well at home.
4. What other ways does Machiavelli mention which gain a prince prestige?
    He can also gain prestige for being a faithful friend or a declared enemy, by esteeming and encouraging talent, and by honoring those who excel. He must also encourage the citizens to do their work well and peaceably, and he should entertain the people periodically with shows and festivities.

XXII

1. On what is the first opinion of a ruler's intelligence based?
    It is based on the quality of people in his service.
2. What are the three kinds of intelligence?
    - The first understands things for itself
    - The second appreciates what others can understand
    - The third doesn't understand for itself nor does it understand through others
3. What must a good minister's focus be?
    His focus must be what is good for the prince, not for himself.

Words to Know:

sagacity: wisdom, shrewdness

acumen: insight, good judgment, intelligence

surfeit: excess, surplus

XXIII

1. What kind of men are to be avoided by the prince?
    The prince must avoid flatterers.
2. Whose advice should a prince seek?
    He should only seek the advise of trusted councilors.
3. Why should a prince confer honors on his ministers?
    He rewards their faithfulness and creates a dependency of them on himself, because they fear losing what he can provide.

XXIV

Why did the Italian princes who lost their states fail?
> They relied on the arms of others, they didn't keep the good favor of the people and/or the nobles, and they failed in planning for the future by becoming complacent with temporary peace.

XXV

1. What does Machiavelli say about the role of fortune?
   > He says that it may be the arbiter of half of the things that men do, but the other half is controlled by men themselves because of free will.
2. What must guide the prince in his choice of action?
   > He must be guided by the times and circumstances in which he finds himself.
3. What quality did Pope Julius have which led to his success?
   > He was impetuous.
4. According to Machiavelli, which prince is more likely to succeed: one who is impetuous or one who is circumspect?
   > He would favor the impetuous one because he would take advantage of what fortune would seem to place before him.

Words to Know:

impetuous: rash, impulsive

circumspect: cautious, guarded

XXVI

1. Does Machiavelli believe he lives in a time which would favor a new ruler in Italy?
   > Yes he does.
2. To whom is Machiavelli addressing this work?
   > He is addressing it to Lorenzo dé Medici.
3. Why does Machiavelli believe Italy is ready for a new prince?
   > He believes Italy is ready because she has been ravaged and reduced to a state of disorder.
4. What does Machiavelli say Lorenzo must do?
   > He must emulate the men praised in this work and raise a citizen army.
5. Who would help a new prince?
   > God would help him.
6. What is Machiavelli's dream?
   > His dream is to see a united Italy.

Questions for Further Thought

A. What is Machiavelli's portrayal of mankind?
   > He portrays mankind as self-serving and fickle. Man generally is interested in his own welfare rather than that of others or of the state.
B. What is the role of virtue in Machiavelli's thought?
   > Virtue is important and desirable in a leader. However, it must not get in the way of his doing what will preserve himself and his state, because the prince will deal with others who are not virtuous. To maintain his virtuous standards at all costs is to commit political suicide.

Unit 3: Philosophy

C. What is the role of fortune in Machiavelli's view?
   Fortune appears to be equated with God. Machiavelli acknowledges that God, or fortune, presents opportunities, but they do not control the outcome of human events. Man must act on the opportunities presented to him. At the same time, Césare Borgia was very successful, but his success was cut short by "fortune." (or perhaps by God's will)?
D. Do you agree with Machiavelli's belief that a prince must always have a strong army? Why or why not?
   Answers will vary.
E. How would you restate the basic themes of *The Prince*?
   The basic themes of *The Prince* are:
   - The state is the most important entity and must be served above everything else.
   - The state is founded on a strong military.
   - Virtue is found in the ability of the ruler to use his intelligence to rule his state. It includes personal ability, courage, talent and quickness of action.
   - Fortune presents opportunities upon which men must act. It is the action of the prince (what Machiavelli would term "virtue") which determines whether or not success will follow on opportunity.
F. Why is it necessary for anybody who desires to rule to have a good grasp of history?
   It is necessary to have a good grasp of history so that one can learn from the successes and mistakes of others. Human nature hasn't changed throughout the centuries, and a study of history shows this fact. It also shows how wise and not-so-wise men have dealt with it. Machiavelli clearly had a knowledge of history from which he drew his advice for the new prince of his time.

For Further Research:

Research Savonarola and see why he is used as an example of an unarmed prophet who failed.

Novel
Unit Four

Don Quixote

by Miguel de Cervantes Saavedra
Translation: Walter Starkie
Mentor Book

About the Author

Miguel de Cervantes was born in September of 1547 into a poor family. From his years of privation he learned the life-lessons of charitable and humane behavior and the necessity of cooperation within the family. When he was 22 he entered the armed forces of Spain and took part in the Battle of Lepanto in 1571. That battle, in which the Turks were defeated by the fleet of Don John of Austria, left him wounded, but he continued to serve and fight against the Turks. When he was returning home, he and his brother Rodrigo were captured by pirates and imprisoned in Algiers for five years. During that time of imprisonment, he attempted to escape four times and managed to hide for five months before he was caught again. He was brave and honest while facing his jailers and they admired him.

He was ransomed by the Trinitarian Friars, and in 1580 he returned home with the intention of working in the Spanish bureaucracy and writing. He was not particularly successful in either endeavor. He married in 1584 and could only modestly support his family, and he was jailed for misappropriating funds. Before his fortunes would change, he would undergo a second incarceration and move to Valladolid.

Cervantes wrote a number of plays and novels, but the one that brought him the fame he sought was *Don Quixote*, Part One, published in 1605. Within six months his work was acclaimed all over Spain and beyond. However, he did not get rich from the book, and a few years later, another author wrote a counterfeit sequel to it. *Don Quixote*, Part Two was not published until 1615, just a year before he died. His death was on April 23, 1616, just 10 days before William Shakespeare died.

Don Quixote

Don Quixote, the first modern novel, is known as a picaresque novel, meaning that it is a style of prose, developed in Spain, which recounts the adventures of a wayward hero in a series of usually humorous or satiric episodes that often depict, in realistic detail, the everyday life of the common people. At the time it was written, novels about chivalry were prevalent, and this one would poke fun at that genre of literature. *Don Quixote* is classic literature because it addresses universal themes relating to human existence. It reflects on right and wrong, on valor, piety, courtesy, strength and honor. It was written during a time of rapid change in Renaissance Spain when influences from Southern as well as Northern Europe, the Moors and the Jews were impacting Spanish culture. Those elements form the backdrop of the story.

The hero is a knight-errant, one who wanders in search of adventures to prove himself as a knight. Underneath the surface story of a knight seeking adventure is the spiritual journey toward salvation. Don Quixote makes three such journeys, or sallies, and is returned to his home in La Mancha after each one. He dedicates his wanderings to Dulcinea, whom we will learn is anything but a lady. His story is an interplay between reality and imagination and is a reflection of Cervantes' Christian beliefs.

Unit 4: Novel

Part One

I. The quality and manner of life of that famous gentleman Don Quixote of La Mancha

1. What was the name of the village from which Don Quixote came?
    The poet does not wish to name it.
2. What was the primary interest of the gentleman described?
    His primary interest was reading books about chivalry.
3. What happened to the gentleman's ability to reason? What was the cause and what was the result?
    He lost the ability to reason due to endless reading, and his fantasy world became more real than reality.
4. What did the gentleman decide to do?
    He decided to become a knight-errant.
5. What did he name his horse?
    He named the horse Rozinante.
6. Who was to be Don Quixote de la Mancha's lady?
    She was to be Aldonza Lorenzo, soon to be called Dulcinea del Toboso.

Words to Know:

jerkin: close-fitting, sleeveless jacket with extended shoulders, worn over a doublet and secured with a belt, worn by men of the 1500s

doublet: padded underwear reinforced with mail, worn under armor

puce: brownish purple color

morion: a metal helmet with a crest and a curved peak, worn by soldiers in the 16th and 17th centuries

II. Our imaginative hero's first sally from his home

1. What was the purpose of the knight's sally?
    His purpose was to rectify grievances, right the wrongs he perceived, redress harms done to others, reform abuses about which he was aware, and discharge debts.
2. What was the one thing lacking for Don Quixote to be able to lawfully undertake his adventure?
    He had not been dubbed a knight.

Words to Know:

list: place of combat

wench: peasant girl or servant, wanton woman

beaver: a piece of armor attached to a helmet to protect the mouth and chin

III. The amusing way in which he is dubbed a Knight

1. What did the innkeeper advise Don Quixote to always carry?
    He advised him to always carry money, lint and ointments for his wounds, and clean shirts.

2. Why did Don Quixote attack the muleteers?
    They removed his arms from the trough to water their animals.
3. Why were his attackers terrified?
    They were terrified because he spoke and acted boldly toward them.
4. Who dubbed Don Quixote a knight?
    The innkeeper did so, assisted by the two wenches.

WORD TO KNOW:

caitiff: despicable coward

IV. What happened to our Knight after leaving the inn

1. Why did Don Quixote return to his village?
    He returned to get the items the innkeeper had told him to carry on his journeys, and to get himself a squire.
2. Whom did Don Quixote rescue on his way back to his village?
    He rescued a young boy who was being flogged by his master for losing his animals. The boy said that the master refused to pay him his wages.
3. What does the expression "every man is the son of his own works" mean?
    It means that each person determines who he is by his own actions and choices.
4. What happened after Don Quixote left the scene of the flogging with a promise from the master to pay the debt?
    The master tied the boy up again and almost killed him.
5. To what did Don Quixote attribute his misfortune at the hand of the traders?
    He attributed it to his horse which stumbled and threw him to the ground.

WORDS TO KNOW:

skinflint: miser

real: name of Spanish currency until the second half of the 19th century, when it was replaced with the peseta. The real was 1/4th of a peseta.

V. Wherein is continued the account of our Knight's mishap

1. Why did the peasant who picked Don Quixote up wait until after dark to return to the village?
    He was a decent fellow and wanted to protect him from the gaze of the villagers.
2. Who was at Dox Quixote's house when they arrived?
    His niece and housekeeper, as well as the barber and parish priest were there.
3. What did Don Quixote's niece call the books he had read?
    She called them "excommunicated volumes."
4. Whom did Don Quixote ask for to heal his wounds?
    He asked for the witch Urganda.

QUESTION FOR FURTHER THOUGHT

In trying to right himself, Don Quixote recalls a story from his books. The author said the story was familiar to everybody, yet no truer than the "miracles of Mahomet." What did he mean, and why the reference?
    He meant that Mahomet (Mohammed) did not work any miracles. This was a time in Spanish history when the Moors (Moslems) had been expelled from Spain. (Remember, Cervantes had fought against the Turks (Moslems) at the Battle of Lepanto in 1571).

Unit 4: Novel

VI. The high and mighty inquisition held by the curate and the barber on the library, and the second sally of our good Knight Don Quixote

1. While Don Quixote slept, what did the others do?
    They went through his books and threw most of them into the courtyard to be burned.
2. What did they agree to tell him when he asked about his books?
    They agreed to tell him that an enchanter had taken the books.
3. What was the name of the man Don Quixote chose as his squire?
    His name was Sancho Panza (panza is a belly).
4. What did Don Quixote promise Sancho?
    He promised him a governorship, or possibly a kingship over whatever lands he would conquer.

Question for Further Thought

What did the author mean when he described Don Quixote's neighbor as "an honest fellow (if such a title can be given to one who is poor)?"
    He meant that often the poor were not honest in their pursuit of the necessities of life, so there was an assumption that they were not always trustworthy.

Word to Know:

alacrity: cheerful willingness

VII. The Terrifying and unprecedented adventure of the Windmills, and the stupendous battle between the gallant Biscayan and the puissant Manchegan

1. What did Don Quixote think the windmills were?
    He thought they were giants.
2. What did Don Quixote say about the windmills after he attacked one?
    He said that the same enchanter who had stolen his books had turned the giants into windmills.
3. Why did Sancho try to take the monk's robe?
    He said it was the spoil of the battle his master had just won.
4. What happened to Don Quixote during his fight with the squire?
    Part of his ear was cut off and his helmet was broken.
5. What did Don Quixote demand of the frightened ladies after he battered their squire?
    He demanded that the knight go to El Toboso and present himself to Dulcinea (Aldonza).
6. What was Sancho willing to trade his promised governorship of an island for?
    He was willing to trade it for the formula for a balsam which would cure any wound. Don Quixote had read about such a balsam in one of his books.

Words to Know:

puissant: powerful, mighty

Manchegan: a man from the area of La Mancha

Biscayan: a Basque, person from the northern area of Spain inhabited by the Basque people

VIII. Don Quixote and the goatherds, and the calamity that overtook him in connection with certain heartless Yanguesan carriers

1. Who shared food with Don Quixote and Sancho?
    Some goatherds in a field shared their food.
2. What did Don Quixote speak about at length during dinner?
    He spoke about man's Golden Age when man was almost perfect and life was ideal.
3. Why did Don Quixote and Sancho attack the Yanguesans?
    Rozinante mixed himself into their herd of mares and they attacked the horse. Don Quixote had to take revenge on them, but he and Sancho were soundly beaten by the 20 or so carriers.
4. Why did Don Quixote accept the blame for what happened?
    He had gone to battle with men who were not knights and was punished for breaking the laws of chivalry as he understood them.
5. How did he advise Sancho to respond in the future?
    He told him to raise his sword against men who were not knights, and he would only join in if the attackers were knights.
6. How did Sancho respond?
    He said that he was a peaceful man with family obligations and would pardon any future insults, but he would not raise the sword to others.

QUESTION FOR FURTHER THOUGHT

What did we learn about the practices of knighthood in this chapter?
    We learned that knights ate and drank sparingly, the didn't spend much time sleeping, they only fought with other knights, and they protected the innocent.

IX. What befell our imaginative gentleman in the inn he supposed to be a castle

1. What excuse did Don Quixote give the innkeeper's wife for not talking about himself?
    He said that self-praise is debasing and that his squire would speak for him.
2. What did Don Quixote say about Dulcinea?
    He said she was ungrateful and beautiful.
3. Who was beat up when Maritornes went to lie with the carrier?
    Don Quixote, Sancho and Maritornes were all beaten.
4. What put an end to the scuffle?
    The officer from the Holy Brotherhood of Toledo thought somebody had been killed, and he ordered the door of the inn to be locked so he could investigate. The innkeeper and Maritornes left in the dark and the carrier returned to his bed.

X. An account of the countless troubles that came upon Don Quixote and his squire in the inn that, to his sorrow, the former took for a castle

1. How did Don Quixote interpret the events of the preceding night?
    He said the beautiful daughter of the castle lord had visited him but was snatched away by a monstrous giant because she is reserved for somebody else, her treasure being held by an enchanted Moor.
2. What are *aves, salves and credos*?
    They are prayers—the Hail Mary, the Hail Holy Queen and the Creed.
3. What happened when Don Quixote swallowed the balsam?
    He vomited violently, sweated profusely, and then slept; waking up feeling better.

Unit 4: Novel

4. Did the balsam work the same for Sancho?
    No, it made him violently ill.
5. What did Don Quixote tell the innkeeper as he was leaving?
    He told him that he had received many favors there and offered to avenge any wrongs the innkeeper may have suffered.
6. Why did Don Quixote say he could not pay the innkeeper?
    He said knights-errant never paid for the lodging because it was due them for their deeds and suffering.
7. What happened to Sancho?
    He tried to give the same reason for not paying, but some guests took him and tossed him up and down, catching him in the blanket.
8. What did the innkeeper take for payment?
    He took Sancho's saddlebags.

Word to Know:

balsam: ointment, balm

XI. The conversation that took place between Sancho Panza and his master Don Quixote, together with some adventures worth recording

1. What was Don Quixote's excuse for not avenging Sancho's treatment?
    He said the rules of chivalry prohibited knights from fighting those who weren't knights.
2. To what did Don Quixote attribute his inability to mount the surrounding wall or alight from his horse?
    He attributed them to enchantment.
3. What did Sancho propose?
    He proposed that they return home and abandon these misadventures.
4. What did Don Quixote mistake for two armies?
    He mistook two flocks of sheep for armies.
5. What did Don Quixote lose?
    He lost his grinding teeth.

XII. The adventure of the corpse, and the never-seen and unheard-of-adventure that Don Quixote terminated with less danger to himself than ever did a famous knight in the world

1. What did Sancho and Don Quixote see approaching as they rode along the King's road?
    They saw lights approaching.
2. What was the source of the lights?
    There were about 20 people dressed in white and riding on horses, carrying torches.
3. What kind of a procession was it?
    It was a funeral procession.
4. How did the people react to Don Quixote's questions?
    They told him they had no time to speak as it was late and they had to press on.
5. What did Don Quixote do?
    He charged at them with his lance and unhorsed one of the riders, scattering them all across the fields.
6. What name did Sancho give Don Quixote?
    He called him the Knight of the Rueful Figure.
7. As they approached a waterfall, what did they hear?
    They heard thuds and the sounds of irons and chains.
8. Sancho admitted that he left his wife and family for what end?
    He was covetous of a higher position in life.

9. Why was he afraid?
   Don Quixote told him to wait for him for three days while he went in search of adventures, and Sancho didn't want to be left alone in an unknown place.
10. What did Don Quixote tell Sancho he had done for him?
    He told him that he had provided for him in his will.
11. What was the source of the thuds they had heard?
    They heard fulling-hammers.
12. How did Don Quixote react to Sancho's laughter when they discovered the source of the frightful noise?
    He beat him and admonished him to respect him as a father.

Words to Know:

rueful: full of woe, mournful

sumpter: pack animal

fulling-hammers: hammers used to beat and thicken cloth fibers

XIII. *The noble adventure and rich prize of Mambrino's helmet, and the liberation by the Knight of a number of ne'er-do-wells*

1. What did Don Quixote say about proverbs?
   He said he was sure they were all true, as they came to be because of experience.
2. What was the origin of the helmet of Mambrino?
   It was originally made for the Saracen king named Mambrino and was then captured by one Rinaldo.
3. Whom did Don Quixote mistake for a knight with the golden helmet?
   He mistook the barber wearing his basin on his head for a knight.
4. What did barbers do during this time?
   They not only cut hair and beards, but they also let blood.
5. How did Don Quixote acquire the "helmet?"
   He knocked the barber off his horse and the frightened man ran away, leaving his basin behind.
6. What were the crimes of the prisoners they met along the road?
   Some were thieves, another a pimp and a wizard, and another a gambler.
7. What did the slaves do while the guards were attacking Don Quixote?
   They freed themselves of their chains.
8. What became of the guards?
   They ran away.
9. What did Don Quixote command the criminals to do?
   He commanded them to go to El Toboso and commend his service to Dulcinea and to relate the adventure to her.
10. What did Ginés de Pasamonte tell him?
    He said they couldn't travel the roads together and that they would pray for him instead of going to Dulcinea.
11. After Don Quixote threatened Ginés, what happened?
    The freed prisoners beat him up and stripped him and Sancho of most their clothing. Then they took off in different directions.
12. Why was Don Quixote bewildered?
    He couldn't understand why he received such rough treatment after rendering such great service to them.

Word to Know:

truculent: hostile, defiant

XIV. Don Quixote's strange adventure in the Sierra Morena

1. Why did Sancho want to hide in the Sierra Morena for a few days?
    He wanted to hide from the Holy Brotherhood after Don Quixote had freed the prisoners.
2. Who found them sleeping in the Sierra?
    Ginés de Pasamonte, whom they had freed, found them, and he stole Sancho's donkey.
3. What did Don Quixote find on the ground?
    He found a locked *portmanteau* with holland shirts and linen garments, as well as some gold crowns.
4. What else did they find in the *portmanteau*?
    They found a little book in which were written some sonnets.
5. Why did Don Quixote want to find the owner of the *portmanteau*?
    He wanted to return it and its contents to him.
6. Did Sancho desire the same thing?
    No, he had already claimed the contents and didn't want to give them back.
7. Who had seen the owner of the *portmanteau*?
    A goatherd had seen him six months earlier.
8. What condition was the owner of the *portmanteau* in?
    He was mad and acting wild, saying he was doing penance for his sins.
9. While the young man, Cardenio, was telling his story, what did he say about young men and love?
    He said young men lust rather than love.
10. What mistake had Cardenio made with regard to Don Fernando?
    He had confided too much, even to the virtues of the woman he loved named Luscinda.
11. What angered Don Quixote?
    Cardenio said that Master Elisabat was the paramour of Queen Madasima, a character in a book about chivalry.
12. What happened?
    Both men were in a fit of rage and Cardenio beat Don Quixote, then Sancho and finally, the goatherd, soundly. Then Cardenio took off.
13. What did Don Quixote want?
    He wanted to find Cardenio so he could finish his story of woe.

Word to Know:

portmanteau: a large leather suitcase that opens into two hinged compartments.

paramour: adulterous lover

XV. The continuation of the adventure in the Sierra Morena

1. What had Don Quixote commanded of Sancho?
    He had commanded him to refrain from speaking.
2. What rule of chivalry was Don Quixote following when he defended Queen Madasima?
    He was following the rule of defending the honor of women.
3. What did Don Quixote decide to do in the wilderness?
    He decided to imitate Amadis of Gaul and act insane for the love of Dulcinea. He would have Sancho deliver a letter to her and would remain in the wilderness as a madman until she answered.

4. What does Don Quixote say about their adventures?
   He says that they appear to be illusions, follies and dreams, but they turn out otherwise because of the work of enchanters.
5. What does Don Quixote say when Sancho refers to the Purgatory he is going to experience?
   Don Quixote says it is better to call it Hell, because it will be terrible.
6. Even though Sancho tells Don Quixote about who "Lady Dulcinea" (Aldonza) really is, what is his response?
   He says that it is enough for him to believe she is beautiful and chaste, and her lineage is irrelevant.
7. In addition to the letter, what does Don Quixote give to Sancho?
   He gives an order for three donkey colts to be given to Sancho by his niece.

QUESTIONS FOR FURTHER THOUGHT

A. Is Don Quixote completely mad? Why do you say so?
   Don Quixote appears to be on the verge of insanity, yet he has lucid moments. It is difficult to distinguish his fantastic role-playing from the actions of a madman. He is able to draw others in, as he did Sancho. While we look at people with a critical eye, he sees the good in everybody. He is idealistic to a fault, and he knows how to placate Sancho to keep him in his service.
B. How does Sancho seek to comfort himself from the blows and abuse he takes from others?
   He seeks solace in food and drink. As long as his stomach (panza) is full, he is momentarily placated. That is in direct contrast to Don Quixote who is moderate in his use of both food and drink.
C. In what other major way are Don Quixote and Sancho different?
   Don Quixote is an idealist who is willing to sacrifice himself for his cause, however crazy it may seem. Sancho is the realist. He has practical concerns, like where they will eat and sleep. He sees that the "Golden Helmet of Mambrino" is really a barber's basin, and he sees that the innkeeper is not a castle lord, etc.
D. What is the difference between Purgatory and Hell in the sense that the two are talking?
   Purgatory is a temporary state or place, from which one is released after purification, while there is never any release from Hell.

WORDS TO KNOW:

apostate: traitor, fugitive

prattle: chatter, drivel

missive: letter, communication

XVI. The penance Don Quixote performed in the Sierra Morena, and the plan of the curate and the barber

1. Who demanded to know the whereabouts of Don Quixote?
   The curate and the barber demanded to know.
2. What had happened to the pocket-book in which Don Quixote had written his missive?
   He had forgotten to give it to Sancho.
3. Why was Sancho upset about not having the book?
   The missive also contained Don Quixote's promise of three colts.
4. What plan did they concoct?
   The curate would disguise himself as a distressed maiden and the barber as her squire, and they would go to Don Quixote and ask him to redress an injury which another knight had inflicted upon her. Then they would lead him out of the wilderness.

5. Why did the curate and the barber change roles?
   The curate thought it was beneath his dignity to dress as a woman.
6. Whom did they happen upon while Sancho went to find his master?
   They happened upon Cardenio.
7. What did they talk about?
   Cardenio finished the tale of woe he had been telling Don Quixote and Sancho before Don Quixote and he went into a rage.
8. What treachery did he reveal?
   He revealed the treachery of his "friend" Don Fernando who convinced Luscinda's father to give him her hand in marriage.
9. What did he witness, unnoticed?
   He witnessed Luscinda make the wedding vows and then faint.
10. What did Cardenio do after that?
    He took off for the mountains, betrayed by Luscinda who had told him she would kill herself before she would marry Fernando.
11. In what conditions did Cardenio live?
    He lived aimlessly in the hills, receiving food from charitable shepherds or, in his madness, forcing them to give it to him. He was in and out of sanity.

Questions for Further Thought

A. The curate thought dressing as a woman was beneath his dignity. What other of his actions were beneath the dignity of a priest?
   It was beneath his dignity as a priest to partake in the ruse at all, and he led Sancho to believe that he would write the letter for him, when he had no intention of doing so. He then made up a lie about the letter, saying Dulcinea could not read but had sent a response for him to return immediately.
B. What did Cervantes say about Sancho's character?
   He said that he was a covetous fool.

Words to Know:

shindy: row, commotion

curate: cleric in charge of a parish

alacrity: eagerness, enthusiasm

XVII. The quaint and delightful adventure that befell the curate and the barber in the same Sierra

1. When the young woman disguised as a boy began to speak, what did she tell the curate, the barber and Cardenio about her family?
   She said they were wealthy honest farmers, vassals to a Duke, who were "rusty Christians," and their lack of a title is why she was in dire straits.
2. How did her parents treat her?
   They treated her with great indulgence and love.
3. Whom had she attracted?
   She had attracted the Duke's younger son, Don Fernando.
4. What did the young woman rely upon to resist the advances of Don Fernando?
   She relied upon her virtue and the admonitions of her parents.

5. What did Don Fernando do to Dorothea?
    He entered her room and begged her to be his and pledged to be faithful to her, giving her a ring. Their betrothal would be known once he decided to make it known, but he disappeared and shortly afterward married a woman of his own social stature named Luscinda.
6. What else did Dorothea recount?
    She told about the wedding of Don Fernando and Luscinda and how she had fainted at the wedding and a letter fell from her bosom, saying that she was betrothed to Cardenio and intended to kill herself after the wedding.
7. How did Don Fernando respond to the knowledge?
    He tried to kill Luscinda but was stopped by her parents.
8. What became of him?
    He fled.
9. What happened to Dorothea when she left the city after hearing that Don Fernando was gone?
    She went to the mountains with her servant who tried to take advantage of her.
10. What did she do to him?
    She pushed him over a cliff.
11. How did she come to be a shepherd?
    She disguised herself as a shepherd and found work as one.
12. Why did she leave that employment?
    She left because the shepherd tried to take advantage of her as her servant had done.
13. What did Cardenio promise Dorothea?
    He promised he would be with her until she was back together with Don Fernando.
14. The curate created a plan to take Don Quixote back to El Toboso and Dorothea pretended to be a princess in distress. What do we note about Sancho Panza at this point?
    Sancho is very simple and gullible, and believes the story the curate has told him. He has internalized the insanity of his master.

Words to Know:

palfrey: a riding horse

boon: a favor sought

XVIII. Dorothea's inventiveness and other entertaining matters

1. How did Don Quixote react to praise?
    He asked Dorothea to stop, because he found it offensive to his sensitivities as a knight to be praised.
2. What story did the curate tell Don Quixote?
    He told him about some galley slaves who had been freed and who had robbed him and the barber of their possessions and beards.
3. What is the meaning of *quijote*?
    It refers to the thigh-piece of armor.
4. Why did Sancho want Don Quixote to marry Dorothea?
    She promised him a lordship if Don Quixote killed the dragon and restored her kingdom to her.
5. What did Don Quixote claim was the power behind his arm?
    He claimed that Dulcinea was that power.
6. How did Sancho get his Dapple back?
    As they made their way toward home, they came upon Ginés de Pasamonte riding on Sancho's mule and when he recognized them, he dismounted and fled.

7. What inconsistency did the curate discuss with Dorothea?
    They discussed the apparent madness of Don Quixote in believing the tales of chivalry while at the same time being totally rational about other matters.

WORD TO KNOW:

encomium: expression of high praise

XIX. The delightful conversation between Don Quixote and his squire Sancho Panza, and other happenings

1. How did Don Quixote know that Sancho had not delivered the letter to Dulcinea?
    He found the notebook in which it was written after Sancho left him in the mountains.
2. What did the two talk about?
    They talked about Sancho's imagined meeting with Dulcinea. Don Quixote asked questions about her, always phrasing them in the best possible way, and Sancho answered in his down-to-earth way.
3. What did the boy whom Don Quixote found being whipped report?
    He told Don Quixote that after he had left them, his master resumed whipping him, and that if he had not interfered in their business, it would not have gone so badly for him.
4. What did the boy say as he departed from their company?
    He told Don Quixote to ignore him if he ever saw him again, no matter what condition he might be in; and he cursed him.

XX. Don Quixote and his company at the inn

1. After the party arrived back at the inn and Don Quixote was asleep, Sancho entered the room while the others were speaking. What did he hear them say which caused him distress?
    He heard them say that the time was past when knights-errant were of any use and that stories of knights were fantasy.
2. What did Don Quixote do in his sleep?
    He dreamt that he was slaying the dragon and was actually slashing the wineskins which were hanging in his room, spilling out all the contents.
3. What madness did Sancho reveal?
    He was so caught up in Don Quixote's fantasy world that he was actually searching for the dragon's head which would guarantee him a position in Don Quixote's kingdom.

XXI. Other strange adventures at the inn

1. Who arrived at the inn?
    Four masked men and a masked woman arrived.
2. What was notable about the woman?
    She seemed very unhappy, as they only heard her sigh and moan.
3. Who were the strangers?
    The man whom everybody obeyed was Don Fernando, and the woman was Luscinda.
4. What did Dorothea do?
    She threw herself at Don Fernando's feet and begged him to take her as his wife as he had promised, and thus save her from shame.
5. How did Don Fernando respond?
    He was overcome with remorse and admiration for her, but angry at Cardenio.

6. What did the curate and the others counsel Don Fernando to do?
    They counseled him to leave Luscinda and Cardenio in peace and to conquer his own passion, taking Dorothea as his wife because he was a Christian and a man of honor.
7. Why did Sancho cry?
    He cried because he realized that Dorothea was not a princess, and therefore he would not have a part in a kingdom.

XXII. The story of the famous Princess Micomicona continued, and our Knight's subtle discourse concerning arms and letters

1. Why was the landlady the happiest of the entire party?
    She was the happiest because the curate and Cardenio had promised to pay all the expenses of the evening.
2. To what did Don Quixote attribute all that had happened?
    He attributed it to enchantment.
3. What offer did Don Fernando make?
    He offered to accompany the party with Dorothea still in her role as the princess so they could return Don Quixote to his home.
4. What did Don Quixote say was the end of war?
    Peace was the end, or goal of war.
5. What was the first hardship of a student?
    His first hardship was poverty.
6. Who suffered even greater poverty than the student?
    The man at arms suffered more.
7. Who was rewarded more for his efforts, the student or the soldier?
    The student was rewarded more, and the soldier had to constantly succeed in war in order to be rewarded.
8. What, in addition to poverty, does the soldier face which the student does not?
    He faces the danger of losing his life.
9. Why did Don Quixote scorn the invention of artillery?
    It could kill from a distance and rob the soldier of the glory of dying in face-to-face combat.

Questions for Further Thought

A. In what way was Don Quixote very rational in his discourse?
    He was very rational in laying down the idea of the superiority of arms over letters.
B. Do you agree with his conclusions?
    Answers will vary.

XXIII. Other unheard-of adventures at the inn

1. What trick did Maritornes play on Don Quixote?
    She convinced him to extend his hand to her, and then she tied it to the door. He had to stand on his horse to put his arm through the hole behind which she was waiting to tie him up.
2. Why could Don Quixote not help the landlord who was being beaten up by the two guests after he was given permission by Dorothea?
    He could not raise his hands against men who were not knights, so he called Sancho to do it.
3. How did Don Quixote help?
    He convinced the guests to pay their bill and to stop beating up the landlord.
4. What other guest arrived at the inn?
    The barber with whom Don Quixote had fought for the basin arrived.

5. What did the men of the Holy Brotherhood have in their possession?
    They had a warrant for the arrest of Don Quixote for freeing the galley slaves.
6. How did the curate secure Don Quixote's release?
    He convinced the officials of the Holy Brotherhood that Don Quixote was mad.
7. How did he settle with the barber from whom Don Quixote had won the basin?
    He paid him eight *reales* for it.
8. Who paid for all the damage?
    Don Fernando paid for it.

WORD TO KNOW:

duenna: chaperone, guardian

XXIV. The amazing method of our Knight's enchantment and how he returned to his village

1. What did Sancho tell Don Quixote about Dorothea?
    He told him that she was no more a queen than his own mother.
2. What had Sancho noticed about Don Fernando which Don Quixote had not?
    He had noticed that he was claiming half of everything Dorothea won.
3. How did Don Quixote respond?
    He was furious at Sancho and banished him from his sight.
4. To what does Dorothea "attribute" Sancho's observations?
    She "attributes" them to enchantment.
5. What scheme did the curate devise for returning Don Quixote to his village?
    Dorothea and Don Fernando, as well as the others, dressed in disguise and while Don Quixote slept, bound him and placed him in a cage which was carried away by a waggoner with whom the curate had negotiated.
6. How did Don Quixote interpret the bogus prophecy?
    He interpreted it to mean he would marry Dulcinea.
7. What did Don Quixote attack?
    He attacked a procession of penitents bearing a statue of the Virgin Mary.
8. What happened to Don Quixote?
    One of the litter-bearers struck him with a forked pole and knocked him to the ground.
9. How long did it take for them to reach the village?
    It took six days.
10. What was Sancho's wife's main concern when they arrived?
    She was concerned that their mule was in good shape and that he had brought her gifts.

WORDS TO KNOW:

sicut in principio: as it was in the beginning

gaol: jail

PART TWO

I. Diverting Interviews between Don Quixote, Sancho Panza, the bachelor Samson Carrasco and others

1. What did the curate and the barber determine when they visited Don Quixote after a month?
    They determined that he was once again of sound mind.

2. What threat to Spain did they converse about?
    They conversed about the threat of the Turks and their naval fleet.
3. What did Don Quixote suggest the king should do about the problem of the Turks?
    He suggested that the king call up all the knights'-errant to fight the Turks.
4. What astonished the barber more than the madness of Don Quixote?
    He was more astonished by Sancho's simplicity and trust in Don Quixote.
5. How did Sancho reply to Don Quixote's question about what the people were saying about him?
    He said they thought Don Quixote was a madman and he a simpleton. The gentry thought he was a pretender to knighthood. Others found him amusing, valiant and courteous while at the same time unfortunate and impertinent.
6. What did Don Quixote say about a reputation for virtue?
    He said it was always persecuted.
7. What did Bartholomew Carrasco tell Sancho?
    He told him that the history of Don Quixote and Sancho was already in a book by the name of *The Imaginative Gentleman, Don Quixote of La Mancha*.
8. In what language and by whom was the book supposedly written?
    It had been written in Arabic by a Moor named Cide Hamete Benegeli and then translated into Spanish.
9. What did Don Quixote ask about the book?
    He asked if a second part was planned.
10. What did Don Quixote and Sancho agree to?
    They agreed to make another sally within the week in search of more adventures.

Words to Know:

circumlocution: indirect way of expressing something

droll: amusing, entertaining

colloquy: discussion, dialogue

saturnine: melancholy

II. What passed between Sancho Panza and his wife on one side and Don Quixote, his niece and housekeeper on the other

1. According to Teresa, what is the sauce that flavors food?
    That sauce is hunger, which all the poor suffer and which entices them to eat with gusto.
2. What did she say about their daughter and marriage?
    She said that she was eager to marry and that would be expedient, because even a poor marriage was better than being kept by a man without benefit of marriage. She also said it would be better for her to marry in her own class rather than be out of place among higher-class people.
3. How did Don Quixote distinguish between knight-courtiers and knights-errant?
    He said the courtiers stayed in the court and served their king in comfort while the knights-errant wandered the world suffering from the elements and risking their lives in unequal matches with giants and other enemies.
4. What lessons about chivalry did he reveal in his conversation with his housekeeper and niece?
    He revealed the rules of equality in matches between knights—equal weapons, equal mounts, and even equal position with relation to the sun.
5. According to Don Quixote, how could a poor man prove that he was a gentleman?
    He could prove it by being a man of virtue—that is affable, well-bred, courteous, gentle, helpful, generous and charitable.

Unit 4: Novel

6. Sancho was a practical man who knew he would never get a governorship or island, so what did he propose to Don Quixote?
   He proposed that they settle on a fixed salary which would be paid to him monthly from the estate of Don Quixote.
7. What was Don Quixote's excuse for not giving him a salary?
   It was not the practice of knights-errant to pay their squires in that way.
8. How did Samson surprise the housekeeper?
   He went to Don Quixote's home and encouraged him to set forth on another sally.

Word to Know:

guerdon: reward

III. The fortunes of Don Quixote on the way to his lady-love, the trick devised by Sancho for her enchantment, and the strange adventure of the cart of Death

1. Why did Don Quixote want to go to El Toboso before beginning his new adventure?
   He wanted to receive the blessing and permission of his lady Dulcinea.
2. Why did Sancho's spirits sink when they came upon El Toboso?
   He had lied to Don Quixote about seeing Dulcinea, and he didn't even know where she lived.
3. What did Sancho propose to Don Quixote as dawn arrived?
   He proposed that they leave the town, and he would return in search of Dulcinea. After finding her he would devise a proper manner for his master to meet her.
4. To what did Don Quixote attribute the homeliness of the village girl whom Sancho claimed was Dulcinea?
   He attributed it to enchantment.
5. What did they see on the cart?
   They saw it driven by a demon, Death with a human face, a winged angel and other fantastic figures.
6. Who, in fact, were the figures?
   They were actors who went from town to town performing religious dramas.
7. What happened to Dapple?
   After Rozinante was frightened by the clown, he ran off with Don Quixote and fell. As Sancho ran to help him, the devil/actor ran off with Dapple. He abandoned him further down the way, however, and Dapple returned to Sancho.
8. How was disaster averted when Don Quixote decided to take vengeance on the actors for taking Dapple?
   Sancho pointed out that there was no knight in the company, and Don Quixote could not take up arms against those who weren't knights. For his part, Sancho did not desire vengeance.

Question for Further Thought

What does Don Quixote mean when he says that all the vices except for envy bring certain pleasure?
   He means that the other vices (pride, lust, gluttony, etc) when indulged bring temporary satisfaction, but there is no satisfaction to be gained from envy—only "discord, rancour and rage."

IV. The strange adventure that befell the gallant Don Quixote with the brave Knight of the Mirrors

1. What function did actors perform for the good of the state according to Don Quixote?
   They were like mirrors which reflected back on us the way we really are.

2. How did the Squire of the Wood describe his master?
   He said he was crazy but valiant and more roguish than either.
3. Would Sancho apply the same description to his master?
   No. He said his master was not at all a rogue, but rather was kind and simple.
4. What did the Knight of the Wood tell Don Quixote about his mission?
   He said that his lady, one Casildea de Vandalia, had sent him out on numerous sallies to do almost the impossible, and that each time he returned to her she treated him with scorn and sent him out again. His present mission was to compel all the knights-errant of Spain to proclaim her the most beautiful woman alive.
5. What did he boast?
   He boasted that he had prevailed over Don Quixote de la Mancha who had confessed that Casildea was more beautiful than Dulcinea.
6. What did the two knights agree to?
   They agreed to fight it out in the morning.
7. What did the Squire of the Wood insist upon, and what was Sancho's response?
   He insisted that he and Sancho also fight, but Sancho said he had no reason to do so, and he did not want to fight with somebody with whom he had just eaten and drunk.
8. Why did Don Quixote call the Knight of the Wood the Knight of the Mirrors?
   His coat was covered with many little pieces of reflective glass.
9. When the Knight of the Mirrors fell from his horse, what did Don Quixote discover?
   He discovered that he was actually Samson Carrasco.
10. Who was the squire?
    He was a neighbor of Sancho, Tom Cecial.
11. What scheme was revealed?
    Samson, in league with the curate and the barber had planned the ruse so that once vanquished, Don Quixote would have to be under the control of Samson. Instead, Don Quixote vanquished Samson, and so he and Sancho could continue on their way to Saragossa.
12. What did Tom ask Samson about the sanity of the two "knights?"
    He asked who was crazier—the one who couldn't help being so, or the one who was so because of his own free choice.
13. What was Samson's answer?
    He said that Quixote would be mad forever, while he himself could choose when not to be.
14. What did Samson vow?
    He vowed to get revenge on Don Quixote.

Question for Further Thought:

What "un-squire-like" behavior did the author call attention to in this section?
   Sancho was unusually talkative for a squire, which the Knight of the Wood pointed out.

Words to Know:

rogue: scoundrel, rascal

perforce: forced by circumstances

V. The happily terminated adventure of the lions, and the story of Camacho's wedding feast

1. What would take away any envy Don Quixote had for other knights?
   Finding a way to "disenchant" Lady Dulcinea would accomplish that.

Unit 4: Novel

2. What did Sancho know and Don Quixote would not believe?
    Sancho knew that the knight they just encountered was Samson Carrasco, and his squire was Tom Cecial, Sancho's neighbor.
3. How did Sancho alleviate Don Quixote's anger at finding curds in his helmet?
    He turned the tables on Don Quixote and claimed that the enchanters had put the curds in the helmet in order to make Don Quixote angry with him.
4. What did the lion do when the keeper opened his cage?
    He looked out at Don Quixote and then turned around and laid down inside the cage.
5. What did Don Quixote request of the keeper who would tell the story of his bravery with the lion to the King?
    He requested that he tell him he was the "Knight of the Lions."
6. Where were the students whom Don Quixote and Sancho met going?
    They were going to the wedding of a rich farmer.
7. What was more important than pedigree to these people?
    Money was more important.
8. Why did Don Quixote think the marriage match was unjust?
    He wanted the bride to marry her neighbor Basilio because he was skilled with a sword, and he had loved her since he was a youth.
9. What did Basilio do after he met the wedding party?
    He told them that Quiteria was rightfully his, and then he proceeded to impale himself on his rapier.
10. Under what condition would Basilio agree to confess?
    He would only agree to confess if Quiteria would marry him.
11. What did she do?
    She said that of her own free will she offered her hand to Basilio in marriage.
12. After their marriage was blessed, what did Basilio do?
    He jumped to his feet and pulled the rapier from his body.
13. What had Basilio done?
    He had encased the rapier in a tube full of blood to make them think he had injured himself unto death.
14. How did Don Quixote justify Basilio's actions?
    He said that love and war were equal and that if one could use strategems in war, he could certainly use them in love as well, provided they brought no injury or dishonor to the beloved.
15. What gracious action did Camacho take?
    He allowed the wedding feast to continue, though the wedding party returned to the village with Don Quixote.

Questions for Further Thought

A. What does the expression "scarcely had fair Aurora given shining Phoebus time to dry up the liquid pearls on her golden hair with the heat of his rays" mean?
    It means "right at dawn."
B. In what ways does Sancho display his wisdom?
    He displays it through his use of expressions such as "he preaches well who lives well." Throughout the story, Sancho expresses himself through these sayings which reveal a true understanding of life as it really is.

Words to Know:

appellative: name or title

scrivener: professional copyist, scribe

obsequies: funeral rites

faggot: bundle of sticks used for firewood

VI. The great adventure of the Cave of Montesinos, in the heart of La Mancha, to which our gallant Don Quixote gave a happy termination

1. What did Don Quixote advise Basilio to do?
    He advised him to give up his deceitful ways and seek an honorable living for himself and his new wife.
2. What did Don Quixote say was more important, reputation or fortune?
    He said reputation was more important.
3. What did Don Quixote relate to the others after he returned from the cave?
    He told them a fantastic story of seeing a crystal castle and meeting the governor Montesinos who had been enchanted by Merlin.
4. How long did Don Quixote claim to be in the cave?
    He claimed to have been there for three days.
5. According to Sancho, how long was he there?
    He was there about an hour.
6. What did Sancho tell Don Quixote after he finished telling his story of what he saw?
    He told him that before he entered the cave he was sane and uttered maxims and counsels, but now he was spouting foolishness.
7. What had the Lady Dulcinea requested of Don Quixote while he was in the cave?
    She had asked (through one of her companions) to borrow six *reales* from him.
8. What perplexed him?
    He was perplexed thinking that people of quality could suffer from need.

Questions for Further Thought

A. What did Cervantes mean when he said they considered him "a Cid in arms and a Cicero in eloquence?"
    Don Quixote had convinced Camacho and his followers to stop trying to take vengeance, and he had used both his sword as a deterrent and words to convince them to stop. El Cid was a knight and Cicero was a famous Roman orator known for his eloquent speech.
B. What did Don Quixote say about a beautiful wife to a poor man?
    He said that a beautiful wife was as a jewel to a poor man, and if she could withstand the hardships of poverty, she deserved to be crowned with laurel.

Words to Know:

Cid: knight given the title of Lord

fathom: approximately 1.83 meters, or 2 yards

VII. The charming episode of Master Peter's puppet show

1. What did Don Quixote say about the life of a soldier?
    He said that it was a life of honor, in spite of the hardship it brought.
2. What did Sancho muse about?
    His master had just spoken with such clarity after having spoken the foolishness of his "vision" in the cave.
3. What did Don Quixote tell Sancho about the Devil and Master Peter?
    He told him that the Devil doesn't know the future, only God does, and that Master Peter must have sold his soul to the Devil in order to become rich through the "divination" of the ape.

Unit 4: Novel

4. Why did Don Quixote destroy the puppet show?
    The story line had the Moors chasing the hero and his lady, and Don Quixote went to their rescue.
5. On what did Don Quixote blame his actions?
    He said the enchanter made him see the puppets as real people, and seeing them thus, he had to go to the defense of the characters as a knight-errant.
6. What did he agree to do?
    He agreed to pay for the damage.
7. The note reveals the identity of the puppet master. Who was he?
    He was Ginés de Pasamonte, the galley-slave whom Don Quixote had freed.

Questions for Further Thought

What is ironic about Don Quixote talking about the forming of an order to take care of crippled soldiers? (See the notes)
    What is ironic is that Cervantes, who was himself wounded at Lepanto, died 150 years before there was any program to help ex-soldiers.

Words to Know:

breeches: knee-length pants

bounty: additional pay from commanders to soldiers from good families

livery: uniform worn by members of a group who are servants of feudal retainers

peregrination: pilgrimage

VIII. The Knight's adventure with a fair huntress

1. What did the duchess ask Sancho about Don Quixote?
    She asked him if he wasn't the one about whom a book titled *The Ingenious Gentleman, Don Quixote of La Mancha* had been written.
2. What did the duchess say in response to Don Quixote's comment about Sancho being droll and talkative?
    She said that being droll meant he was shrewd and humorous rather than dull.
3. What did Don Quixote feel for the first time when he was treated so graciously in the duke's castle?
    He felt convinced for the first time that he was actually a knight-errant.
4. What advise did Don Quixote give Sancho?
    He told him to watch his tongue and to talk less, lest he expose himself as a buffoon.
5. How did the ecclesiastic and Don Quixote react to Sancho's story as compared to the duke and duchess?
    They were impatient to hear it ended, while the duke and duchess encouraged him to tell the story in his own way.
6. What did the ecclesiastic come to realize?
    He came to realize that Don Quixote was the character in the books the duke had been reading.
7. How did Don Quixote respond to the ecclesiastic's words?
    He responded with strong words and rebuked him for speaking about things about which he knew nothing. He then told him that his actions were always directed toward virtuous ends, and the duke and duchess would have to say whether or not that made him an idiot.

Question for Further Thought

Why do you think the ecclesiastic in the duke's service was presented as such an unpleasant fellow?
> Perhaps he represented somebody whom Cervantes knew personally. Cervantes was a faithful Catholic, but he was not blind to the vices of the clergy, and this may have been a way of poking fun at them. It was common in this era for nobles to retain their own clergymen, and human nature being what it is, there were no doubt, members of the clergy who lived more like parasites than true spiritual leaders.

Words to Know:

aberrant: unusual, peculiar

seneschal: supervisor of feasts in the home of a nobleman

cynosure: center of attraction

IX. The amusing discourse that passed between the duchess and Sancho, and the disenchantment of Dulcinea

1. What did Sancho say about his master?
   > He said that his master was "stark staring mad" but had moments when he spoke with absolute clarity. It is because he believed that his master was mad that he dared to deceive him about Dulcinea.
2. What did the duchess say about Sancho?
   > She said that if he believed his master was mad and continued to follow him, he must be more crazy than his master. Then she expressed doubt in Sancho's ability to govern others if he could not govern himself.
3. How did Sancho respond?
   > He said that due to loyalty and gratitude, he had to stay with his master. He then philosophized through the use of numerous sayings about the final equality of all men in death.
4. What did she tell Sancho about Dulcinea?
   > She told him that he was the one who was deceived about her, because she actually was enchanted and someday they would all see her as she really was.
5. According to the duke, why was hunting an important activity for dukes and kings?
   > It was important because it mimicked war in the chase, strategies, etc., and also exposed them to discomforts which served to invigorate the body.
6. What did "Merlin" require in order for Dulcinea to be released from her enchanted fate as a homely peasant?
   > Sancho Panza would have to be whipped 3300 times but of his own free will.
7. What did the "silvery nymph" do when Sancho refused?
   > She chastised him and told him that she was Dulcinea, trapped inside the ugly coarse body of a peasant girl.
8. What condition did the duke place upon Sancho's governorship?
   > Sancho either had to lash himself or allow himself to be lashed.

Question for Further Thought

What is odd about the fact that before Sancho starts to speak with the duchess he checks for people hiding behind the curtains?
> The room is filled with the damsels and *duennas* of the duchess, so what he says is likely to be repeated. It is almost as if they aren't there because the duchess says "Now that we are alone, and there is no one here to hear us…"

X. Don Quixote's advice to Sancho Panza, and the latter's departure to his island

1. What did the duchess advise Sancho to use for his lashings and why?
    She told him to use a thorn branch or a knotted cat-o'-nine-tails because it was an act of charity which he was performing. Acts of charity performed half-heartedly brought no merit.
2. What did Sancho tell his wife in the letter he had dictated to her?
    He told her what he had experienced, that he had been given a governorship, that he was sending his hunting suit to be made into clothing for their daughter, and he promised her money in the future.
3. What advise did Don Quixote give Sancho?
    He told him that he had received his post of governor through no merit of his own, so he should give thanks first to God and then to the profession of knight-errantry. He should fear God, know himself, show pride in his humble origins, and act always with virtue.
4. What did Don Quixote say about virtue?
    He said that virtue is acquired, not inherited like a pedigree, and he should always be virtuous in the treatment of his family.
5. What advice did Don Quixote give to Sancho about governing?
    He told him to avoid arbitrariness in his judgments, to treat the poor with compassion, to seek truth in dealing with rich and poor alike, to weigh compassion more than justice, to act without passion toward his enemies, and to refrain from abusing the guilty.
6. What advice did Don Quixote give Sancho about personal grooming and clothing?
    He advised him to be clean and groomed, to keep his nails short, to not wear baggy, unbuttoned clothing, to wear breeches and hose, and a long coat and a longer cloak.
7. What should he do about clothing his servants?
    He should give liveries to his servants which are durable and decent, and clothe the poor, thus guaranteeing himself attendants in heaven as well.
8. What advice did he give Sancho about eating?
    He told him to avoid garlic and onions lest their odor betray his humble birth, to eat little for his own health, to drink with restraint, to not chew on both sides of his mouth at once, and never to belch in the company of others.
9. What further advice did Don Quixote give Sancho about his personal conduct?
    He told him to walk slowly and gravely, to speak with deliberation and to avoid speaking in proverbs, to be moderate in sleep and to ride a horse like a gentleman.
10. To what did Don Quixote attribute being left-handed?
    He said being left-handed or illiterate was due to humble birth or a wayward nature which his teachers could not overcome.
11. Sancho was a poor man. What was the only thing he had?
    He had his proverbs.
12. What did Sancho say that made Don Quixote acknowledge that he would be fit to govern?
    He said that he would rather go to Heaven as plain Sancho than to Hell as a governor.
13. What amazed the duke and duchess?
    They saw the instructions Don Quixote had written for Sancho and were amazed at his good sense as well as at his madness.
14. How did Don Quixote feel when Sancho left?
    He was very sad and retired to his room, asking that he not be disturbed.
15. Why did he grieve?
    He grieved because he tore his stocking and had no silk with which to mend it.
16. What did Don Quixote hear as he stood at the window?
    He heard one of the *duennas* singing a song which revealed her love for him.

17. What did he lament?

He lamented that the women were so attracted to him but he was bound to Dulcinea with whom he could not be.

QUESTIONS FOR FURTHER THOUGHT

A. Do you think the advice Don Quixote gave Sancho was reasonable? Why or why not?
Answers will vary.
B. Which of the points of behavior do you think Sancho would have the most difficulty with?
There are probably two points which would be difficult because they would require a complete change in his way of living. Those are eating little and drinking even less, as well as speaking directly without the use of proverbs. Much of Sancho's focus has been on getting the next meal and even as he responds to Don Quixote's advice, he speaks with proverbs.
C. Does Don Quixote's reference to illiteracy and left-handedness reflect a cultural bias?
Perhaps it does. It is possible that in 16th century Spain, teachers were supposed to train their students to write with the right hand, and left-handedness probably indicated lack of schooling in general.

XI. How Sancho Panza governed his island

1. What was the first order Sancho gave as governor?
His first order was that he not be called Don Sancho Panza, because he thought the Don was pretentious and nobody in his family had used the title.
2. What happened when Sancho sat at dinner?
He was attended by a doctor who had each plate removed before Sancho could eat from it. He said he was there to insure that Sancho only ate what was good for him.
3. What did the doctor recommend that Sancho eat?
He recommended 100 rolled up wafers with a few slices of quince.
4. How did Sancho respond to the doctor?
He ordered him out and threatened violence if he didn't leave on his own. Then he said that the office of governor was not worth having if he were not fed properly.
5. What diverted attention from the doctor?
Sancho received a dispatch from the duke warning him of enemy activity against his island and of a plot to murder him.
6. What did Sancho tell the doctor and the butler?
He told them to serve him plain hearty food and to serve honestly, because he would not accept bribes and would serve fairly.
7. What plan did Sancho reveal for governing the island?
He planned to get rid of the freeloaders, encourage the laborers, preserve the privileges of the gentry, reward the good, reverence religion and honor holy men.
8. How did Sancho deal with the fighting men in the street?
He made the winner of the game pay the picaroon 100 reales and give 30 for the prisoners. Then he banished the picaroon from the island because he was a parasite.
9. What did the notary advise Sancho about the gaming-house frequented by the gentry?
He advised him to leave it alone because it was less corrupt than the others.
10. What did Sancho resolve to do as he continued his rounds of the island?
He resolved to arrange a marriage between his daughter Sanchica and the young man whom the constables had arrested.

Questions for Further Thought

A. To what could you attribute Sancho's wisdom in handling the cases that were brought to him as governor?
    Though not a man of letters, Sancho had learned much from observing others and living life. He had first-hand knowledge of human nature.
B. Why do you suppose Sancho considered the gaming-houses injurious to the state?
    Sancho believed that people should work for a living, and the gaming-houses encouraged parasites like the picaroon who did not work but depended on "gratuities" to make their money. Also, the houses facilitated corruption.

Word to Know:

picaroon: a pirate or one who acts like a pirate

XII. The terrifying cat-and-bell scare experienced by Don Quixote, and the fortunes of the page that carried the letters to Teresa, wife of Sancho Panza

1. How was Don Quixote wounded?
    The duke and duchess played a trick on him and released some cats into his chamber. One of the cats attacked him and scratched his face and bit his nose.
2. What was the gist of the letter to Teresa Panza from the duchess?
    The letter praised Sancho's value as a governor and promised a match for Sanchicha.
3. What did the duchess request of Teresa?
    She asked her to send some of the famous La Mancha acorns to her.
4. How did the page contrast the ladies of Aragon and Castile?
    He said the ladies of Aragon treated their people with less formality and greater familiarity than the ladies of Castile. Therefore, it was not unusual that the duchess would have requested the acorns.
5. What did the curate say about the Panza family?
    He said they were all born with their bellies full of proverbs, because they all used many of them while speaking.
6. What was done with the letters Teresa sent to her husband and the duchess?
    They were both read by the duke and duchess, much to their amusement.

XIII. The violent end of Sancho's governorship, and his adventures leading to his meeting with Don Quixote

1. How had Sancho spent his time as governor to this point?
    He had judged cases, given opinions, made statutes and issued proclamations.
2. What happened on the seventh night?
    As he was falling asleep, he was disturbed with loud noises and men brandishing their swords, claiming the island had been invaded by the enemy.
3. What did he tell the men to do?
    He told them to get Don Quixote because he himself knew nothing of fighting.
4. What did the men put on Sancho?
    They put two shields tightly on his front and back over his shirt.
5. What happened?
    The people, all of whom were in on the joke, fought a mock war with the "enemy" and trampled over Sancho who could not stand because of the rigid shields around his body.
6. When victory was declared, what did Sancho do?
    He returned to his room and dressed, then he went out and saddled Dapple.

7. What parting words did he have for the steward, the secretary, the butler and the doctor?
   He said he was going to return to the life he had left because that was the life for which he was best suited. He also said he was leaving without anything, just as he had come.
8. To whom would Sancho render an account of his administration?
   He would render an account to the duke.
9. Why was the "pilgrim" Ricote forced to leave the village where he lived?
   Between 1609 and 1613, the Moors were expelled from Spain.
10. What nationality did the "pilgrims" pretend to be?
    They pretended to be Germans.
11. What wisdom did Ricote demonstrate about the condition of the Moors?
    He said that though not all were guilty of conspiracy against the state, enough were that the king had to take action against all of them. His words were "it was not safe for Spain to nurse the serpent in its bosom."
12. How did the pilgrims to Spain fare materially?
    They were given food and drink and generally enough money to return home with a hundred or more crowns worth of gold hidden in their staves or clothing.
13. What was Ricote's plan?
    He wanted to return to his village to recover a treasure he had hidden in its outskirts, and then he planned to recover his wife and daughter to take them to Germany.
14. Did Sancho accept Ricote's offer of a part of his treasure?
    No, again Sancho showed wisdom in not accepting it by saying "well-got wealth may meet disaster, but ill-got wealth destroys its master."
15. What happened to Sancho as he rode back to rejoin his master?
    He fell into a pit.
16. What did Don Quixote think when he heard Sancho call from the pit?
    He thought he was a voice from Purgatory.
17. What did Sancho tell the Duke and Duchess about his governorship?
    He told them that he had governed as he should and that he left with no more than he took, which was nothing. He also said he had accepted no bribes.

Words to Know:

Moor: Moslems who invaded Spain in the 8th century and established a civilization that lasted until the late 15th century.

penury: poverty, destitution

XIV. Of what befell Don Quixote and his squire on their way to Barcelona, and an adventure which caused greater sorrow to the former than any yet

1. What did Don Quixote tell Sancho were two of Heaven's greatest gifts?
   Two of Heaven's greatest gifts were liberty and honor.
2. Why did Don Quixote find it difficult to enjoy the luxury of the castle?
   It was difficult because it came, not from Heaven, but from others, and that put him in their debt.
3. What did Don Quixote remind Sancho to do?
   He reminded him that he had to lash himself in order to free Dulcinea of her enchantment.
4. What did Don Quixote hear as he sat to eat in the inn?
   He heard the people in the next room discussing the second part of the story of Don Quixote, and then one of them saying that what he didn't like in the second part was that Don Quixote no longer loved Dulcinea.
5. How did he react on hearing that?
   He was full of rage and proclaimed that Don Quixote was constant in his love for her.

Unit 4: Novel

6. Why did Don Quixote decide not to continue on to Saragossa?
   He wanted to prove that the writer of the second part of his story was a fraud, because he had written about Don Quixote in Saragossa.
7. Why was Don Quixote sad when he met the bandit captain Rocque Guinart?
   He was sad because he had been surprised with his horse unbridled and was not on guard for danger.
8. How did Don Quixote view the misfortunes he suffered as a knight-errant?
   He saw them as penances for his sins.
9. What did Don Quixote, Sancho and Rocque witness in the sea by Barcelona?
   They saw galley ships involved in a mock battle.
10. What limits did Don Quixote's host place upon himself?
    Though he would jest with him, he would do no harm to his person.
11. What did the Knight of the White Moon require of Don Quixote when he vanquished him in the match?
    He required that he return to his home, but did not insist that he denounce his belief that Dulcinea was the most beautiful woman.
12. Who was the Knight of the White Moon, and why did he pursue Don Quixote?
    He was Samson Carrasco, and his goal was to help Don Quixote recover from his madness by spending a year at home without arms.
13. Why did Don Antonio object to Carrasco's plan?
    He objected because Don Quixote's cure would take away from the mirth he brought to mankind which was so amused by his madness.

Words to Know:

swarthy: dark skinned

hautboy: oboe

XV. How Don Quixote and Sancho returned to their village

1. To what did Don Quixote attribute his defeat?
   He attributed his defeat to his unhappy fate.
2. What did Don Quixote acknowledge about fortune?
   He acknowledged that everything that happened was due to the "special disposition of Providence." Every man creates his own fortune by the actions he takes and the decisions he makes. Only he was to blame for what had happened.
3. Why did he agree to spend the required year at home?
   He was a man of honor and had given his word he would do so if he lost the match.
4. What did Don Quixote propose to Sancho about disenchanting Dulcinea?
   He proposed that he pay Sancho to lash himself as Merlin had required.
5. What change came over Don Quixote as they approached an inn?
   He recognized the inn as an inn and not as a castle. In other words, his sanity had returned.
6. What claim did Don Alvaro Tarfe make to Don Quixote?
   He claimed to be the closest friend of the Don Quixote written about in the second part of the book and that he had ridden with him to Saragossa, the city to which Don Quixote refused to go.
7. What deposition did Don Alvaro officially make?
   He deposed that the man he had thought was Don Quixote who was mentioned in *The Second Part of Don Quixote of La Mancha*, written by Avellaneda, was not the same Don Quixote in whose company he now was.
8. How did Don Quixote plan to spend his year?
   He planned to spend it as a shepherd, practicing the virtues of the pastoral life.

9. How did his niece and the housekeeper react to his plan?
    They were horrified that he would think of going out into the wilderness with sheep rather than spend his time as a gentleman at home.

Question for Further Thought

Sancho said that "Great hearts…should be as patient in adversity as they are joyful in prosperity." How would you restate his idea of character?
    Life inevitably brings joy and sorrow, and the man of character is he who accepts both with grace. One must expect that his fortunes can change over time, so he should learn to take them in stride.

Word to Know:

abeyance: suspension, ceasing temporarily

XVI. How Don Quixote fell sick, made his last will and died

1. To what did the people close to Don Quixote attribute his illness?
    They attributed it to his sorrow at having been defeated and to the fact that Dulcinea had not been disenchanted.
2. What did the physician recommend?
    He recommended that they see to Don Quixote's spiritual health—in other words, that they prepare him for death.
3. What insight had Don Quixote received while he slept?
    He realized the folly and fraud of all the books he had read about knight-errantry.
4. What did he say about his life and death?
    He said that though he may have been considered a madman in life, he would not be considered one in death.
5. What was Don Quixote's middle name?
    It was Alonso Quixano, known as the Good.
6. When the priest, the bachelor and the barber heard Don Quixote renounce Amadis of Gaul and all stories of knight-errantry, what was their reaction?
    They were convinced he had fallen into a new madness, and they tried to talk him out of it.
7. What did Don Quixote do for Sancho?
    He declared all their accounts settled and left him whatever money he had in his possession, and he apologized for making Sancho appear as mad as himself.
8. Whom did he appoint as his sole heir?
    He appointed his niece, Antonia Quixano as his sole heiress, on the condition that she would never marry a man who had even read books on knight-errantry.
9. What did he leave the housekeeper?
    He left her salary wages plus twenty ducats for her mourning.
10. Whom did he appoint as the executors of his will?
    He appointed the priest and Carrasco as executors of his will.
11. What did he ask of the executors in regard to the author of The Second Part of the Achievements of Don Quixote de la Mancha?
    He asked that they beg his pardon for having been the cause of his writing such a silly book.
12. How long did Don Quixote live after dictating his last will and testament?
    He lived for three days.
13. Why did the priest want the notary to certify that Don Quixote had died a natural death?
    He didn't want any future writers to resurrect him with further stories of wild adventures.

Unit 4: Novel

14. Why had the author not named the town of Don Quixote's birth?
    He thought it better that the towns of the region of La Mancha should compete for the honor of having given birth to him.
15. What was the meaning of Carrasco's epitaph on Don Quixote's tomb?
    He meant that Don Quixote died a noble death, fitting of a knight, and that though he was considered a fool, he died a wise man.

QUESTIONS FOR FURTHER THOUGHT

A. What kind of a man was Don Quixote at the beginning of the book?
   He was an unmarried gentleman who had enough wealth to be comfortable and to preclude his having to work for a living. He spent his time reading chivalric novels.
B. Why would somebody living comfortably as he did risk taking on the roaming life of a knight-errant with no guarantee of success?
   Perhaps one would do so because he was bored with his life as it was. He was obviously a man of high ideals, and perhaps he wanted to put those ideals to the test.
C. What kind of worldview did Don Quixote hold?
   He saw the world as needing redemption, and it was the function of the knight-errant "to fight for the right, without question or pause, to be willing to march into hell for a heavenly cause…" (*Man of La Mancha* theme song). His worldview was shaped by his Catholicism and by the society in which he lived. He had a tolerance and sympathy for others, including Moslems, but he also believed that people had a hand in their fate. In the end, what mattered was being right with God.
D. Sancho had been described at the beginning as good even though he was poor. What kind of character did he demonstrate throughout the story?
   Sancho was a simple person, a farmer, and he spoke mostly in proverbs. Proverbs always carry a bit of wisdom, and from that standpoint, Sancho reflected an inner wisdom through the sayings. He had a good heart and understood what was required of him by the Church. However, as many of the poor people of the day, he was often concerned about the next meal, and he had learned various ways of making a bit of money on the side. So when he went to work for Don Quixote, he was not above helping himself to whatever was available, and he knew how to take advantage of every opportunity to improve his lot. He was loyal to Don Quixote, even though he saw him as a madman, but he didn't hesitate to deceive him when it suited his purposes (as he did when he claimed to have lashed himself while he had actually lashed the trees).
E. What do you think the role of the duke and duchess was in the novel?
   Answers may vary. Perhaps they were used to show the emptiness of the genteel life. After all, what did they do but spend great expense and effort to amuse themselves at Don Quixote's expense. He never realized that he was the object of their amusement, because he saw only the good in people and took them at face value. But they saw an opportunity to divert themselves for awhile with him and Sancho, and they took advantage of it. This may have been a social commentary on that class of people.

WORDS TO KNOW:

eclogue: poem about a pastoral subject

epitaph: text on a gravestone, often in verse

Glossary:
Words to Know

abashed	embarrassed, ashamed
aberrant	unusual, peculiar
abeyance	suspension, ceasing temporarily
abjure	renounce, reject, give up
absolution	the forgiveness of sins
abstruse	obscure, mysterious
acedia	another name for sloth
acolyte	cleric's assistant
acumen	insight, good judgment, intelligence
adamantine	impenetrably hard mythological substance
alacrity	eagerness, enthusiasm, readiness, speed
alchemy	any apparently magical process of changing ordinary materials into something valuable, such as metal to gold
amain	with full force and speed
ambrosial	tasting delicious, as food of the gods
anachronism	a thing or person belonging to a date or period other than the correct one (a medieval knight in Ancient Greece)
antipathy	hostility, ill-feeling
aphorisms	sayings; clichés
apostate	one who renounces his religious beliefs, traitor, fugitive
apothecary	dispenser of drugs and medicines
appellative	name or title

Glossary: Words to Know

ascetic	austere, severe; one who practices self-denial and self-mortification
audacity	boldness, daring, overconfidence
augury	the art of telling the future by reading signs or omens; fortune-telling
aureole	halo, corona
avarice	greediness, materialism
baldric	a sash worn over one shoulder to the opposite hip to support a sword
balsam	ointment, balm
bane	blight, curse
beaver	a piece of armor attached to a helmet to protect the mouth and chin
benignity	gentle disposition, kindness
Biscayan	a Basque, person from the northern area of Spain inhabited by the Basque people
boon	a favor sought
bounty	additional pay from commanders to soldiers from good families
breeches	knee-length pants
caitiff	despicable coward
calumny	slander, misrepresentation, lies
caparison	ornamental covering for a horse, saddle decoration
carbuncle	a red gemstone, garnet
cenobite	monk; one who lives in a community
censer	vessel which holds charcoal and incense and hangs on the end of a long chain, used during the Mass and other liturgical services and symbolizing the sending of prayers up to Heaven
chamberlain	manager of a royal or noble household
chivalry	gallantry, courtesy, graciousness, loyalty
Cid	knight given the title of Lord
circumlocution	indirect way of expressing something

circumspect	cautious, guarded
colloquy	discussion, dialogue
concupiscence	tendency toward lust
contemplation	concentration of the mind on achieving unity with God
contumacious	flagrantly disobedient or rebellious; refusing to appear in court
contumacy	defiance of authority
cornice	molding or ledge which projects along a wall
courser	a swift horse
covenant	promise, pledge
cowl	monk's hood
crone	a term which insults the age or appearance of a (usually older) woman
cur	person who is seen as mean or cowardly; mongrel
curate	cleric in charge of a parish
cynosure	center of attraction
decree	official order
decretal	papal decree relating to Church law or doctrine
delectation	enjoyment, appreciation
descry	to discover something
diadem	crown, or bright star
dialectic	logical argumentation
diffidence	shyness, reserve
diffident	hesitant, insecure
disquisition	a formal discourse in which a subject is examined and discussed
dissolute	degenerate, immoral

Glossary: Words to Know

doublet	padded underwear reinforced with mail, worn under armor
droll	amusing, entertaining
duenna	chaperone, guardian
eclogue	poem about a pastoral subject
egress	way out, exit
empery	absolute dominion, sovereignty
Empyrean	the sky or heavens, the celestial sphere, believed to be the highest part of Heaven and the dwelling place of God
encomium	expression of high praise
enervate	weaken, debilitate
enmity	hostility, antagonism
enthrall	captivate, beguile
epitaph	text on a gravestone, often in verse
eschew	avoid, give up
Eunoe	memory of good
faggot	bundle of sticks used for firewood
fain	happily, eagerly
fathom	approximately 1.83 meters, or 2 yards
fête	honor, praise, celebrate
franklin	class of landowner, free by birth but not of noble blood
Fulling-hammers	hammers used to beat and thicken cloth fibers
gainsay	deny, contradict
gaol	jail
gaudies	the paternoster or "Our Father" beads on a rosary
geomancer	one who predicts the future based on patterns made by throwing handfuls of dirt on the ground

geometer	one who specializes in geometry
gonfalon	identifying banner suspended from a crossbar
graft	to acquire money by unfair or dishonest means
guerdon	reward
guile	cunning, slyness, deviousness, craftiness
hagiographer	one who writes about the lives of the saints
Halcyon	peaceful, heavenly, quiet
harridan	scolding, ill-tempered woman
hauberk	the chain-mail tunic of a knight
hautboy	oboe
heresy	dissent, unorthodoxy
hermit	recluse, one who lives alone
hostelry	inn
ignominious	humiliating, shameful
ignominy	humiliation, disgrace
Ilium	Troy
imperious	domineering, arrogant, haughty
imperturbability	consistently calm
impetuous	rash, impulsive
incandescence	emission of visible light due to an increase in temperature
inconstancy	unfaithfulness
indigence	poverty, deprivation
indolence	laziness, idleness, inactivity
indolent	lazy, sluggish

Glossary: Words to Know

ingrate	somebody who shows no gratitude
intercessor	one who asks another for something; in religious terms, one who prays to God for the needs of another (as St. Bernard would pray to Mary who would intercede with Christ, her Son)
interdicted	banned by law
jerkin	close-fitting, sleeveless jacket with extended shoulders, worn over a doublet and secured with a belt, worn by men of the 1500s
kalends	in Rome, the first day of each month
league	a unit of distance, about 3 miles
liege	a lord who deserves loyalty and service from his knights
limiter	a begging friar assigned to a specific area so as to limit his activity
limpid	calm, transparent
list	place of combat
livery	uniform worn by members of a group who are servants of feudal retainers
livid	the color of a bruise; ashen blue-black, here symbolizing envy
loquacious	talkative
luminescence	light occurring due to a chemical change at low temperature
mace	club, scepter
magnanimity	nobility, generosity
Manchegan	a man from the area of La Mancha
manciple	one who buys food and supplies for a college or monastery
mille	one who operates a mill, grinding grain into flour
missive	letter, communication
Moor	Moslems who invaded Spain in the 8th century and established a civilization that lasted until the late 15th century.
morion	a metal helmet with a crest and a curved peak, worn by soldiers in the 16th and 17th centuries

mutable	changeable
nefarious	extremely wicked
niggardly	stingy, miserly
nimbus	cloud of light around a deity, halo
obdurate	obstinate, stubborn
obloquy	disgrace, humiliation
obsequies	funeral rites
obsequious	submissive
occident	the west
oligarchy	government in which power is held by a few people
omnipotent	all-powerful, supreme
oriflamme	source of inspiration
orisons	prayers
paean	expression of praise or joy
page	a youthful personal attendant
paladin	medieval champion of a cause
palfrey	a woman's riding horse
pallid	pale, ashen
palmer	medieval pilgrim who carried palm leaves to prove he had been to the Holy Land
pander	cater to or profit from the weaknesses of others, such as procuring clients for prostitutes, etc.
panoply	full ceremonial dress, full armor
paramour	adulterous lover
parricide	murder of a parent or close relative
parse	to analyze grammatical structure of a word or sentence

Glossary: Words to Know

parsimony	frugality, thriftiness, prudence
patrimony	inheritance
Paynim	Muslim
peccant	guilty of sin; sinner
pedagogue	teacher
pennon	long narrow flag carried on a lance
penury	poverty, destitution
peregrination	pilgrimage
perfidy	treachery, betrayal
perforce	forced by circumstances
pernicious	destructive, harmful
picaroon	a pirate or one who acts like a pirate
pithy	condensed, to the point
porphyry	purple stone
portcullis	heavy gate which is suspended from chains and is raised and lowered
portmanteau	a large leather suitcase that opens into two hinged compartments
prattle	chatter, drivel
presage	foretell, portend
proffer	to propose or offer something for consideration
progenitor	ancestor, originator
prone	lying face-down
propitiation	the winning of another's favor
propitious	favorable, encouraging
prostrate	face down

puce	brownish purple color
puissance	power
puissant	powerful, mighty
punctilious	meticulous, conscientious
purlieu	an outlying or neighboring area
pusillanimous	timid, cowardly
quiddity	the essential nature of something
rapacious	greedy, grasping, gluttonous
rapacity	greed, selfishness, miserliness
rapine	plunder; use of force to take another's property
ravin	plunder or prey
real	name of Spanish currency until the second half of the 19th century, when it was replaced with the peseta. The real was 1/4th of a peseta.
reeve	steward or other minor estate official; the intermediary between a lord and his serfs
reprobate	degenerate, rascal
rhetoric	public speaking
rill	rivulet, brook
rogue	scoundrel, rascal
rueful	full of woe, mournful
sagacious	wise, clever
sagacity	wisdom, shrewdness
sanguine	cheerful, optimistic
satrap	governor of a province in ancient Persia
saturnine	melancholy
screed	lengthy piece of writing or speech

Glossary: Words to Know

scrivener	professional copyist, scribe
sedulous	doing something with great care and concentration
sempiternal	everlasting
seneschal	supervisor of feasts in the home of a nobleman
sequent	following
shindy	row, commotion
sicut in principio	as it was in the beginning
simoniac	one who sells spiritual things such as relics, sacraments, church offices, etc.
sinister	evil, ominous; (from the left side)
skinflint	miser
sloth	apathy, laziness, indolence
smite	slice, cut
sophist	one skilled in devious argumentation
squire	apprentice to a knight
stone	British unit of measure—one stone equals approximately 14 pounds
subsume	to include into something larger
succor	help, assistance
sufferance	patient endurance
summoner	one who called sinners to trial in church court
sumpter	pack animal
supine	lying on the back, face up
suppliant	humbly entreating
surcease	a temporary stoppage of an action (like a truce)
surfeit	excess, surplus

suzerainty	a nation which controls the international affairs of a dependent nation but allows it to control its own internal affairs
swart	dark and weathered complexion
swarthy	dark skinned
swathing	wrapping of a person in bandages or cloth
swoon	faint, lose consciousness
sylvan	wooded, full of trees
synod	a church council to discuss religious issues
temporize	to delay acting in order to gain time
thrall	one whose life is completely controlled by another
timorous	nervous, frightened
tonsure	ceremonial shaving of the head of a monk, sometimes in the form of a cross
transmutations	changes, transformations
treason	treachery, betrayal
tribute	tax
truce	temporary cessation of fighting
truculent	hostile, defiant
usury	the practice of lending money at an exorbitant rate of interest
victuals	food
vitiate	to make something defective
vouchsafe	to allow or promise
wain	wagon
wanton	reckless, willful
wench	peasant girl or servant, wanton woman
wraith	ghost, spirit, phantom particularly the spectral image of a person in his exact likeness

Glossary: Words to Know

wrath	anger, rage
yeoman	a loyal servant

SOURCES CONSULTED

Alighieri, Dante. 2003. *The Divine Comedy*, trans. John Ciardi. New York. New American Library.

Cervantes, Miguel de. 1957. *Don Quixote*, trans. Walter Starkie. New York. Mentor Books.

Chaucer, Geoffrey. 1952. *The Canterbury Tales*, ed. Maynard Hutchins. Chicago. Great Books of the Western World, Encyclopedia Britannica.

Cowen, Louise and Os Guinness. 1998. *Invitation to the Classics*. Grand Rapids. Baker Books.

Crabb, Daniel M, Ph.D. n.d. *Don Quixote Notes*. Toronto. Coles Notes.

Einhard. 1969. *Two Lives of Charlemagne*, trans. Lewis Thorpe. London. Penguin Books.

Hillegass, C.K. 1966. *Beowulf*. Lincoln. Cliffs Notes.

Hillegass, C.K. 1990. *Chaucer's Canterbury Tales*. Lincoln. Cliffs Notes.

Hillegass, C.K. 1967. *Machiavelli's The Prince*. Lincoln. Cliffs Notes.

Machiavelli, Niccolò. 2004. *The Prince*. New York. Penguin Books.

Milton, John. 2000. *Paradise Lost,* ed. John Leonard. New York. Penguin Books.

St. Benedict. 1975. *The Rule of Saint Benedict*, trans. Anthony Meisel and M. L. Del Mastro. New York. Image Books.

Stravisnskas, Peter M. J., PhD, S.T.L., ed. 1991. *Catholic Encyclopedia*. Huntington. Our Sunday Visitor.

_____. 1963. *Beowulf*, trans. Burton Raffel. New York. Mentor Books.

_____. 1967. *The Song of Roland*, trans. Frederick Bliss Luquiens. New York. Collier Books.

http://www.sparknotes.com/poetry/paradiselost/section6.rhtml

About the Author

Fran Rutherford was the primary educator of her children for 16 years, during which time she taught the Classics using a couple of the programs available to homeschool parents. When she began, the curricula available did not flesh out the readings or provide an analysis of the works studied. Deciding to read the books before the children, Fran began to write questions which would help the children to focus on the main ideas put forth, and the result is three study guides, covering the readings of most classical curricula for high school students.

Those study guides are now available in both Student Guides and Teacher Guides. They are: *Greek Classics*, *Ancient Rome*, and *Old World Europe*. They have proven to be very helpful for both students and their teachers in understanding

the works which form the foundation of Western Civilization.

Fran has been a speaker at various homeschooling conferences and gatherings and encourages parents to educate their children through the high school years. She is available to speak on topics relating to classical curricula, as well as the "how-to" of actually doing it. Her latest talk "Beauty and the Beast" explored the notion of beauty and how the classics help incorporate it into our lives.

Fran can be reached through her blog or at Classicstudyguides.com with any questions relative to Questions for the Thinker Study Guides© or Questions for the Thinker Ebook Study Guides©, as well as to schedule talks.

About the Illustrator

James Rutherford was born in Albuquerque, New Mexico, the third child of Larry and Fran Rutherford. He showed an extraordinary aptitude for music and drawing at a young age. After completing the fifth grade, his parents decided to educate him at home and afford him the time to not only get a rigorous education, but also to have the time to spend on his music and art. He studied the Classics of Greece and Rome, Europe and America when he was in high school and accompanied his assignments with beautiful illustrations of the gods and other subjects of interest.

James attended the University of Dallas, graduating *cum laude* with a Bachelor's Degree in Art and Sculpture. He is the Sr. Operations Designer for Aquinasandmore.com and is also the organist for a Catholic church in Denver. He is the illustrator for the Questions for the Thinker Study Guides© series.

www.ingramcontent.com/pod-product-compliance
Lightning Source LLC
Chambersburg PA
CBHW082038230426
43670CB00016B/2695